Betty Crocker

outdoor
food

100 Recipes for the Way You Really Cook

WILEY

Wiley Publishing, Inc.

Copyright © 2008 by General Mills, Minneapolis, Minnesota. All rights reserved.

Published by John Wiley & Sons, Inc., Hoboken, New Jersey

Published simultaneously in Canada

For general information on our other products and services or for technical support, please contact our Customer Care Department within the United States at (800) 762-2974, outside the United States at (317) 572-3993 or fax (317) 572-4002.

Wiley also publishes its books in a variety of electronic formats. Some content that appears in print may not be available in electronic books. For more information about Wiley products, visit our web site at www.wiley.com.

Library of Congress Cataloging-in-Publication Data:

Betty Crocker outdoor food : 100 recipes for the way you really cook.
  p. cm.
 Includes index.
 ISBN 978-0-470-27879-6 (cloth : alk. paper)
 1. Outdoor cookery. I. Crocker, Betty.
 TX823.B486 2008
 641.5'78—dc22

                              2007046852

General Mills

Publisher, Cookbooks: **Maggie Gilbert/Lynn Vettel**

Manager, Cookbooks: **Lois Tlusty**

Recipe Development and Testing:
Betty Crocker Kitchens

Photography and Food Styling: **General Mills Photography Studios**

Wiley Publishing, Inc.

Publisher: **Natalie Chapman**

Executive Editor: **Anne Ficklen**

Project Editor: **Adam Kowit**

Editor: **Lauren Brown**

Production Manager: **Leslie Anglin**

Cover Design: **Suzanne Sunwoo**

Art Director: **Tai Blanche**

Layout: **Indianapolis Composition Services**

Manufacturing Manager: **Kevin Watt**

Manufactured in China

10 9 8 7 6 5 4 3 2 1

Cover photo: Baby Burgers
(page 38)

Our Betty Crocker Kitchens seal guarantees success in your kitchen. Every recipe has been tested in America's Most Trusted Kitchens™ to meet our high standards of reliability, easy preparation and great taste.

Dear Friends,

Surf, sand and sun are not the only things that come to mind when we think of summer. The great foods you enjoy at a barbecue, a picnic or an outdoor party help to create the fun and festive mood that accompanies the nice weather. The bounty of fresh fruits, vegetables and herbs that are grown in the summer makes the perfect addition to these great recipes.

You'll find chapters on appetizers and party foods, grilling, picnic-perfect foods, sumptuous side dishes and refreshing drinks. Whether you are feeding your family or the entire block, you will be prepared to please. Brie Quesadillas with Mango Guacamole, Shrimp Deviled Eggs, Chipotle Salsa Ribs, Mediterranean Potato Salad and Frosty Guava-Peach Sippers are just a few of the delicious dishes you can make.

Get ready to enjoy the warm sun and the cool breeze with a feast at your fingertips!

Warmly,

Betty Crocker

contents

Summertime Produce

Treat Yourself to the Season's Best

Summertime is the perfect time to eat plenty of fruits and vegetables. With the amazing palette of colors, plus the crisp and juicy choices available, every eating occasion can be an especially tasty one.

Health experts recommend that we eat five to nine servings of fruits and vegetables each day. Choosing an assortment of these foods gives us a variety of vitamins, minerals and phytonutrients as well as fiber. Together, getting enough of these substances can offer a better chance at better health.

4 Ways to Fit in These All-Stars

- **As a topper:** Slice and diced fruits make terrific toppings for yogurt, cereal, frozen yogurt, angel food cake and pancakes. Roasted or steamed vegetables spruce up baked potatoes, pasta and rice. Top burgers and sandwiches with lettuce and sliced tomatoes or bell peppers.

- **As a mixer:** Toss a handful (or two) of lightly cooked chopped veggies into soups, scrambled eggs, pasta and rice dishes. Add fruit pieces to salads and smoothies.

- **As a side dish:** Forget the chips. Brighten your plate with bite-size berries, sliced cantaloupe or mango or bright green broccoli. Have already-cut produce on hand for afternoon snacks, afterwork munchies or predinner nibbles.

- **As the main event:** Mix favorite fruits or vegetables with light salad dressing, and wrap them up in a whole-grain tortilla or spoon into a pita bread.

Produce That Packs a Punch

Every fruit and vegetable—even iceberg lettuce—has something good to offer, though some pack more nutrition than others. Here are a few of summer's best.

Blueberries: Ranked by the USDA as a top fruit in terms of antioxidant power. Phytonutrient-wise, what's inside may neutralize free radicals and may also help maintain urinary tract health.

Broccoli: Offers calcium, potassium and folate. An excellent source of vitamin C. Contains antioxidants that may neutralize free radicals and disarm some cancer-causing agents.

Cantaloupe: One cup contains 100% of the recommended daily amount of vitamin A (beta-carotene) and vitamin C. Beta-carotene helps keep cells healthy. Some evidence suggests it may help protect the skin from sun damage.

Papaya: Rich in vitamin C and a good source of folate and potassium.

Red bell pepper: An excellent source of vitamin A. Contains more than 100% of the recommended daily amount of vitamin C in ½ cup.

Romaine lettuce: A good source of vitamin C, vitamin A (beta-carotene) and folate. Phytonutrients include zeaxanthin, which may help protect eyes against age-related changes.

Strawberries: 1 cup of whole berries contains 100% of the recommended daily amount of vitamin C. Phytonutrients may help neutralize free radicals and keep cells healthy.

In-Season Herbs

These small garden treasures are packed with distinctive flavors and fragrant aromas that make everyday fare simply extraordinary. Here's a sampler of summer herb favorites.

Basil

Characteristics:

- Intense sweet and spicy flavor, often described as a blend of licorice and cloves.

- Signature herb in Mediterranean and Italian cuisines.

- Available in other varieties, such as lemon, clove, cinnamon and Thai Basil.

Herb Ideas:

- Toss chopped basil with mixed salad greens.

- Sprinkle sliced tomatoes with chopped basil, Parmesan cheese and olive oil.

- Add chopped basil to pasta along with fresh mozzarella and cherry tomatoes.

Chives

Characteristics:

- Bright green with hollow stems.

- Delicate onion flavor.

- Heating chives diminishes their flavor, so add right before serving.

Herb Ideas:

- Sprinkle over grilled or roasted vegetables.

- Stir into cream cheese or cottage cheese.

- Top salads with finely chopped chives.

Cilantro

Characteristics:

- Extremely aromatic with a pungent, acidic flavor.

- Sometimes referred to as Mexican parsley or Chinese parsley.

- This flat-leaf parsley look-alike is a global herb used in Mexican, Indian, Middle Eastern and Asian cuisines.

Herb Ideas:

- Stir into sour cream, salsa or dips.

- Add to chicken salad.

- Top grilled fish with chopped or whole cilantro and lemon or lime juice.

Ginger-Lime Tuna Steaks, page 94

Mint

Characteristics:

- Strong, sweet flavor and cool aftertaste.

- Although "mint" encompasses numerous varieties of this herb, peppermint and spearmint are the most notable.

- Adventurous cooks may want to try chocolate, pineapple and apple mint.

- Peppermint has large, bright green leaves and spearmint has small, dustier gray-green leaves.

Herb Ideas:

- Slightly bruise leaves, and add to your favorite beverage (teas, lemonade, sparkling water).

- Stir chopped mint into chocolate sauce or hot fudge sauce, and serve over cake or ice cream.

- Add chopped mint to fresh peas cooked with butter.

Parsley

Characteristics:

- Distinctive tangy, peppery flavor.

- Most popular in the U.S. is curly leaf parsley, which has small, curly dark green leaves. In most of Europe, however, flat-leaf parsley or Italian parsley, with its flat, dark green leaves, is more popular.

Herb Ideas:

- Stir chopped parsley into tuna salad or egg salad filling for sandwiches.

- Toss with melted butter or olive oil and cooked vegetables.

- Make a parsley pesto by using half basil and half parsley in your favorite pesto recipe.

Cranberry-Mint Iced Tea,
page 130

Sage Advice

- Homegrown fresh herbs should be picked early in the morning after the dew has evaporated but before the sun is too strong. Pick the tops of the herbs (about 2 to 3 inches) because those leaves contain the most oils.

- Most fresh herbs can be stored in the refrigerator. Wrap stems of fresh herbs in damp paper towel, then put the herbs in a plastic bag and refrigerate.

- For herbs like mint, parsley and cilantro, fill a small jar or glass with about 2 inches of water. Place the stems in the water, and place a plastic bag over the herbs. Secure with a rubber band around the neck of the jar.

- Experimenting with a new herb or adding fresh herbs to a recipe? Use 1 teaspoon of fresh herbs for every four servings the recipe makes. Taste the recipe to decide if you have enough herbs. If you'd like a little more, add a little at a time until the flavor is right.

- Fresh herbs can't be beat, but if you'd like to (or need to) use dried herbs, substitute in a 3-to-1 ratio: for every 3 teaspoons of fresh herbs, you'll need 1 teaspoon of dried herbs.

Herb Blends

The best way to combine different herbs is to experiment, starting with two or three and then adding from there, depending on the recipe. Start with these tried-and-true herb mixtures.

Fines Herbes is terrific for delicately flavored foods like green salads, eggs and cream sauces. Make this with equal parts of summer favorites such as chives, chervil, parsley and tarragon.

Bouquet Garni is a French-inspired herb combination used to flavor soups, stews, casseroles and even rice and grains. Wrap a whole bay leaf, thyme sprig and several parsley sprigs in a small piece of cheesecloth or linen, and tie with string; simmer in the liquid or mixture that you are preparing.

Mixed Herbs are a bit stronger than Fines Herbes so they're used with more robustly flavored foods like meat, fish and some vegetables. Make with equal parts of sage, thyme, marjoram and parsley.

Cheese Tray with Olive Rosemary Skewers

Bread and Spreads Platter

Peachy Cream Cheese–Jalapeño Spread

Five-Layer Mexican Dip

Guacamole-Cheese Crisps

Brie Quesadillas with Mango Guacamole

Taco Mozzi Sticks

Mini Corn Dogs on a Stick

Pesto-Salmon Roulades

Mini Crab Points

Layered Shrimp Spread

Spicy Grilled Shrimp Platter

Planked Salmon Platter

Seafood Salad Tartlets

Basil-Turkey Mini Focaccia Sandwiches

Light Lemon-Dijon Chicken Salad

Cashew Curry Shrimp Salad

Baby Burgers

Mini Barbeque Pizza Wedges

Key Lime Bars

S'mores Chocolate Chip Ice-Cream Sandwiches

Tiramisu Cheesecake Dessert

1

breezy party food

Cheese Tray with Olive Rosemary Skewers

Prep Time: 45 min ▪ Start to Finish: 45 min ▪ 24 Servings

1 round (7 oz) Gouda or Edam cheese
48 to 96 assorted large pitted or stuffed olives (such as kalamata and large
    pimiento-stuffed green olives), drained
24 sprigs rosemary, each 4 inches long
1½ lb assorted cheeses (such as Colby–Monterey Jack, dill Havarti, sharp
    Cheddar and pepper Jack)
Assorted crackers

1 Remove paper and wax from cheese round. On center of 12- to 14-inch platter, place cheese round. Thread 2 to 4 olives on each rosemary sprig. Insert sprigs into cheese round.

2 Cut assorted cheeses into slices and shapes, such as triangles, squares, cubes and sticks; arrange around cheese round. Serve with crackers.

Use thick rosemary sprigs for the skewers so that they won't break. You also can use 3- to 4-inch party picks.

1 Serving: Calories 200 (Calories from Fat 140); Total Fat 15g (Saturated Fat 8g); Cholesterol 40mg; Sodium 400mg; Total Carbohydrate 6g (Dietary Fiber 0g); Protein 9g

Bread and Spreads Platter

Prep Time: 20 min ▪ Start to Finish: 20 min ▪ 18 Servings

2 containers (8 oz each) chives-and-onion cream cheese spread
¼ cup diced drained roasted red bell peppers (from 7-oz jar)
¼ cup chopped pimiento-stuffed green olives
2 tablespoons refrigerated basil pesto (from 7-oz container)
Leaf lettuce leaves
1 loaf (20 inch) baguette French bread (12 oz), cut into ¼-inch slices

1 Among 3 small bowls, divide cream cheese. Stir red peppers into cream cheese in 1 bowl. Stir olives into cream cheese in another bowl. Stir pesto into cream cheese in third bowl.

2 Line serving platter with lettuce leaves. Mound 3 spreads on lettuce leaves. Surround with bread slices.

Make little paper flags identifying the three spreads. Then, attach them to toothpicks and place in the spreads.

1 Serving: Calories 140 (Calories from Fat 80); Total Fat 9g (Saturated Fat 5g); Cholesterol 25mg; Sodium 330mg; Total Carbohydrate 11g (Dietary Fiber 0g); Protein 4g

Peachy Cream Cheese–Jalapeño Spread

Prep Time: 15 min ▪ Start to Finish: 15 min ▪ 8 Servings (2 tablespoons spread and 3 crackers each)

¼ cup peach or apricot preserves
½ red jalapeño chile, seeded, finely chopped
½ green jalapeño chile, seeded, finely chopped
1 package (8 oz) cream cheese, cut in half
Assorted crackers and/or cocktail pumpernickel or rye bread

1 In small bowl, mix preserves and chiles. On small serving plate, place blocks of cream cheese. Spoon preserves mixture over cream cheese.

2 Serve with crackers or cocktail bread.

The remaining chiles can be kept in the refrigerator for several days. Dice a few into taco meat or almost any casserole to add a bit of flavor and heat.

1 Serving: Calories 190 (Calories from Fat 120); Total Fat 13g (Saturated Fat 7g); Cholesterol 30mg; Sodium 190mg; Total Carbohydrate 15g (Dietary Fiber 0g); Protein 3g

Five-Layer Mexican Dip

Prep Time: 20 min ■ Start to Finish: 20 min ■ 20 Servings (¼ cup dip and 6 chips each)

1 can (16 oz) refried beans
2 tablespoons chunky-style salsa
1 ½ cups sour cream
1 cup guacamole
1 cup shredded Cheddar cheese (4 oz)
2 medium green onions, chopped (2 tablespoons)
Tortilla chips

1 In medium bowl, mix refried beans and salsa. On 12- or 13-inch serving plate or pizza pan, spread bean mixture in thin layer.

2 Spread sour cream over bean mixture, leaving about 1-inch border of beans around edge. Spread guacamole over sour cream, leaving border of sour cream showing.

3 Sprinkle cheese over guacamole. Sprinkle onions over cheese. Serve immediately, or cover and refrigerate until serving. Serve with tortilla chips.

1 Serving: Calories 150 (Calories from Fat 90); Total Fat 10g (Saturated Fat 4g); Cholesterol 20mg; Sodium 250mg; Total Carbohydrate 13g (Dietary Fiber 2g); Protein 4g

Guacamole-Cheese Crisps

Prep Time: 25 min ▪ Start to Finish: 25 min ▪ 16 Appetizers

1 cup finely shredded Cheddar-Jack with jalapeño peppers cheese blend (from
    8-oz package)
1 ripe avocado, pitted, peeled and chopped
1 tablespoon lime juice
1 clove garlic, finely chopped
3 tablespoons sour cream
3 tablespoons chunky-style salsa

1 Heat oven to 400°F. Line cookie sheet with parchment paper. For each cheese crisp, spoon 2 teaspoons cheese onto paper-lined cookie sheet; pat into 2-inch round. Bake 6 to 8 minutes or until edges are light golden brown. Immediately remove from cookie sheet to wire rack. Cool 5 minutes or until crisp.

2 In small bowl, place avocado, lime juice and garlic; mash avocado with fork and mix with ingredients. Spoon 1½ teaspoons avocado mixture on each cheese crisp; top with about ½ teaspoon each sour cream and salsa.

You can prepare the crisps up to 4 hours ahead of time. Just store them tightly covered at room temperature, then add the topping just before serving.

1 Appetizer: Calories 50 (Calories from Fat 40); Total Fat 4.5g (Saturated Fat 2g); Cholesterol 10mg; Sodium 55mg; Total Carbohydrate 1g (Dietary Fiber 0g); Protein 2g

Brie Quesadillas with Mango Guacamole

Prep Time: 35 min ▪ Start to Finish: 35 min ▪ 24 Servings

Guacamole

1 medium avocado, pitted, peeled and quartered

½ small jalapeño chile, seeded, finely chopped

1 small clove garlic, finely chopped

2 tablespoons lime juice

¼ cup chopped fresh cilantro

⅛ teaspoon salt

½ medium mango, cut in half lengthwise, seed removed, peeled and diced

Quesadillas

6 flour tortillas (8 inch)

1 round (6 to 7 oz) Brie cheese, cut into ⅛-inch strips (not wedges)

¼ lb thinly sliced cooked ham (from deli)

1 tablespoon vegetable oil

1 In food processor, place all guacamole ingredients except mango. Cover; process with 3 or 4 on/off turns until coarsely chopped. Place in small bowl; stir in mango. Set aside.

2 Top half of each tortilla with cheese and ham. Fold tortilla over and press down. Brush top with oil.

3 Heat 12-inch skillet over medium-high heat. Place 3 quesadillas, oil side down, in skillet. Brush tops with half of remaining oil. Cook 2 to 3 minutes, turning once, until both sides are golden brown and cheese is melted. Repeat with remaining quesadillas and oil. Cut each into 4 wedges. Serve with guacamole.

1 Serving: Calories 80 (Calories from Fat 45); Total Fat 5g (Saturated Fat 2g); Cholesterol 10mg; Sodium 190mg; Total Carbohydrate 7g (Dietary Fiber 0g); Protein 3g

If you prefer, you can mash the guacamole ingredients with a fork instead of using a food processor.

Taco Mozzi Sticks

Prep Time: 40 min ▪ Start to Finish: 1 hr 10 min ▪ 8 Servings (2 cheese sticks and 2 teaspoons sauce each)

3 tablespoons milk
3 tablespoons all-purpose flour
1 package (8 oz) mozzarella string cheese (8 sticks), cut crosswise in half
1 egg
3 cups cheese-flavored tortilla chips, crushed (¾ cup crushed)
1 tablespoon taco seasoning mix (from 1.25-oz package)
¾ cup vegetable oil
⅓ cup taco sauce, warmed

1 Line 15×10×1-inch pan with waxed paper. In shallow bowl, place milk. In another shallow bowl, place flour. Dip each stick of string cheese in milk, then coat with flour.

2 Beat egg into remaining milk mixture with fork. In another shallow bowl, mix crushed chips and taco seasoning mix. Dip coated cheese sticks in egg mixture, then coat with chip mixture. Place in pan. Freeze at least 30 minutes but no longer than 8 hours.

3 In 12-inch skillet, heat oil over medium-high heat until 375°F. Cook frozen cheese sticks in oil 1 to 2 minutes on each side, gently turning once or twice, until light golden brown and cheese is warm. Do not overcook or cheese will melt. Serve immediately with warmed taco sauce.

To keep mess to a minimum, place the tortilla chips in a plastic food-storage bag and crush with a rolling pin.

1 Serving: Calories 210 (Calories from Fat 130); Total Fat 14g (Saturated Fat 5g); Cholesterol 40mg; Sodium 380mg; Total Carbohydrate 11g (Dietary Fiber 0g); Protein 9g

Mini Corn Dogs on a Stick

Prep Time: 30 min ▪ Start to Finish: 45 min ▪ 40 Servings (1 corn dog each)

40 wooden toothpicks
1 package (16 oz) cocktail wieners (about 40 pieces)
1 can (12 oz) refrigerated flaky biscuits (10 biscuits)
1 egg, beaten
1 tablespoon milk
½ cup cornmeal
1 tablespoon sugar
¾ cup ketchup
¾ cup yellow mustard

1 Heat oven to 400°F. Grease cookie sheet with shortening or spray with cooking spray. Insert toothpick into narrow end of each wiener. Separate dough into 10 biscuits; carefully divide each biscuit horizontally into 4 rounds. Wrap sides and top of each wiener with dough round, pinching edges to seal.

2 In pie plate, mix egg and milk. On a plate, mix cornmeal and sugar. Roll each wrapped wiener in egg mixture, then roll lightly in cornmeal mixture. Place seam side down on cookie sheet.

3 Bake 10 to 12 minutes or until tops are light golden brown and bottoms are golden brown. Remove from cookie sheet with spatula. Serve with ketchup and mustard.

Don't worry if the dough doesn't wrap perfectly around the hot dogs; it will come together during baking.

1 Serving: Calories 80 (Calories from Fat 40); Total Fat 4.5g (Saturated Fat 1.5g); Cholesterol 10mg; Sodium 310mg; Total Carbohydrate 7g (Dietary Fiber 0g); Protein 2g

Pesto-Salmon Roulades

Prep Time: 15 min ▪ Start to Finish: 15 min ▪ 28 Roulades

1 package (6 oz) smoked salmon lox
⅓ cup refrigerated basil pesto (from 7-oz container)
½ cup drained roasted red bell peppers (from 7-oz jar), cut into thin strips
28 roasted-garlic bagel chips (from 5.5-oz bag)

1 Cut each salmon piece in half lengthwise so that it is about ¾ inch wide. Spread each with about ½ teaspoon of the pesto; top with roasted bell pepper strip. Carefully roll up.

2 Place each roulade on bagel chip. Serve immediately.

Salmon lox is sliced very thinly, so handle the slices carefully to avoid tearing them.

1 Roulade: Calories 30 (Calories from Fat 20); Total Fat 2g (Saturated Fat 0g); Cholesterol 0mg; Sodium 80mg; Total Carbohydrate 1g (Dietary Fiber 0g); Protein 2g

Mini Crab Points

Prep Time: 15 min ▪ Start to Finish: 15 min ▪ 16 Servings

¼ cup mayonnaise or salad dressing
1 small clove garlic, finely chopped
1 can (6 oz) crabmeat, well drained, flaked
¼ cup finely chopped celery
2 tablespoons diced red bell pepper
2 medium green onions, thinly sliced (2 tablespoons)
¼ teaspoon seafood seasoning (from 6-oz container)
4 slices whole wheat bread, toasted
Chopped fresh parsley

1 In medium bowl, mix mayonnaise and garlic. Stir in crabmeat, celery, bell pepper, onions and seafood seasoning.

2 Top toasted bread with crab mixture. Cut diagonally into quarters. Sprinkle with parsley. Serve immediately.

These garlicky crab appetizers are similar to crab or lobster rolls, sandwiches that are popular across the eastern seaboard.

1 Serving: Calories 50 (Calories from Fat 30); Total Fat 3g (Saturated Fat 0.5g); Cholesterol 10mg; Sodium 100mg; Total Carbohydrate 4g (Dietary Fiber 0g); Protein 3g

Layered Shrimp Spread

Prep Time: 15 min ▪ Start to Finish: 15 min ▪ 16 Servings

1 container (8 oz) pineapple cream cheese spread
½ cup peach or apricot preserves
2 tablespoons cocktail sauce
1 bag (4 oz) frozen cooked salad shrimp, thawed, drained
2 medium green onions, thinly sliced (2 tablespoons)
¼ cup coconut chips
Assorted crackers

1 On 10- to 12-inch serving plate, spread cream cheese to within 1 inch of edge of plate. In small bowl, mix preserves and cocktail sauce. Spread over cream cheese.

2 Top evenly with shrimp. Sprinkle with onions and coconut. Serve with crackers.

Coconut chips are larger than flaked or shredded coconut, so they add more flavor and texture. Look for coconut chips in the baking aisle. You can substitute flaked or shredded coconut, if necessary.

1 Serving: Calories 150 (Calories from Fat 80); Total Fat 8g (Saturated Fat 4g); Cholesterol 25mg; Sodium 240mg; Total Carbohydrate 15g (Dietary Fiber 0g); Protein 4g

Spicy Grilled Shrimp Platter

Prep Time: 20 min ■ Start to Finish: 1 hr 20 min ■ 10 Servings (3 shrimp each)

4 cups water
2 tablespoons kosher (coarse) salt
2 tablespoons sugar
1 tablespoon crushed red pepper
    flakes
3 cloves garlic, sliced
1 teaspoon paprika

30 uncooked deveined peeled shrimp
    (1¼ lb of 26–30 count size), thawed
    if frozen, tail shells removed
⅓ cup cocktail sauce
⅓ cup refrigerated honey mustard dressing
⅓ cup spicy hot peanut sauce (from 7-oz
    bottle)

1 In 2-quart saucepan, heat 1 cup of the water to boiling. Add salt, sugar, red pepper flakes, garlic and paprika; stir to dissolve salt.

2 Remove from heat. Add remaining 3 cups cold water. Place shrimp in large resealable food-storage plastic bag. Pour brine mixture over shrimp. Seal bag, pushing out air. Place bag in dish or plastic container. Refrigerate 1 hour.

3 Heat gas or charcoal grill. Remove shrimp from brine mixture; discard brine. On each of 6 (12-inch) metal skewers, thread shrimp, leaving ¼-inch space between each.

4 Place shrimp on grill. Cover grill; cook over medium heat 5 to 6 minutes, turning once, until shrimp are pink.

5 In 3 separate small bowls, place cocktail sauce, dressing and peanut sauce. Arrange bowls on platter; add shrimp to platter.

To broil shrimp, set oven control to broil. Place shrimp on rack in broiler pan. Broil with tops 6 inches from heat 6 to 8 minutes, turning once, until shrimp are pink.

If using bamboo skewers, be sure to soak them in water at least 30 minutes before using so they won't burn during grilling.

1 Serving: Calories 100 (Calories from Fat 45); Total Fat 5g (Saturated Fat 1g); Cholesterol 80mg; Sodium 440mg; Total Carbohydrate 4g (Dietary Fiber 0g); Protein 10g

Planked Salmon Platter

Prep Time: 50 min ▪ Start to Finish: 1 hr 50 min ▪ 16 Servings

Salmon

1 untreated cedar plank, 12×6 inches

1 salmon fillet, about 1 inch thick (1 lb)

2 tablespoons mayonnaise or salad
   dressing

2 teaspoons Dijon mustard

1 teaspoon grated lemon peel

Accompaniments

½ cup sour cream

1 teaspoon chopped fresh or ½
   teaspoon dried dill weed

1 jar (3.5 oz) small capers, drained

¼ cup spicy brown mustard

2 hard-cooked eggs, finely chopped

1 cup thinly sliced cucumber

32 slices cocktail rye bread

1 Soak cedar plank in water 1 to 2 hours.

2 Heat gas or charcoal grill for indirect-heat cooking as directed by manufacturer. Place salmon, skin side down, on plank. In small bowl, mix mayonnaise, mustard and lemon peel. Brush generously over salmon.

3 Place plank with salmon on grill for indirect cooking. Cover grill; cook over medium heat 25 to 30 minutes or until salmon flakes easily with fork.

4 Remove salmon from plank to platter, using large spatula, or leave salmon on plank and place on large wood cutting board or platter.

5 In small bowl, mix sour cream and dill weed. Place remaining accompaniments except bread in individual small bowls. Place sour cream mixture and remaining accompaniments around salmon. Serve salmon and accompaniments with bread.

To broil salmon, set oven control to broil. Place salmon, skin side down, on rack in broiler pan. (Do not use cedar plank.) Broil with top 6 inches from heat about 15 minutes or until salmon flakes easily with fork.

1 Serving: Calories 120 (Calories from Fat 50); Total Fat 6g (Saturated Fat 2g); Cholesterol 50mg; Sodium 270mg; Total Carbohydrate 8g (Dietary Fiber 0g); Protein 8g

Seafood Salad Tartlets

Prep Time: 15 min ▪ Start to Finish: 15 min ▪ 30 Tartlets

1 can (6.5 oz) lump crabmeat, drained
1 jar (6.5 oz) marinated artichoke hearts, well drained, finely chopped
    (about 1 cup)
¼ cup chives-and-onion cream cheese spread (from 8-oz container)
2 tablespoons mayonnaise or salad dressing
2 tablespoons chopped red onion
½ teaspoon seafood seasoning
2 packages (2.1 oz each) frozen mini fillo dough shells (30 shells)
30 tiny shrimp (from 4-oz can), rinsed, patted dry
Fresh parsley sprigs

1 In medium bowl, mix crabmeat, artichoke hearts, cream cheese, mayonnaise, onion and seafood seasoning.

2 Just before serving, spoon 1 scant tablespoon crabmeat mixture into each fillo dough shell. Garnish each tartlet with shrimp and parsley.

The frozen fillo dough shells thaw quickly, so there's no need to defrost them ahead.

1 Tartlet: Calories 35 (Calories from Fat 15); Total Fat 1.5g (Saturated Fat 0.5g); Cholesterol 10mg; Sodium 80mg; Total Carbohydrate 3g (Dietary Fiber 0g); Protein 2g

Basil-Turkey Mini Focaccia Sandwiches

Prep Time: 20 min ▪ Start to Finish: 1 hr 5 min ▪ 40 Mini Sandwiches

Focaccia
1 can (13.8 oz) refrigerated pizza crust dough
1 tablespoon olive or vegetable oil
½ teaspoon garlic powder
½ teaspoon Italian seasoning
¼ cup shredded Parmesan cheese (1 oz)

Filling
1 container (6.5 oz) garlic-and-herbs spreadable cheese, softened
2 medium plum (Roma) tomatoes, thinly sliced
1 package (1 oz) fresh basil leaves, stems removed
½ lb thinly sliced smoked turkey breast (from deli)

1 Heat oven to 400°F. Grease large cookie sheet with shortening or cooking spray. Unroll pizza crust dough; press into 12×8-inch rectangle on cookie sheet. With end of handle of wooden spoon, press indentations in top, about 1 inch apart. Brush dough with oil. Sprinkle with garlic powder, Italian seasoning and Parmesan cheese.

2 Bake 10 to 13 minutes or until golden brown. Cool 30 minutes; cut in half horizontally.

3 Spread cut side of bottom of focaccia with spreadable cheese. Top with single layer of tomatoes and basil. Layer turkey evenly over basil. Place top of focaccia, cut side down, over turkey; press down. Pierce through all layers with toothpicks, placing them every 1 ½ inches over focaccia. With long serrated knife, cut between toothpicks into squares.

1 Sandwich: Calories 50 (Calories from Fat 25); Total Fat 2.5g (Saturated Fat 1.5g); Cholesterol 10mg; Sodium 160mg; Total Carbohydrate 5g (Dietary Fiber 0g); Protein 2g

Use purchased focaccia bread, if you prefer. Most store-bought focaccia bread is round, so the number of appetizers will vary.

Light Lemon-Dijon Chicken Salad

Prep Time: 20 min ▪ Start to Finish: 20 min ▪ 4 Servings

Lemon-Dijon Dressing
¼ cup reduced-fat mayonnaise or salad dressing
2 tablespoons lemon juice
2 teaspoons Dijon mustard
1 clove garlic, finely chopped

Chicken Salad
4 cups shredded romaine lettuce
2 cups shredded cooked chicken breasts
¼ cup sliced drained oil-packed sun-dried tomatoes
1 hard-cooked egg, chopped
2 medium green onions, sliced (2 tablespoons)
¼ cup shredded Parmesan cheese, if desired

1 In small bowl, mix all dressing ingredients with wire whisk.

2 Arrange lettuce, chicken, tomatoes and egg on individual serving plates. Spoon dressing over top. Sprinkle with onions and cheese.

To easily remove the skin from a garlic clove, press the clove firmly with the broad side of a chef's knife, then slice off the ends. The skin will pop right off.

1 Serving: Calories 210 (Calories from Fat 100); Total Fat 11g (Saturated Fat 2g); Cholesterol 115mg; Sodium 260mg; Total Carbohydrate 6g (Dietary Fiber 2g); Protein 24g

Cashew Curry Shrimp Salad

Prep Time: 15 min ▪ Start to Finish: 2 hrs 15 min ▪ 4 Servings

Curry Dressing

½ cup reduced-fat mayonnaise or salad dressing

2 tablespoons lemon juice

1 tablespoon milk

1 teaspoon curry powder

⅛ teaspoon pepper

Shrimp Salad

1 cup frozen sweet peas

1 package (12 oz) frozen cooked deveined peeled shrimp, thawed, drained, tail
   shells removed

2 medium stalks celery, thinly sliced

1 can (1.75 oz) shoestring potatoes

½ cup cashew halves

1 head Belgian endive

1 In small bowl, mix all dressing ingredients with wire whisk.

2 Cook and drain peas as directed on bag. In medium bowl, place peas, shrimp and celery. Add dressing; toss to coat. Cover; refrigerate at least 2 hours to blend flavors.

3 Just before serving, gently stir shoestring potatoes and cashews into shrimp mixture. Arrange endive leaves around edge of medium serving platter. Spoon shrimp mixture into center of platter.

1 Serving: Calories 390 (Calories from Fat 210); Total Fat 23g (Saturated Fat 4.5g); Cholesterol 175mg; Sodium 470mg; Total Carbohydrate 21g (Dietary Fiber 4g); Protein 24g

Baby Burgers

Prep Time: 30 min ■ Start to Finish: 30 min ■ 16 Appetizer Burgers

1 lb lean (at least 80%) ground beef
2 teaspoons dried minced onion
1 teaspoon parsley flakes
¾ teaspoon seasoned salt
4 slices (1 oz each) American cheese,
    cut into quarters
8 slices white bread, toasted, crusts
    removed, cut into quarters

16 thin slices plum (Roma) tomatoes
    (2 small), if desired
16 thin hamburger-style dill pickle
    slices, if desired
Ketchup, if desired
Mustard, if desired

1 Heat gas or charcoal grill. In medium bowl, mix beef, onion, parsley flakes and seasoned salt. Divide into 16 portions. Shape each portion into a ball and flatten to ½-inch-thick patty, about 1 ½ inches in diameter. On each of 4 (12-inch) metal skewers, thread 4 patties horizontally, leaving space between each.

2 Place patties on grill. Cover grill; cook over medium heat 8 to 10 minutes, turning once, until patties are no longer pink in center (160°F).

3 Top each burger with cheese piece. Place each burger on toast square. Top with tomato slice and another toast square. Place pickle slice on top; spear with toothpick to hold layers together. Serve with ketchup and mustard for dipping.

To broil patties, set oven control to broil. Thread patties on skewers as directed. Place patties on rack in broiler pan. Broil with tops 6 inches from heat 8 to 10 minutes, turning once, until no longer pink in center.

These cute little burgers can be mixed and shaped ahead of time. Just cover and refrigerate them until you are ready to grill.

1 Burger: Calories 110 (Calories from Fat 50); Total Fat 6g (Saturated Fat 2.5g); Cholesterol 25mg; Sodium 270mg; Total Carbohydrate 7g (Dietary Fiber 0g); Protein 8g

Mini Barbecue Pizza Wedges

Prep Time: 10 min ■ Start to Finish: 20 min ■ 12 Wedges (2 pizzas)

1 package (10 oz) prebaked Italian pizza crusts (6 inch)
¼ cup barbecue sauce
½ cup chopped cooked chicken
1 tablespoon chopped red onion
1 cup finely shredded mozzarella cheese (4 oz)
6 cherry tomatoes, thinly sliced (⅛ cup)

1 Heat gas or charcoal grill for indirect-heat cooking as directed by manufacturer. Top pizza crusts with remaining ingredients in order given.

2 Place pizzas on grill for indirect cooking. Cover grill; cook over medium heat 8 to 10 minutes, rotating pizzas occasionally, until cheese is melted and pizzas are hot. Cut each into 6 wedges.

1 Wedge: Calories 110 (Calories from Fat 35); Total Fat 4g (Saturated Fat 2g); Cholesterol 15mg; Sodium 230mg; Total Carbohydrate 13g (Dietary Fiber 0g); Protein 7g

Key Lime Bars

Prep Time: 15 min ▪ Start to Finish: 4 hrs 20 min ▪ 36 Bars

1½ cups graham cracker crumbs (24 squares)
⅓ cup butter or margarine, melted
3 tablespoons sugar
1 package (8 oz) cream cheese, softened
1 can (14 oz) sweetened condensed milk
1 tablespoon grated lime peel
¼ cup Key lime juice or regular lime juice
Additional lime peel, if desired

1 Heat oven to 350°F. Grease bottom and sides of 9-inch square pan with shortening or cooking spray.

2 In small bowl, mix cracker crumbs, butter and sugar thoroughly with fork. Press evenly in bottom of pan. Refrigerate while preparing cream cheese mixture.

3 In small bowl, beat cream cheese with electric mixer on medium speed until light and fluffy. Gradually beat in milk until smooth. Beat in lime peel and lime juice. Spread over layer in pan.

4 Bake about 35 minutes or until center is set. Cool 30 minutes. Cover loosely; refrigerate at least 3 hours until chilled. For bars, cut into 6 rows by 6 rows. Garnish with additional lime peel. Store covered in refrigerator.

1 Bar: Calories 90 (Calories from Fat 45); Total Fat 5g (Saturated Fat 3g); Cholesterol 15mg; Sodium 65mg; Total Carbohydrate 10g (Dietary Fiber 0g); Protein 2g

S'Mores Chocolate Chip Ice-Cream Sandwiches

Prep Time: 15 min ▪ Start to Finish: 3 hr 15 min ▪ 8 Sandwiches

About 3 tablespoons marshmallow creme
16 fudge-covered graham cookies (1½ × 1¾ inches each)
½ cup chocolate chip ice cream

1 Spoon about 1 teaspoon marshmallow creme on 1 cookie. Top with about ½ tablespoon ice cream. Top with another cookie, pressing gently. Place in shallow pan; immediately place in freezer. Repeat for remaining sandwiches, placing each in freezer as made.

2 Freeze at least 3 hours until firm. Wrap individually in plastic wrap or waxed paper.

These frozen treats make a fun summer dessert. To serve a crowd, make a double or triple batch.

1 Sandwich: Calories 100 (Calories from Fat 40); Total Fat 4.5g (Saturated Fat 3.5g); Cholesterol 0mg; Sodium 50mg; Total Carbohydrate 13g (Dietary Fiber 0g); Protein 0g

Tiramisu Cheesecake Dessert

Prep Time: 20 min ▪ Start to Finish: 2 hrs 25 min ▪ 24 Servings

2 cups crushed vanilla wafer cookies (about 40 cookies)
⅛ cup butter or margarine, melted
2 tablespoons whipping cream
2 tablespoons instant espresso coffee granules
3 packages (8 oz each) cream cheese, softened
¾ cup sugar
3 eggs
1 oz bittersweet baking chocolate, grated
Chocolate-covered espresso beans, if desired

1 Heat oven to 350°F. Line 13×9-inch pan with foil; spray with cooking spray. In small bowl, mix crushed cookies and melted butter with fork. Press mixture in bottom of pan. Refrigerate while continuing with recipe.

2 In small bowl, mix whipping cream and coffee granules with fork until coffee is dissolved; set aside.

3 In large bowl, beat cream cheese with electric mixer on medium speed 2 to 3 minutes, scraping bowl occasionally, until smooth and creamy. On low speed, beat in sugar, eggs and coffee mixture, about 30 seconds. Beat on medium speed about 2 minutes longer or until ingredients are well blended. Using rubber spatula, spread cream cheese filling over crust. Bake 25 to 35 minutes or until center is set.

4 Cool 30 minutes. Sprinkle with grated chocolate or top with espresso beans. Refrigerate about 1 hour or until completely chilled. For servings, cut into 6 rows by 4 rows, using sharp knife dipped in water.

1 Serving: Calories 200 (Calories from Fat 140); Total Fat 15g (Saturated Fat 9g); Cholesterol 65mg; Sodium 140mg; Total Carbohydrate 12g (Dietary Fiber 0g); Protein 4g

In a hurry?

Sift unsweetened baking cocoa over the tiramisu bars instead of grating chocolate.

Sweet and Salty Snack Mix

Ranch Pretzel Nibblers

Chilly Garden Pizza

Caesar Vegetable Dip

Shrimp Deviled Eggs

Tiny Meat and Cheese Bites

Chicken Salad Roll-Ups

Dilly Ham and Cheese Sandwiches

Caesar Focaccia Subs

Curried Egg Salad Sandwiches

Italian Country Sandwich

Italian Chicken Salad

Deli Beef and Bean Tossed Salad

Beef Fajita Pitas

Fresh Fruit Medley

Angel Berry Summer Pudding

Malted Milk Ball Cupcakes

Nutty Chocolate Chip Picnic Cake

Make sure leftovers are refrigerated in a cold cooler within 2 hours of cooking or removal from the refrigerator. If not, throw them out.

2

picnic portables

Sweet and Salty Snack Mix

Prep Time: 10 min　　Start to Finish: 10 min　　20 Servings (¼ cup each)

1 package (8 oz) yogurt-covered raisins (1 cup)
2 cups roasted salted soy nuts
1 cup candy-coated peanut butter and chocolate candies
1 cup teddy bear-shaped chocolate graham snacks

1 Mix all ingredients in large bowl or resealable plastic food-storage bag.

You can make this crunchy snack up to one month ahead of time. Store it in small resealable plastic food-storage bags or in an airtight container.

1 Serving: Calories 160 (Calories from Fat 60); Total Fat 7g (Saturated Fat 3g); Cholesterol 0mg; Sodium 50mg; Total Carbohydrate 19g (Dietary Fiber 2g); Protein 5g

Ranch Pretzel Nibblers

Prep Time: 5 min » Start to Finish: 45 min » 16 Servings (½ cup each)

1 package (14 oz) sourdough pretzel nuggets (about 5 cups)
3 cups checkerboard pretzels or mini-pretzel twists
⅓ cup vegetable oil
1 package (1 oz) ranch dressing mix

1 Heat oven to 325°F. In ungreased 15×10×1-inch pan, place pretzels. In small bowl, mix oil and dressing mix. Pour over pretzels; stir to coat.

2 Bake 10 minutes, stirring once. Cool completely, about 30 minutes. Store tightly covered.

1 Serving: Calories 170 (Calories from Fat 50); Total Fat 6g (Saturated Fat 1g); Cholesterol 0mg; Sodium 680mg; Total Carbohydrate 27g (Dietary Fiber 1g); Protein 3g

Chilly Garden Pizza

Prep Time: 15 min   Start to Finish: 15 min   6 Servings

1 container (6.5 oz) 50%-less-fat garlic-and-herbs spreadable cheese
1 package (10 oz) prebaked thin Italian pizza crust (12 inch)
¾ cup chopped fresh spinach
½ cup diced seeded cucumber
1 large tomato, chopped (1 cup)
½ cup sliced fresh mushrooms
1 tablespoon chopped fresh basil leaves
¼ teaspoon salt
⅛ teaspoon pepper
¾ cup shredded carrot

1 Spread cheese over pizza crust.

2 Top with spinach, cucumber, tomato, mushrooms and basil. Sprinkle with salt and pepper. Top with carrot.

Enjoy the bounty of your garden and get your vitamins and minerals, too. Spinach is loaded with vitamin A, and tomatoes are a vitamin C powerhouse.

1 Serving: Calories 220 (Calories from Fat 80); Total Fat 8g (Saturated Fat 4g); Cholesterol 15mg; Sodium 420mg; Total Carbohydrate 29g (Dietary Fiber 2g); Protein 7g

Caesar Vegetable Dip

Prep Time: 5 min   Start to Finish: 35 min   10 Servings

½ cup sour cream
¼ cup mayonnaise or salad dressing
¼ cup creamy Caesar dressing
¼ cup shredded Parmesan cheese
1 leaf romaine lettuce
3 tablespoons slightly crushed croutons (about 6)
Assorted raw vegetables

1 In small bowl, mix sour cream, mayonnaise and Caesar dressing until smooth. Stir in cheese. Cover and refrigerate 30 minutes to blend flavors.

2 Line serving bowl with lettuce leaf. Spoon dip into bowl. Sprinkle with crushed croutons. Serve with vegetables.

Keep this dip chilled while serving, place the serving bowl on a bed of ice.

1 Serving: Calories 70 (Calories from Fat 40); Total Fat 4.5g (Saturated Fat 2g); Cholesterol 10mg; Sodium 180mg; Total Carbohydrate 5g (Dietary Fiber 2g); Protein 3g

Shrimp Deviled Eggs

Prep Time: 40 min ▌ Start to Finish: 50 min ▌ 12 Appetizers

6 eggs
2 medium green onions, thinly sliced (2 tablespoons)
¼ cup reduced-fat mayonnaise or salad dressing
1 tablespoon white vinegar
¼ teaspoon salt
¼ teaspoon red pepper sauce
½ cup coarsely chopped cooked salad shrimp, thawed if frozen
1 tablespoon cocktail sauce

1 Place eggs in single layer in 2-quart saucepan; add enough cold water so it is at least 1 inch above eggs. Heat to boiling; remove from heat. Cover and let stand 18 minutes. Drain; rinse with cold water. Let stand in ice water 10 minutes.

2 Peel eggs; cut in half lengthwise. Slip out yolks; place in medium bowl. Mash yolks with fork until smooth. Reserve 1 teaspoon green part of onions for garnish. Stir mayonnaise, vinegar, salt, pepper sauce and remaining green onions into mashed yolks. Fold in shrimp.

3 Fill egg whites with yolk mixture, heaping it lightly. Just before serving, top with cocktail sauce and reserved green onions.

To keep your eggs from tipping over when you serve them, cut a very thin slice from the rounded bottom of each egg half. This will make the eggs more stable. If transporting these deviled eggs, prepare ahead and refrigerate 2 hours or until thoroughly chilled. Then, place in an insulated cooler with plenty of ice packs.

1 Appetizer: Calories 80 (Calories from Fat 60); Total Fat 6g (Saturated Fat 1.5g); Cholesterol 130mg; Sodium 150mg; Total Carbohydrate 1g (Dietary Fiber 0g); Protein 5g

Tiny Meat and Cheese Bites

Prep Time: 40 min   Start to Finish: 40 min   40 Appetizers

1 cup pickled vegetable mix (from 16-oz jar), drained
40 cubes (½ inch) hard salami (about ½ lb)
40 cubes (½ inch) Swiss cheese (about ¼ lb)

1 Cut larger pieces of vegetable mix into ½-inch pieces.

2 Alternate pieces of salami, vegetables and cheese on toothpicks.

1 Appetizer: Calories 35 (Calories from Fat 25); Total Fat 2.5g (Saturated Fat 1g); Cholesterol 5mg; Sodium 115mg; Total Carbohydrate 0g (Dietary Fiber 0g); Protein 2g

Chicken Salad Roll-Ups

Prep Time: 35 min   Start to Finish: 1 hr 35 min   24 Appetizers

2 cups chopped cooked chicken
3 medium green onions, chopped (3 tablespoons)
¼ cup chopped walnuts
½ cup creamy poppy seed dressing
½ cup cream cheese spread (from 8-oz container)
2 flour tortillas (10 inch)
6 leaves Bibb lettuce
½ cup finely chopped strawberries

1 In food processor bowl, mix chicken, onions and walnuts. Cover and process by using quick on-and-off motions until finely chopped. Add ½ cup of the poppy seed dressing; process only until mixed. In small bowl, mix remaining dressing and the cream cheese with spoon until smooth.

2 Spread cream cheese mixture evenly over entire surface of tortillas. Remove white rib from lettuce leaves. Press lettuce into cream cheese, tearing to fit and leaving top 2 inches of tortillas uncovered. Spread chicken mixture over lettuce. Sprinkle strawberries over chicken.

3 Firmly roll up tortillas, beginning at bottom. Wrap each roll in plastic wrap. Refrigerate at least 1 hour. Trim ends of each roll. Cut rolls into ½- to ¾-inch slices.

If transporting this appetizer, place the slices in a covered container in an insulated cooler with plenty of ice packs to keep them cold until ready to serve.

1 Appetizer: Calories 70 (Calories from Fat 35); Total Fat 4g (Saturated Fat 1.5g); Cholesterol 20mg; Sodium 50mg; Total Carbohydrate 5g (Dietary Fiber 0g); Protein 4g

Dilly Ham and Cheese Sandwiches

Prep Time: 45 min ░ Start to Finish: 45 min ░ 32 Appetizers

1 cup garlic-and-herbs spreadable cheese (from 6.5-oz container)
32 slices cocktail pumpernickel bread
½ lb shaved or very thinly sliced baked ham (from deli)
1 seedless cucumber, very thinly sliced
Fresh dill weed, if desired

1 Spread about 1½ teaspoons cheese on each bread slice. Top with ham, folded to fit, and 2 cucumber slices.

2 Garnish with tiny sprigs of dill.

Make these sandwiches a day ahead, then store them in a single layer in a totable container. Keep them in your fridge until you're ready to go.

1 Appetizer: Calories 50 (Calories from Fat 25); Total Fat 2.5g (Saturated Fat 1.5g); Cholesterol 10mg; Sodium 150mg; Total Carbohydrate 4g (Dietary Fiber 0g); Protein 3g

Caesar Focaccia Subs

Prep Time: 25 min   Start to Finish: 25 min   24 Servings

3 round Italian focaccia breads (about 10 inches in diameter)
1 cup Caesar dressing
12 to 20 leaves romaine lettuce
12 oz thinly sliced smoked turkey
12 oz thinly sliced salami
12 oz sliced smoked provolone cheese

1 Cut each bread in half horizontally. Drizzle dressing evenly over cut sides of bottom and top halves of bread.

2 Layer lettuce, turkey, salami and cheese on bottom halves. Top with top halves. Secure loaves with toothpicks or small skewers. Cut each loaf into 8 wedges.

For a flavor boost, try preparing subs with specialty focaccia bread, such as sun-dried tomato or spinach-Parmesan.

1 Serving: Calories 310 (Calories from Fat 160); Total Fat 18g (Saturated Fat 5g); Cholesterol 30mg; Sodium 810mg; Total Carbohydrate 24g (Dietary Fiber 1g); Protein 13g

Curried Egg Salad Sandwiches

Prep Time: 15 min » Start to Finish: 15 min » 2 Sandwiches

3 hard-cooked eggs, chopped
¼ cup fat-free mayonnaise or salad dressing
¼ teaspoon salt
¼ teaspoon curry powder
¼ cup shredded carrot
2 tablespoons finely chopped onion
2 tablespoons coarsely chopped cashews
4 slices whole-grain bread

1 In small bowl, stir together all ingredients except bread.

2 Spread egg mixture on 2 slices bread. Top with remaining bread.

Prepare these perfectly portable sandwiches in advance. Make the egg salad the night before, and assemble sandwiches in the morning. Add an ice pack to your lunch box or picnic basket, and you're ready to go.

1 Sandwich: Calories 340 (Calories from Fat 140); Total Fat 15g (Saturated Fat 4g); Cholesterol 320mg; Sodium 960mg; Total Carbohydrate 36g (Dietary Fiber 5g); Protein 17g

Italian Country Sandwich

Prep Time: 10 min   Start to Finish: 10 min   4 Servings

    1 uncut loaf (1 lb) Italian peasant-style rustic bread or ciabatta bread
    ⅓ cup rosemary-flavored or plain olive oil
    ¼ lb hard salami, thinly sliced
    ¼ lb sliced provolone cheese
    ¼ lb thinly sliced prosciutto
    1 small red onion, thinly sliced

1 Cut bread loaf in half horizontally. Drizzle oil over cut sides of bread.

2 Layer salami, cheese, prosciutto and onion on bottom of bread; add top of bread. Cut loaf into 4 pieces.

Make your own rosemary olive oil: In a small saucepan, warm 1 cup olive oil with 1 or 2 sprigs of washed and dried fresh rosemary for 8 to 10 minutes. Cool; discard rosemary. Pour oil into a jar with a tight-fitting lid. Store in refrigerator up to 2 weeks.

1 Serving: Calories 740 (Calories from Fat 380); Total Fat 42g (Saturated Fat 13g); Cholesterol 60mg; Sodium 1860mg; Total Carbohydrate 60g (Dietary Fiber 3g); Protein 30g

Italian Chicken Salad

Prep Time: 10 min   Start to Finish: 10 min   24 Servings (¾ cup each)

4 cups cut-up cooked chicken
2 bags (10 oz each) ready-to-eat Italian-blend salad greens
2 cans (14 oz each) artichoke hearts, drained, chopped
2 cans (4.25 oz each) chopped ripe olives
½ cup zesty Italian dressing

1 In very large (9-quart) bowl, mix all ingredients except dressing.

2 Toss salad with dressing until coated.

Keep salad cold during transporting by placing the covered bowl in an insulated cooler with plenty of ice packs. Place on serving table just before serving.

1 Serving: Calories 100 (Calories from Fat 45); Total Fat 5g (Saturated Fat 1g); Cholesterol 20mg; Sodium 230mg; Total Carbohydrate 5g (Dietary Fiber 2g); Protein 8g

Deli Beef and Bean Tossed Salad

Prep Time: 10 min   Start to Finish: 10 min   6 Servings

1 bag (10 oz) mixed salad greens
1 can (15 oz) three-bean salad, chilled, or 1 pint (2 cups) three-bean salad (from deli)
¼ lb cooked roast beef (from deli), cut into julienne strips (¾ cup)
1 cup shredded Cheddar or Swiss cheese (4 oz)
12 cherry tomatoes, cut in half

1 In large bowl, toss all ingredients.

1 Serving: Calories 170 (Calories from Fat 80): Total Fat 9g (Saturated Fat 5g): Cholesterol 30mg: Sodium 420mg: Total Carbohydrate 12g (Dietary Fiber 3g): Protein 11g

Beef Fajita Pitas

Prep Time: 10 min   Start to Finish: 10 min   4 Servings

¼ cup chunky-style salsa
2 pita breads (6 inch), cut in half to form pockets
¾ lb thinly sliced cooked roast beef (from deli)
1 small red bell pepper, cut into ¼-inch strips
4 slices (1 oz each) Monterey Jack cheese

1 Spoon salsa into pita bread halves.

2 Fill pita breads with beef, bell pepper and cheese.

For a more authentic Mexican flavor, sprinkle the pitas with chopped fresh cilantro.

1 Serving: Calories 340 (Calories from Fat 120); Total Fat 13g (Saturated Fat 7g); Cholesterol 95mg; Sodium 440mg; Total Carbohydrate 19g (Dietary Fiber 1g); Protein 37g

Fresh Fruit Medley

Prep Time: 20 min · Start to Finish: 20 min · 12 Servings

Honey-Poppy Seed Dressing
¼ cup vegetable oil
3 tablespoons honey
2 tablespoons lemon juice
1½ teaspoons poppy seed

Fruits
2 nectarines or apricots, sliced
1 orange, peeled, sliced
1 medium pineapple, peeled, cored and cut into 1-inch pieces
1 small bunch seedless grapes, each cut in half (2 cups)

1 In tightly covered container, shake all dressing ingredients. Shake again before pouring over fruits.

2 In large bowl, toss fruits and dressing. Cover and refrigerate until ready to serve.

Use a mixture of red and green grapes to add color to the fruit medley.

1 Serving: Calories 110 (Calories from Fat 45); Total Fat 5g (Saturated Fat 0.5g); Cholesterol 0mg; Sodium 0mg; Total Carbohydrate 16g (Dietary Fiber 1g); Protein 0g

Angel Berry Summer Pudding

Prep Time: 25 min   Start to Finish: 4 hrs 25 min   12 Servings

2 boxes (4-serving size each) vanilla instant pudding and pie filling mix
4 cups milk
¾ teaspoon rum extract
1 round angel food cake (10 inch), torn into bite-size pieces
4 cups sliced fresh strawberries
2 cups fresh raspberries
Frozen (thawed) whipped topping, if desired

1 Make pudding mixes as directed on package for pudding, using 4 cups milk and adding rum extract.

2 In 13×9-inch glass baking dish, spoon ⅓ of the pudding. Layer with half of the cake pieces and half of the berries. Repeat layers, ending with remaining pudding.

3 Cover and refrigerate at least 4 hours. Garnish each serving with a dollop of whipped topping.

This recipe is perfect to tote to a casual picnic. Place the covered container in an insulated cooler with plenty of ice packs to keep it cold until serving time.

1 Serving: Calories 260 (Calories from Fat 20); Total Fat 2g (Saturated Fat 1g); Cholesterol 5mg; Sodium 650mg; Total Carbohydrate 57g (Dietary Fiber 3g); Protein 7g

Malted Milk Ball Cupcakes

Prep Time: 20 min   Start to Finish: 1 hr 25 min   24 Cupcakes

Cupcakes

1 box yellow cake mix

1 cup malted milk balls, coarsely crushed

¼ cup natural-flavor malted milk powder

1¼ cups water

⅓ cup vegetable oil

3 eggs

Frosting and Garnish

¼ cup butter or margarine, softened

2 cups powdered sugar

2 tablespoons natural-flavor malted milk powder

1 tablespoon unsweetened baking cocoa

2 tablespoons milk

1⅔ cups malted milk balls, coarsely crushed

1 Heat oven to 350°F. Place paper baking cup in each of 24 regular-size muffin cups. In large bowl, mix cake mix, 1 cup malted milk balls and ¼ cup malted milk powder. Add water, oil and eggs. Beat with electric mixer on low speed 2 minutes. Divide batter evenly among muffin cups.

2 Bake 18 to 23 minutes or until toothpick inserted in center comes out clean. Cool 10 minutes; remove from pan to wire rack. Cool completely, about 30 minutes.

3 In medium bowl, beat all frosting ingredients except malted milk balls on medium speed until smooth. Frost cupcakes. Sprinkle with 1⅔ cups malted milk balls.

1 Cupcake: Calories 240 (Calories from Fat 90); Total Fat 10g (Saturated Fat 4.5g); Cholesterol 30mg; Sodium 190mg; Total Carbohydrate 37g (Dietary Fiber 0g); Protein 2g

Nutty Chocolate Chip Picnic Cake

Prep Time: 15 min Start to Finish: 1 hr 50 min 15 Servings

½ cup miniature semisweet chocolate chips
⅓ cup packed brown sugar
⅓ cup chopped pecans
1 box devil's food cake mix
Water, oil and eggs called for on cake mix box

1 Heat oven to 350°F. Lightly grease bottom only of 13×9-inch pan with shortening or cooking spray.

2 In small bowl, mix chocolate chips, brown sugar and pecans; set aside. Make cake mix as directed on box, using water, oil and eggs. Pour into pan. Sprinkle with chocolate chip mixture.

3 Bake 30 to 35 minutes or until toothpick inserted in center comes out clean. Cool completely, about 1 hour. Store tightly covered.

For an extra dose of decadence, drizzle the cake with caramel or hot fudge topping. Or decorate with your favorite frosting.

1 Serving: Calories 290 (Calories from Fat 130); Total Fat 14g (Saturated Fat 3.5g); Cholesterol 40mg; Sodium 280mg; Total Carbohydrate 37g (Dietary Fiber 2g); Protein 3g

Italian Sausage Burgers

Backyard Beer Burgers

Veggie Burger and Grilled Pepper Sandwiches

Summertime Mushroom-Tomato Kabobs

Greek Pork Kabobs

Buffalo Chicken Kabobs

Jerk Shrimp Kabobs

Summer Herb Steaks

Grilled Jerk Flank Steak

Chipotle Salsa Ribs

Apple-Maple Brined Pork Tenderloin

Fiery Pork Tenderloin with Pineapple Salsa

Hoisin-Glazed Pork Chops

Southwestern Pork Chops

Chicken with Oregano-Peach Sauce

Three-Herb Chicken

Lemon Chicken with Grilled Fennel and Onions

Ginger-Lime Tuna Steaks

Dill Salmon

Grilled Salmon with Fresh Lime Cream

3

great
for the
grill

Italian Sausage Burgers

Prep Time: 10 min ▪ Start to Finish: 25 min ▪ 6 Sandwiches

1 lb lean ground beef
½ lb bulk mild or hot Italian sausage
2 tablespoons Italian-style bread crumbs
6 slices (¾ oz each) mozzarella cheese
12 slices Italian bread, ½ inch thick
½ cup sun-dried tomato mayonnaise
1 cup shredded lettuce
1 medium tomato, thinly sliced

1 Heat coals or gas grill for direct heat. In large bowl, mix beef, sausage and bread crumbs. Shape mixture into 6 patties, about ½ inch thick and 3½ inches in diameter.

2 Cover and grill patties 4 to 6 inches from medium heat 12 to 15 minutes, turning once, until meat thermometer inserted in center reads 160°F. Top patties with cheese. Cover and grill about 1 minute longer or until cheese is melted. Add bread slices to side of grill for last 2 to 3 minutes of grilling, turning once, until lightly toasted.

3 Spread toasted bread with mayonnaise; top 6 bread slices with lettuce, tomato and patties. Top with remaining bread slices.

You can make your own sun-dried tomato mayonnaise by combining ⅓ cup mayonnaise with about 2 tablespoons chopped sun-dried tomatoes. Plain mayonnaise works fine here, too.

1 Sandwich: Calories 490 (Calories from Fat 280); Total Fat 31g (Saturated Fat 10g); Cholesterol 85mg; Sodium 750mg; Total Carbohydrate 25g (Dietary Fiber 2g); Protein 29g

Backyard Beer Burgers

Prep Time: 10 min ▪ Start to Finish: 25 min ▪ 6 Sandwiches

1½ lb ground beef
1 small onion, finely chopped (¼ cup)
¼ cup regular or nonalcoholic beer
1 tablespoon Worcestershire sauce
1 teaspoon salt
¼ teaspoon pepper
2 cloves garlic, finely chopped
6 rye or whole wheat hamburger buns, split
Ketchup, if desired
Pickle planks, if desired

1 Heat coals or gas grill for direct heat. Mix all ingredients except buns, ketchup and pickles. Shape mixture into 6 patties, about ¾ inch thick.

2 Grill patties uncovered about 4 inches from medium heat 10 to 15 minutes, turning once, until no longer pink in center and juice is clear. Add buns, cut sides down, for last 4 minutes of grilling or until toasted.

3 Top burgers with ketchup and pickle planks; serve on buns.

Don't be tempted to press down on the hamburgers with a spatula while they're cooking, or you'll squeeze out the flavorful juices! Using a meat thermometer will ensure that you cook grilled foods to the correct temperature before serving. Ground beef patties should reach 160°F to be thoroughly cooked.

1 Sandwich: Calories 320 (Calories from Fat 130); Total Fat 14g (Saturated Fat 5g); Cholesterol 70mg; Sodium 620mg; Total Carbohydrate 24g (Dietary Fiber 2g); Protein 24g

Veggie Burger and Grilled Pepper Sandwiches

Prep Time: 10 min ▪ Start to Finish: 25 min ▪ 4 Sandwiches

4 frozen soy-protein burgers
½ teaspoon salt
4 slices (¾ oz each) mozzarella cheese
4 whole-grain sandwich buns, split
¼ cup roasted-garlic mayonnaise
1 cup roasted bell peppers
1 medium tomato, sliced

1 Heat coals or gas grill for direct heat. Sprinkle burgers with salt.

2 Cover and grill burgers 4 to 6 inches from medium heat 8 to 10 minutes, turning once or twice, until thoroughly heated. Top each burger with cheese. Cover and grill about 1 minute or just until cheese is melted.

3 Spread cut sides of buns with garlic mayonnaise. Thinly slice bell peppers. Layer tomato, burger and bell peppers on each bun.

1 Sandwich: Calories 450 (Calories from Fat 210); Total Fat 24g (Saturated Fat 6g); Cholesterol 20mg; Sodium 1190mg; Total Carbohydrate 38g (Dietary Fiber 4g); Protein 21g

Summertime Mushroom-Tomato Kabobs

Prep Time: 15 min ▪ Start to Finish: 25 min ▪ 4 Kabobs

4 fresh portabella mushroom caps (about 3 oz each)
6 red cherry or miniature plum (Roma) tomatoes
6 yellow cherry tomatoes
6 medium green onions, cut into 2-inch pieces
¼ cup red wine vinaigrette or Greek vinaigrette dressing

1 Heat coals or gas grill for direct heat. Scrape underside of mushroom caps, using small spoon, to remove dark gills and stems. Cut each cap into 6 pieces.

2 Thread mushroom pieces, red and yellow tomatoes and onion pieces alternately on each of four 14- to 15-inch metal skewers.

3 Cover and grill kabobs 4 to 6 inches from medium heat 8 to 10 minutes, turning and brushing with vinaigrette occasionally, until mushrooms are tender. Place on serving plate. Drizzle with any remaining dressing.

When threading the veggies on the skewers, leave about a ¼-inch space between the pieces so they cook evenly.

1 Kabob: Calories 110 (Calories from Fat 60); Total Fat 7g (Saturated Fat 0.5g); Cholesterol 0mg; Sodium 140mg; Total Carbohydrate 9g (Dietary Fiber 2g); Protein 4g

Greek Pork Kabobs

Prep Time: 15 min ■ Start to Finish: 30 min ■ 4 Servings

½ cup Greek vinaigrette dressing
1 tablespoon chopped fresh parsley
1 lb boneless pork loin, cut into 1-inch cubes
1 red onion, cut into 8 wedges
1 large red or green bell pepper, cut into 8 pieces

1 Heat coals or gas grill for direct heat. In large bowl, mix dressing and parsley; stir in pork, onion and bell pepper. Thread pork, onion and bell pepper alternately on each of four 15-inch metal skewers, leaving ¼-inch space between each piece. Reserve remaining vinaigrette in bowl.

2 Cover and grill kabobs 4 to 6 inches from medium heat 10 to 15 minutes, turning kabobs 2 or 3 times and brushing with vinaigrette during last 5 minutes of grilling, until pork is no longer pink in center. Discard any remaining vinaigrette.

Skewers with flat sides (rather than round) hold ingredients more securely and keep pieces in place when you turn the kabobs.

1 Serving: Calories 300 (Calories from Fat 150); Total Fat 17g (Saturated Fat 3.5g); Cholesterol 75mg; Sodium 280mg; Total Carbohydrate 9g (Dietary Fiber 1g); Protein 26g

Buffalo Chicken Kabobs

Prep Time: 20 min ▪ Start to Finish: 40 min ▪ 4 Servings

1 lb boneless, skinless chicken breasts, cut into 24 cubes
24 (about 1 ½ cups) refrigerated new potato wedges (from 1-lb 4-oz bag)
24 pieces (about 1 inch) celery
2 tablespoons olive or vegetable oil
1 teaspoon red pepper sauce
½ teaspoon black and red pepper blend
½ teaspoon seasoned salt
6 cups torn romaine lettuce
½ cup shredded carrot
½ cup blue cheese dressing

1 Heat coals or gas grill for direct heat. Thread chicken, potatoes and celery alternately on each of eight 8- to 10-inch metal skewers, leaving ¼-inch space between each piece. Mix oil and pepper sauce; brush over chicken and vegetables. Sprinkle with pepper blend and seasoned salt.

2 Cover and grill kabobs 4 to 6 inches from medium heat 15 to 20 minutes, turning occasionally, until chicken is no longer pink in center and potatoes are tender.

3 Arrange romaine and carrot on 4 individual serving plates. Top each with 2 kabobs. Serve with dressing.

This is a super one-dish entrée salad, so all you need to add is warm garlic bread. Wrap the bread in foil, then heat it on the grill for 5 to 10 minutes.

1 Serving: Calories 430 (Calories from Fat 210); Total Fat 24g (Saturated Fat 3g); Cholesterol 75mg; Sodium 590mg; Total Carbohydrate 26g (Dietary Fiber 5g); Protein 29g

Jerk Shrimp Kabobs

Prep Time: 20 min ▪ Start to Finish: 35 min ▪ 4 Kabobs

2 tablespoons olive or vegetable oil
2 teaspoons Caribbean jerk seasoning (dry)
¼ teaspoon salt
1 ½ lb uncooked peeled deveined large shrimp (21 to 30) or extra-large shrimp
    (16 to 20), thawed if frozen, tail shells removed
16 chunks (about 1 inch) fresh pineapple
1 red bell pepper, cut into 16 pieces
¼ cup pineapple preserves
2 tablespoons lime juice

1 Heat coals or gas grill for direct heat. In large bowl, mix oil, jerk seasoning and salt. Add shrimp, pineapple and bell pepper; toss to coat. Thread shrimp, pineapple and bell pepper alternately on each of four 12- to 15-inch metal skewers, leaving ¼-inch space between each piece. Mix preserves and lime juice; set aside.

2 Cover and grill kabobs 4 to 6 inches from medium heat 4 minutes. Turn kabobs; brush with preserves mixture. Cover and grill 4 to 8 minutes longer or until shrimp are pink and firm.

Although the ingredients in Caribbean jerk seasoning vary, the most common combination is a blend of chiles, thyme, sweet spices, garlic and onions. Traditionally, jerk seasoning is used to flavor grilled meats.

1 Kabob: Calories 250 (Calories from Fat 60); Total Fat 7g (Saturated Fat 1g); Cholesterol 240mg; Sodium 430mg; Total Carbohydrate 22g (Dietary Fiber 2g); Protein 27g

Summer Herb Steaks

Prep Time: 25 min ▪ Start to Finish: 35 min ▪ 4 Servings

¼ cup Dijon mustard
2 teaspoons chopped fresh or ½ teaspoon dried rosemary leaves, crumbled
1 teaspoon coarsely ground pepper
2 cloves garlic, finely chopped
4 beef top loin steaks, about 1 inch thick (about 1 lb)

1 Heat coals or gas grill for direct heat. In small bowl, mix mustard, rosemary, pepper and garlic; spread on both sides of beef.

2 Cover and grill beef over medium heat 1 minute on each side to seal in juices. Cover and grill 8 to 9 minutes longer for medium doneness, turning once.

Top loin is one of the lower-fat cuts of beef. Other "skinny" cuts include eye round, top round, round tip, tenderloin and sirloin.

1 Serving: Calories 190 (Calories from Fat 80); Total Fat 9g (Saturated Fat 3g); Cholesterol 65mg; Sodium 430mg; Total Carbohydrate 2g (Dietary Fiber 0g); Protein 25g

Grilled Jerk Flank Steak

Prep Time: 15 min ▪ Start to Finish: 4 hrs 30 min ▪ 6 Servings

3 tablespoons teriyaki marinade and sauce (from 10-oz bottle)
1 tablespoon canola or vegetable oil
2 teaspoons pumpkin pie spice
½ teaspoon dried thyme leaves
½ teaspoon salt
¼ teaspoon pepper
2 cloves garlic, finely chopped
1 jalapeño chile with seeds, finely chopped
1½ lb beef flank steak

1 Place all ingredients except beef in heavy-duty resealable plastic food-storage bag. Add beef steak; seal bag and turn to coat beef. Refrigerate at least 4 hours but no longer than 24 hours.

2 Heat coals or gas grill for direct heat. Remove beef from marinade; discard marinade.

3 Cover and grill beef 4 to 5 inches from hot heat about 10 minutes, turning once, until slightly pink when cut in center. Let stand 5 minutes. To serve, cut across grain into thin slices.

To broil: Place marinated steak on broiler pan. Broil with top 4 to 5 inches from heat using times in recipe as a guide, turning once.

Pumpkin pie spice is a combination of cinnamon, nutmeg, cloves, ginger and sometimes mace—all common spices in Caribbean cooking.

1 Serving: Calories 180 (Calories from Fat 80); Total Fat 9g (Saturated Fat 3g); Cholesterol 65mg; Sodium 240mg; Total Carbohydrate 0g (Dietary Fiber 0g); Protein 25g

Chipotle Salsa Ribs

Prep Time: 10 min ▪ Start to Finish: 6 hrs 10 min ▪ 6 Servings

Southwestern Rub

1 tablespoon packed brown sugar

1 teaspoon chili powder

1 teaspoon paprika

½ teaspoon ground cumin

½ teaspoon seasoned salt

½ teaspoon garlic-pepper blend

¼ teaspoon ground ginger

Ribs

4 lb pork loin back ribs (not cut into serving pieces)

½ cup chipotle salsa

¼ cup chili sauce

2 tablespoons orange marmalade

1 In small bowl, prepare rub by mixing all ingredients. Rub mixture over ribs. Wrap tightly in plastic wrap and refrigerate at least 4 hours but no longer than 12 hours.

2 If using charcoal grill, place drip pan directly under grilling area, and arrange coals around edge of firebox. Heat coals or gas grill for indirect heat. Cover and grill ribs over drip pan or over unheated side of gas grill and 4 to 6 inches from medium heat 1 hour 30 minutes to 2 hours, turning occasionally, until tender.

3 In small bowl, mix salsa, chili sauce and marmalade. Brush over ribs during last 10 to 15 minutes of grilling. Heat remaining salsa mixture to boiling; boil and stir 1 minute. Cut ribs into serving-size pieces. Serve salsa mixture with ribs.

1 Serving: Calories 610 (Calories from Fat 400); Total Fat 44g (Saturated Fat 16g); Cholesterol 175mg; Sodium 500mg; Total Carbohydrate 11g (Dietary Fiber 1g); Protein 43g

When food is cooked away from the heat source, it's called "indirect-heat" grilling. This is the best way to cook large cuts or long-cooking foods because the indirect heat won't burn or overcook the food.

Apple-Maple Brined Pork Tenderloin

Prep Time: 15 min ▪ Start to Finish: 8 hrs 40 min ▪ 6 Servings

4 cups cold water
2 cups apple cider
½ cup maple-flavored or real maple syrup
¼ cup salt
2 pork tenderloins (about 1 lb each)
1 tablespoon chopped fresh rosemary leaves
½ teaspoon coarsely ground pepper
¼ teaspoon garlic powder

1 In large container or stockpot, stir water, cider, maple syrup and salt until salt is dissolved. Add pork to brine mixture. Cover and refrigerate at least 8 hours but no longer than 12 hours.

2 Heat coals or gas grill for direct heat. Remove pork from brine mixture; rinse thoroughly under cool running water and pat dry. Discard brine. Sprinkle pork with rosemary, pepper and garlic powder.

3 Cover and grill pork 4 to 6 inches from medium heat 20 to 25 minutes, turning occasionally, until pork has slight blush of pink in center and meat thermometer inserted in center reads 160°F.

Brining is an age-old process for preserving meats. Today, this simple method of soaking meat in a saltwater solution makes it exceptionally moist, juicy and flavorful.

1 Serving: Calories 190 (Calories from Fat 50); Total Fat 6g (Saturated Fat 2g); Cholesterol 95mg; Sodium 460mg; Total Carbohydrate 2g (Dietary Fiber 0g); Protein 34g

Fiery Pork Tenderloin with Pineapple Salsa

Prep Time: 40 min ▪ Start to Finish: 40 min ▪ 4 Servings

Pork

2 teaspoons canola or soybean oil

2 pork tenderloins (¾ lb each)

1 teaspoon black pepper

¼ to ½ teaspoon ground red pepper (cayenne)

½ teaspoon salt

Pineapple Salsa

1 can (8 oz) pineapple tidbits, drained

4 medium green onions, sliced (¼ cup)

¼ cup chopped red bell pepper

2 tablespoons chopped fresh or 2 teaspoons dried mint leaves

½ teaspoon grated lime peel

2 teaspoons lime juice

¼ teaspoon salt

1 Brush grill rack with oil. Heat coals or gas grill for direct heat. Rub 1 teaspoon oil onto each pork tenderloin; sprinkle with peppers and ½ teaspoon salt.

2 Cover and grill pork over medium heat 20 to 30 minutes, turning 3 times, until pork has slight blush of pink in center and meat thermometer inserted in center reads 160°F.

3 Meanwhile, in medium bowl, mix all salsa ingredients. Cut pork into ½-inch slices. Serve with salsa.

Serve fresh green beans, roasted or steamed, as an easy, healthy side dish.

1 Serving: Calories 270 (Calories from Fat 80); Total Fat 9g (Saturated Fat 2.5g); Cholesterol 110mg; Sodium 520mg; Total Carbohydrate 10g (Dietary Fiber 1g); Protein 39g

Hoisin-Glazed Pork Chops

Prep Time: 10 min ▪ Start to Finish: 25 min ▪ 4 Servings

½ cup barbecue sauce
¼ cup hoisin sauce
2 tablespoons dry sherry, if desired
1 tablespoon honey
4 boneless pork loin chops, about ½ inch thick (about 1 lb)
½ teaspoon garlic-pepper blend
¼ teaspoon salt
¼ teaspoon ground ginger

1 Heat coals or gas grill for direct heat. In 1-quart saucepan, mix barbecue sauce, hoisin sauce, sherry and honey. Cook over medium heat about 5 minutes, stirring occasionally, until flavors are blended.

2 Sprinkle pork with garlic pepper, salt and ginger. Cover and grill pork 4 to 6 inches from medium heat 10 to 12 minutes, turning frequently and brushing with hoisin glaze during last 5 minutes of grilling, until pork is no longer pink in center.

3 Heat remaining glaze to boiling; boil and stir 1 minute. Serve pork with remaining glaze.

Hoisin is a thick, reddish brown sauce with a spicy-sweet flavor that's often used in Chinese cooking. It's a blend of soybeans, garlic, chiles and spices. Look for it in the ethnic-foods section of the grocery store.

1 Serving: Calories 260 (Calories from Fat 80); Total Fat 9g (Saturated Fat 3g); Cholesterol 65mg; Sodium 760mg; Total Carbohydrate 22g (Dietary Fiber 0g); Protein 24g

Southwestern Pork Chops

Prep Time: 10 min ▪ Start to Finish: 1 hr 20 min ▪ 8 Servings

8 pork loin or rib chops, about ½ inch thick (about 2 lb)
1 tablespoon chili powder
1 teaspoon ground cumin
¼ teaspoon ground red pepper (cayenne)
¼ teaspoon salt
1 large clove garlic, finely chopped

1 Trim excess fat from pork. In small bowl, mix remaining ingredients; rub evenly on both sides of pork. Cover and refrigerate 1 hour to blend flavors.

2 Heat coals or gas grill for direct heat. Cover and grill pork 4 to 6 inches from medium heat 8 to 10 minutes, turning frequently, until no longer pink when cut near bone.

To keep food from sticking and to make cleanup a breeze, brush the grill rack with vegetable oil or spray with cooking spray before heating the grill.

1 Serving: Calories 170 (Calories from Fat 70); Total Fat 8g (Saturated Fat 3g); Cholesterol 65mg; Sodium 125mg; Total Carbohydrate 0g (Dietary Fiber 0g); Protein 23g

Chicken with Oregano-Peach Sauce

Prep Time: 15 min ▪ Start to Finish: 35 min ▪ 4 Servings

½ cup peach preserves
¼ cup raspberry vinegar
2 tablespoons chopped fresh oregano leaves
4 boneless, skinless chicken breast halves (1¼ lb)
½ teaspoon garlic-pepper blend
½ teaspoon seasoned salt

1 Heat coals or gas grill for direct heat. In 1-quart saucepan, heat preserves and vinegar to boiling, stirring constantly, until preserves are melted. Spoon about ¼ cup mixture into small bowl or custard cup for brushing on chicken. Stir oregano into remaining mixture and reserve to serve with chicken.

2 Sprinkle chicken with garlic pepper and seasoned salt.

3 Cover and grill chicken 4 to 6 inches from medium heat 15 to 20 minutes, turning once and brushing with preserves mixture during last 10 minutes of grilling, until juice of chicken is no longer pink when centers of thickest pieces are cut. Discard any remaining preserves mixture brushed on chicken. Serve chicken with reserved preserves mixture with oregano.

When buying fresh oregano, look for bright-green bunches with no sign of wilting or yellowing. Store it in the refrigerator in a plastic bag for up to three days.

1 Serving: Calories 220 (Calories from Fat 35); Total Fat 4g (Saturated Fat 1g); Cholesterol 75mg; Sodium 250mg; Total Carbohydrate 19g (Dietary Fiber 0g); Protein 27g

Three-Herb Chicken

Prep Time: 10 min ▪ Start to Finish: 1 hr 25 min ▪ 4 Servings

Herb Marinade
½ cup vegetable oil
½ cup lime juice
2 tablespoons chopped fresh or 2 teaspoons dried basil leaves
2 tablespoons chopped fresh or 2 teaspoons dried oregano leaves
2 tablespoons chopped fresh or 2 teaspoons dried thyme leaves
1 teaspoon onion powder
¼ teaspoon lemon-pepper seasoning

Chicken
4 chicken thighs (about 1 lb)
4 chicken drumsticks (about 1 lb)

1 Prepare marinade by mixing all ingredients in shallow glass, plastic dish or resealable plastic food storage bag. Add chicken thighs and drumsticks to marinade; turn to coat. Cover dish or seal bag and refrigerate, turning chicken occasionally, at least 30 minutes but no longer than 24 hours.

2 Heat coals or gas grill for direct heat. Remove chicken from marinade; reserve marinade. Cover and grill chicken, skin sides down, 5 to 6 inches from medium heat 8 to 10 minutes. Turn chicken; brush with marinade. Cover and grill 25 to 35 minutes longer, turning occasionally and brushing with marinade, until juice of chicken is no longer pink when centers of thickest pieces are cut. Discard any remaining marinade.

1 Serving: Calories 430 (Calories from Fat 300); Total Fat 33g (Saturated Fat 7g); Cholesterol 100mg; Sodium 95mg; Total Carbohydrate 1g (Dietary Fiber 0g); Protein 31g

Lemon Chicken with Grilled Fennel and Onions

Prep Time: 40 min ■ Start to Finish: 55 min ■ 6 Servings

6 bone-in chicken breasts (about 3 lb)
¼ cup olive or vegetable oil
1 teaspoon grated lemon peel
¼ cup lemon juice
2 tablespoons chopped fresh or 2 teaspoons dried oregano leaves
½ teaspoon salt
2 medium fennel bulbs, cut into ½-inch slices
1 medium red onion, cut into ½-inch slices

1 Place chicken in shallow glass or plastic dish. In small bowl, mix oil, lemon peel, lemon juice, oregano and salt; pour over chicken. Cover and let stand 15 minutes.

2 Heat coals or gas grill for direct heat. Remove chicken from marinade; reserve marinade. Brush fennel and onion with marinade.

3 Cover and grill chicken (skin sides down), fennel and onion over medium heat 15 to 20 minutes, turning once and brushing frequently with marinade, until juice of chicken is no longer pink when centers of thickest pieces are cut. Discard any remaining marinade.

For an easy summer meal, serve this lemony chicken with fresh tomato slices and angel hair pasta.

1 Serving: Calories 240 (Calories from Fat 100); Total Fat 11g (Saturated Fat 2g); Cholesterol 75mg; Sodium 310mg; Total Carbohydrate 8g (Dietary Fiber 3g); Protein 28g

Ginger-Lime Tuna Steaks

Prep Time: 10 min ■ Start to Finish: 1 hr 25 min ■ 4 Servings

1½ lb tuna steaks, ¾ to 1 inch thick
¼ cup lime juice
2 tablespoons olive or vegetable oil
2 teaspoons finely chopped gingerroot
½ teaspoon salt
⅛ teaspoon ground red pepper (cayenne)
2 cloves garlic, crushed
Lime wedges, if desired

1 If fish steaks are large, cut into 6 serving pieces. In shallow glass or plastic dish or resealable plastic food-storage bag, mix remaining ingredients except lime wedges. Add fish; turn to coat. Cover dish or seal bag and refrigerate, turning fish once, at least 1 hour but no longer than 24 hours.

2 Heat coals or gas grill for direct heat. Remove fish from marinade; reserve marinade. Cover and grill fish about 4 inches from medium heat 11 to 15 minutes, brushing 2 or 3 times with marinade and turning once, until fish flakes easily with fork and is slightly pink in center. Discard any remaining marinade. Serve fish with lime wedges.

For variety, try this recipe using swordfish or halibut steaks instead of the tuna steaks.

1 Serving: Calories 280 (Calories from Fat 120); Total Fat 13g (Saturated Fat 3g); Cholesterol 65mg; Sodium 270mg; Total Carbohydrate 0g (Dietary Fiber 0g); Protein 40g

Dill Salmon

Prep Time: 10 min ▪ Start to Finish: 40 min ▪ 6 Servings

1 large salmon fillet (about 2 lbs)
1 tablespoon vegetable oil
¼ teaspoon pepper
½ cup dill dip
2 tablespoons milk

1 Heat coals or gas grill for direct heat. Place fish on 24-inch piece of heavy-duty foil. Brush fish with oil; sprinkle with pepper. Wrap foil securely around fish.

2 Cover and grill fish 4 to 6 inches from medium heat 20 to 30 minutes or until fish flakes easily with fork.

3 Mix dill dip with milk until smooth. Serve salmon with dill sauce.

For the safest possible picnic, remember that perishable food should be consumed within two hours (or one hour if the outside temperature is over 90°F).

1 Serving: Calories 270 (Calories from Fat 140); Total Fat 15g (Saturated Fat 3.5g); Cholesterol 90mg; Sodium 210mg; Total Carbohydrate 1g (Dietary Fiber 0g); Protein 31g

Grilled Salmon with Fresh Lime Cream

Prep Time: 30 min ▪ Start to Finish: 1 hr 5 min ▪ 6 Servings

Salmon

1 teaspoon grated lime peel

¼ cup lime juice

2 tablespoons honey

1 tablespoon chopped fresh or 1 teaspoon dried dill weed

2 teaspoons canola or soybean oil

1¼ lb salmon fillets, cut into 6 serving pieces

½ teaspoon salt

Lime Cream

⅓ cup fat-free mayonnaise

1 teaspoon grated lime peel

2 teaspoons lime juice

1 In small bowl, mix 1 teaspoon lime peel, ¼ cup lime juice, honey, dill weed and oil.

2 In 8-inch square (2-quart) glass baking dish, arrange salmon pieces, skin sides up, in single layer. Pour marinade over salmon; turn in marinade to cover all sides. Cover with plastic wrap and refrigerate 20 to 30 minutes.

3 Brush grill rack with oil. Heat coals or gas grill for direct heat. Remove salmon from marinade; discard marinade. Sprinkle salmon with salt. Place skin sides down on grill. Cover and grill over medium heat 10 to 15 minutes or until salmon flakes easily with fork.

4 Meanwhile, in small bowl, mix all lime cream ingredients with wire whisk. Serve with salmon.

1 Serving: Calories 180 (Calories from Fat 70); Total Fat 7g (Saturated Fat 2g); Cholesterol 75mg; Sodium 370mg; Total Carbohydrate 4g (Dietary Fiber 0g); Protein 24g

Neptune Pasta Salad

Roasted Sweet Pepper Pasta Salad
with Herbs and Feta

Mediterranean Quinoa Salad

Confetti Rice

Black Bean Chili Salad

Fiesta Taco Salad with Beans

Grilled Potato Wedges with
Barbeque Dipping Sauce

Caesar and Bacon Potato Salad

Garlic Oven Fries

Easy Grilled Vegetables

Grilled Corn with Chile-Lime Spread

Portabella Mushrooms with Herbs

Dilled Cucumber-Tomato Salad

Lime-Mint Melon Salad

Asian Slaw

Tortellini, Brocoli and Bacon Salad

Picnic Pasta Salad

Mediterranean Potato Salad

Smoked Sausage Baked Beans

California Citrus Broccoli Slaw

4

sumptuous sides

Neptune Pasta Salad

Prep Time: 25 min ▪ Start to Finish: 25 min ▪ 4 Servings

1 box Caesar pasta salad mix
¼ cup cold water
3 tablespoons vegetable oil
1 package (8 oz) refrigerated flake-style imitation crabmeat
1½ cups broccoli florets

1 Fill 3-quart or larger saucepan ⅔ full of water. Heat to boiling. Add contents of pasta pouch to boiling water. Gently boil about 12 minutes, stirring occasionally, until pasta is tender; drain. Rinse with cold water until chilled; drain.

2 In large bowl, mix seasoning mix, water and oil. Stir in pasta mixture, imitation crabmeat and broccoli. Toss with croutons and parmesan topping just before serving.

Add 1 cup cherry tomato halves for a burst of color and vine-ripe flavor!

1 Serving: Calories 350 (Calories from Fat 110); Total Fat 12g (Saturated Fat 1.5g); Cholesterol 15mg; Sodium 1220mg; Total Carbohydrate 43g (Dietary Fiber 2g); Protein 16g

Roasted Sweet Pepper Pasta Salad with Herbs and Feta

Prep Time: 35 min   Start to Finish: 35 min   8 Servings (1¼ cups each)

2 large red or yellow bell peppers, cut into 1-inch pieces
1 medium red onion, cut into wedges (about 2 cups)
Cooking spray
3 cups uncooked penne pasta (10 oz)
1 cup sliced 70%-less-fat turkey pepperoni (about 3 oz), cut in half
½ cup crumbled feta cheese
½ cup fat-free Italian dressing
2 tablespoons chopped fresh basil leaves
1 tablespoon chopped fresh mint leaves

1 Heat oven to 450°F. Spray 13×9×2-inch pan with cooking spray. Place bell peppers and onion in single layer in pan. Spray vegetables with cooking spray. Bake uncovered 15 to 20 minutes or until vegetables are lightly browned and tender.

2 Meanwhile, cook and drain pasta as directed on package. Rinse with cold water; drain.

3 In large bowl, toss bell peppers, onion, pasta and remaining ingredients. Serve immediately, or refrigerate 1 to 2 hours.

1 Serving: Calories 220 (Calories from Fat 45); Total Fat 5g (Saturated Fat 2g); Cholesterol 20mg; Sodium 540mg; Total Carbohydrate 33g (Dietary Fiber 3g); Protein 10g

Mediterranean Quinoa Salad

Prep Time: 30 min ▪ Start to Finish: 1 hr 35 min ▪ 4 Servings

1 cup uncooked quinoa
2 cups roasted garlic-seasoned chicken broth (from two 14-oz cans)
½ cup chopped drained roasted red bell peppers (from 7-oz jar)
½ cup cubed provolone cheese
¼ cup chopped kalamata olives
2 tablespoons chopped fresh basil leaves
2 tablespoons fat-free Italian dressing

1 Rinse quinoa under cold water 1 minute; drain.

2 In 2-quart saucepan, heat quinoa and broth to boiling; reduce heat. Cover and simmer 15 to 20 minutes or until quinoa is tender; drain. Cool completely, about 45 minutes.

3 In large serving bowl, toss quinoa and remaining ingredients. Serve immediately, or refrigerate 1 to 2 hours before serving.

Quinoa is a popular grain in South American cuisine and is gaining popularity in the United States.

1 Serving: Calories 260 (Calories from Fat 80); Total Fat 9g (Saturated Fat 3.5g); Cholesterol 10mg; Sodium 820mg; Total Carbohydrate 33g (Dietary Fiber 3g); Protein 13g

Confetti Rice

Prep Time: 10 min   Start to Finish: 30 min   8 Servings (½ cup each)

1¼ cups water
1 can (14 oz) 33%-less-sodium chicken broth
1 teaspoon salt-free seasoning blend
1 cup uncooked converted rice
1 cup chopped broccoli
½ cup shredded carrot (about 1 medium)
1 jar (2 oz) diced pimientos, drained

1 In 3-quart saucepan, heat water, broth and seasoning blend to boiling. Stir in rice; reduce heat to low. Cover and simmer 15 minutes.

2 Stir in broccoli and carrot. Cover and cook about 5 minutes or until rice and broccoli are tender. Stir in pimientos. Let stand 5 minutes.

Frozen cut broccoli can be substituted for the fresh. Just be sure to chop up any large pieces.

1 Serving: Calories 100 (Calories from Fat 5); Total Fat 0.5g (Saturated Fat 0g); Cholesterol 0mg; Sodium 115mg; Total Carbohydrate 22g (Dietary Fiber 0g); Protein 3g

Black Bean Chili Salad

Prep Time: 10 min   Start to Finish: 10 min   4 Servings

Chili Vinaigrette Dressing

¼ cup red wine vinegar

2 tablespoons vegetable oil

½ teaspoon chili powder

¼ teaspoon ground cumin

1 small clove garlic, finely chopped

Salad

1 cup frozen whole kernel corn (from 1-lb bag), thawed, drained

1 cup diced jicama

1 medium tomato, seeded, chopped (¾ cup)

2 medium green onions, sliced (2 tablespoons)

2 cans (15 oz each) black beans, rinsed, drained

1 In large glass or plastic bowl, mix all dressing ingredients.

2 Stir in all salad ingredients.

1 Serving: Calories 390 (Calories from Fat 70); Total Fat 8g (Saturated Fat 1.5g); Cholesterol 0mg; Sodium 10mg; Total Carbohydrate 62g (Dietary Fiber 15g); Protein 18g

Fiesta Taco Salad with Beans

Prep Time: 15 min   Start to Finish: 20 min   5 Servings (2 cups each)

1 can (15 oz) black beans, rinsed, drained
½ cup taco sauce
6 cups lettuce, torn into bite-size pieces
1 medium green bell pepper, cut into strips
2 medium tomatoes, cut into wedges
½ cup pitted ripe olives, drained
1 cup corn chips
1 cup shredded Cheddar cheese (4 oz)
½ cup reduced-fat Thousand Island dressing

1 In 2-quart saucepan, cook beans and taco sauce over medium heat 4 to 5 minutes, stirring occasionally, until thoroughly heated.

2 In large bowl, toss lettuce, bell pepper, tomatoes, olives and corn chips. Spoon bean mixture over lettuce mixture; toss. Sprinkle with cheese. Serve immediately with dressing.

You can cut back on the fat and calories in this recipe by using reduced-fat Cheddar cheese and fat-free Thousand Island dressing.

1 Serving: Calories 350 (Calories from Fat 130): Total Fat 15g (Saturated Fat 6g): Cholesterol 25mg: Sodium 980mg: Total Carbohydrate 40g (Dietary Fiber 8g): Protein 15g

Grilled Potato Wedges with Barbecue Dipping Sauce

Prep Time: 45 min   Start to Finish: 45 min   4 Servings

4 medium white potatoes
Cooking spray
1 teaspoon Cajun seasoning
½ cup reduced-fat sour cream
2 tablespoons barbecue sauce

1 Heat coals or gas grill for direct heat. Cut each potato lengthwise into 8 wedges; pat dry with paper towels. Spray potato wedges thoroughly with cooking spray. Sprinkle with Cajun seasoning. Place in grill basket (grill "wok").

2 Cover and grill potato wedges over medium heat 30 to 40 minutes, stirring every 10 minutes, until tender.

3 In small bowl, mix sour cream and barbecue sauce. Serve with potato wedges.

If Cajun seasoning isn't available, make your own seasoning, using ½ teaspoon chili powder, ¼ teaspoon ground oregano and ¼ teaspoon onion or garlic salt.

1 Serving: Calories 160 (Calories from Fat 40); Total Fat 4g (Saturated Fat 2.5g); Cholesterol 10mg; Sodium 240mg; Total Carbohydrate 30g (Dietary Fiber 3g); Protein 4g

Caesar and Bacon Potato Salad

Prep Time: 35 min ▌ Start to Finish: 1 hr 50 min ▌ 6 Servings

6 unpeeled small red potatoes, cut into ½-inch cubes (3 cups)
1 cup frozen cut green beans (from 1-lb bag)
2 hard-cooked eggs
½ cup Caesar dressing
2 tablespoons chopped fresh basil leaves
½ teaspoon salt
⅛ teaspoon coarse pepper
4 slices cooked bacon, chopped
2 cups romaine lettuce, torn into bite-size pieces
Additional chopped fresh basil leaves, if desired

1 In 2-quart saucepan, place potatoes; add enough water to cover potatoes. Heat to boiling; reduce heat to medium. Cook 5 minutes. Add green beans. Cook 4 to 6 minutes or until potatoes and beans are tender; drain. Cool 15 minutes. Peel and chop one of the eggs.

2 In medium bowl, mix dressing, 2 tablespoons basil, salt and pepper. Add potatoes, beans, chopped egg and bacon; stir gently to mix. Cover and refrigerate 1 hour.

3 Line serving plate with lettuce. Spoon salad onto lettuce. Peel and coarsely chop remaining egg; sprinkle over salad. Garnish with additional basil.

1 Serving: Calories 220 (Calories from Fat 140); Total Fat 16g (Saturated Fat 3g); Cholesterol 75mg; Sodium 520mg; Total Carbohydrate 16g (Dietary Fiber 3g); Protein 6g

Garlic Oven Fries

Prep Time: 10 min ‖ Start to Finish: 30 min ‖ 4 Servings

4 medium red potatoes (2½ to 3 inch), each cut in 8 wedges
2 teaspoons olive or vegetable oil
1 teaspoon dried basil leaves
1 teaspoon garlic salt

1 Heat oven to 500°F. Spray 15×10×1-inch pan with cooking spray. In medium bowl, toss potatoes with oil to coat. Sprinkle with basil and garlic salt. Arrange in single layer in baking pan.

2 Bake uncovered 15 to 18 minutes, stirring once, until potatoes are tender but crisp on outside.

Red potatoes have a slightly waxy texture and retain their shape better when cooked than russet potatoes do.

1 Serving: Calories 130 (Calories from Fat 20); Total Fat 2.5g (Saturated Fat 0g); Cholesterol 0mg; Sodium 250mg; Total Carbohydrate 26g (Dietary Fiber 3g); Protein 2g

Easy Grilled Vegetables

Prep Time: 25 min   Start to Finish: 1 hr 25 min   6 Servings

12 pattypan squash, about 1 inch in diameter
2 medium red or green bell peppers, each cut into 6 pieces
1 large red onion, cut into ½-inch slices
⅓ cup reduced-fat Italian dressing
Freshly ground pepper, if desired

1 In 13×9-inch (3-quart) glass baking dish, place squash, bell peppers and onion. Pour dressing over vegetables. Cover and let stand 1 hour to blend flavors.

2 Heat coals or gas grill for direct heat. Remove vegetables from marinade; reserve marinade. Place vegetables in grill basket (grill "wok") or directly on grill rack.

3 Cover and grill vegetables over medium heat 10 to 15 minutes, shaking basket or turning vegetables and brushing with marinade 2 or 3 times, until crisp-tender. Sprinkle with pepper.

You can use one medium zucchini, cut into 1-inch pieces, in place of the pattypan squash. If you like mushrooms, go ahead and add them for the last 10 minutes of grilling.

1 Serving: Calories 80 (Calories from Fat 25); Total Fat 3g (Saturated Fat 0g); Cholesterol 0mg; Sodium 170mg; Total Carbohydrate 11g (Dietary Fiber 3g); Protein 2g

Grilled Corn with Chile-Lime Spread

Prep Time: 25 min   Start to Finish: 30 min   8 Servings

½ cup butter or margarine, softened
½ teaspoon grated lime peel
3 tablespoons lime juice
1 to 2 teaspoons ground red chiles or chili powder
8 ears fresh corn with husks

1 Heat coals or gas grill. In small bowl, mix all ingredients except corn.

2 Remove large outer husks from each ear of corn; gently pull back inner husks and remove silk. Spread each ear of corn with about 2 teaspoons butter mixture; reserve remaining butter mixture. Pull husks up over ears.

3 Place corn on grill. Cook uncovered over medium heat 10 to 15 minutes, turning frequently, until tender. Let stand 5 minutes. Serve corn with remaining butter mixture.

1 Serving: Calories 230 (Calories from Fat 120); Total Fat 13g (Saturated Fat 8g); Cholesterol 30mg; Sodium 105mg; Total Carbohydrate 26g (Dietary Fiber 4g); Protein 4g

Portabella Mushrooms with Herbs

Prep Time: 20 min ‖ Start to Finish: 1 hr 30 min ‖ 4 Servings

2 tablespoons olive or vegetable oil
1 tablespoon balsamic vinegar
1 teaspoon chopped fresh or ¼ teaspoon dried oregano leaves
1 teaspoon chopped fresh or ¼ teaspoon dried thyme leaves
⅛ teaspoon salt
1 clove garlic, finely chopped
4 fresh portabella mushroom caps (about 4 inches in diameter)
¼ cup crumbled feta cheese with herbs

1 In large glass or plastic bowl or resealable plastic food-storage bag, mix oil, vinegar, oregano, thyme, salt and garlic. Add mushrooms; turn to coat. Cover dish or seal bag and refrigerate 1 hour.

2 Heat coals or gas grill for direct heat. Remove mushrooms from marinade (mushrooms will absorb most of the marinade). Cover and grill mushrooms over medium heat 8 to 10 minutes or until tender. Sprinkle with cheese.

This is a great side dish to serve with almost any grilled meat. Or serve it as a first course.

1 Serving: Calories 110 (Calories from Fat 80); Total Fat 9g (Saturated Fat 2.5g); Cholesterol 10mg; Sodium 180mg; Total Carbohydrate 4g (Dietary Fiber 0g); Protein 3g

Dilled Cucumber-Tomato Salad

Prep Time: 15 min ▮ Start to Finish: 15 min ▮ 5 Servings (½ cup each)

¼ cup plain yogurt

1 small clove garlic, finely chopped

1½ teaspoon chopped fresh or ½ teaspoon dried dill weed

¼ teaspoon sugar

⅛ teaspoon salt

3 large plum (Roma) tomatoes, seeded, diced (1½ cups)

1 medium cucumber, peeled, seeded and cubed (1 cup)

1 In medium bowl, mix yogurt, garlic, dill weed, sugar and salt.

2 Fold in tomatoes and cucumber. Serve immediately.

1 Serving: Calories 25 (Calories from Fat 0); Total Fat 0g (Saturated Fat 0g); Cholesterol 0mg; Sodium 75mg; Total Carbohydrate 4g (Dietary Fiber 0g); Protein 1g

Lime-Mint Melon Salad

Prep Time: 20 min ※ Start to Finish: 2 hrs 20 min ※ 6 Servings

1½ cups ½-inch cubes honeydew melon (½ medium)
1½ cups ½-inch cubes cantaloupe (½ medium)
1 teaspoon grated lime peel
3 tablespoons lime juice
2 tablespoons chopped fresh or 1 tablespoon dried mint leaves
1 teaspoon honey
¼ teaspoon salt

1 In medium glass or plastic bowl, toss all ingredients.

2 Cover and refrigerate about 2 hours or until chilled.

Select cantaloupe and honeydew melon by smelling the soft stem end. A sweet fruity fragrance means the melon is ripe. Store both varieties of melon at room temperature until ripe, then keep them in the refrigerator.

1 Serving: Calories 40 (Calories from Fat 0): Total Fat 0g (Saturated Fat 0g): Cholesterol 0mg: Sodium 110mg: Total Carbohydrate 9g (Dietary Fiber 0g): Protein 0g

Asian Slaw

Prep Time: 15 min   Start to Finish: 45 min   6 Servings (½ cup each)

4 cups thinly sliced Chinese (napa) cabbage
½ medium red bell pepper, thinly sliced
½ medium cucumber, seeded, thinly sliced
¼ cup citrus vinaigrette dressing
2 tablespoons low-sodium teriyaki sauce

1 In large bowl, mix cabbage, bell pepper and cucumber.

2 In small bowl, mix dressing and teriyaki sauce. Pour over cabbage mixture; toss to coat. Refrigerate at least 30 minutes before serving.

If low-sodium teriyaki sauce is not available, use low-sodium soy sauce.

1 Serving: Calories 40 (Calories from Fat 15); Total Fat 1.5g (Saturated Fat 0g); Cholesterol 0mg; Sodium 300mg; Total Carbohydrate 6g (Dietary Fiber 1g); Protein 1g

Tortellini, Broccoli and Bacon Salad

Prep Time: 25 min   Start to Finish: 1 hr 25 min   24 Servings (about ½ cup each)

2 bags (19 oz each) frozen cheese-filled tortellini
4 cups broccoli florets
2 cups cherry tomatoes, each cut in half
2 tablespoons chopped fresh chives
1 cup reduced-fat coleslaw dressing
1 lb bacon, crisply cooked, crumbled
¼ cup sunflower nuts

1 Cook and drain tortellini as directed on package. Rinse with cold water; drain.

2 In very large (4-quart) bowl, mix tortellini, broccoli, tomatoes, chives and dressing. Cover and refrigerate at least 1 hour to blend flavors.

3 Just before serving, stir in bacon. Sprinkle with nuts.

1 Serving: Calories 160 (Calories from Fat 80); Total Fat 9g (Saturated Fat 2.5g); Cholesterol 45mg; Sodium 340mg; Total Carbohydrate 14g (Dietary Fiber 1g); Protein 6g

Picnic Pasta Salad

Prep Time: 20 min // Start to Finish: 2 hrs 20 min // 26 Servings (½ cup each)

1 package (16 oz) bow-tie (farfalle) pasta
1 can (8 oz) tomato sauce
1 cup Italian dressing
1 tablespoon chopped fresh or 1 teaspoon dried basil leaves
1 tablespoon chopped fresh or 1 teaspoon dried oregano leaves
1 cup sliced fresh mushrooms (3 oz)
5 plum (Roma) tomatoes, coarsely chopped (1½ cups)
1 large cucumber, coarsely chopped (1½ cups)
1 medium red onion, chopped (1½ cups)
1 can (2.25 oz) sliced ripe olives, drained

1 Cook and drain pasta as directed on package. Rinse with cold water; drain.

2 In large bowl, mix tomato sauce, dressing, basil and oregano. Add pasta and remaining ingredients; toss. Cover and refrigerate at least 2 hours until chilled but no longer than 48 hours.

1 Serving: Calories 120 (Calories from Fat 40); Total Fat 4.5g (Saturated Fat 0g); Cholesterol 0mg; Sodium 220mg; Total Carbohydrate 17g (Dietary Fiber 2g); Protein 3g

Don't like mushrooms? Go ahead and use roasted red bell pepper slices instead.

Mediterranean Potato Salad

Prep Time: 25 min // Start to Finish: 25 min // 12 Servings (½ cup each)

1½ lb medium red potatoes, cut in half
3 slices bacon
¾ cup red or yellow grape tomatoes
¼ cup chopped onion
¼ cup sliced ripe olives
½ cup fat-free Italian dressing
1 tablespoon cider vinegar
1 tablespoon chopped fresh Italian parsley, if desired

1 In 3-quart saucepan, heat 1 inch water to boiling. Add potatoes. Cover and heat to boiling; reduce heat. Cover and simmer 10 to 15 minutes or until tender; drain. Cool slightly. Cut potatoes into ¾-inch cubes; place in large bowl.

2 Meanwhile, line microwavable plate with microwavable paper towel. Place bacon on paper towel; top with another microwavable paper towel. Microwave on High 2 to 3 minutes or until bacon is crisp. Crumble bacon.

3 Stir bacon, tomatoes, onion and olives into warm cubed potatoes. In small bowl, mix dressing and vinegar; pour over potato mixture, stirring gently to coat vegetables. Sprinkle with parsley. Serve warm or cool.

Serve this delicious side with grilled turkey or chicken sausage for an easy summer meal!

1 Serving: Calories 60 (Calories from Fat 15); Total Fat 1.5g (Saturated Fat 0g); Cholesterol 0mg; Sodium 170mg; Total Carbohydrate 12g (Dietary Fiber 2g); Protein 2g

Smoked Sausage Baked Beans

Prep Time: 10 min ‖ Start to Finish: 1 hr 10 min ‖ 24 Servings

2 cans (5.5 oz each) baked beans
1 ring (1 lb) fully cooked smoked sausage, cubed
2 jalapeño chiles, seeded, finely chopped
1 tablespoon ground cumin
1 tablespoon chili powder

1 Heat oven to 350°F. In ungreased 4-quart casserole or nonstick Dutch oven, mix all ingredients.

2 Bake uncovered 45 to 60 minutes or until thoroughly heated and bubbly.

You can make these beans in advance, using a slow cooker, then bring it along to keep the beans warm. In 5- to 6-quart slow cooker, mix all ingredients. Cover and cook on Low heat setting 4 to 5 hours (or High heat setting 2 to 2½ hours) until thoroughly heated and desired consistency.

1 Serving: Calories 180 (Calories from Fat 60); Total Fat 7g (Saturated Fat 2.5g); Cholesterol 20mg; Sodium 750mg; Total Carbohydrate 26g (Dietary Fiber 7g); Protein 9g

California Citrus Broccoli Slaw

Prep Time: 20 min   Start to Finish: 20 min   12 Servings

Broccoli Slaw

1 bag (16 oz) broccoli slaw

1 small jicama, peeled, cut into julienne strips (2 cups)

3 oranges

1 small red onion, cut in half, thinly sliced (1 cup)

²⁄₃ cup chopped fresh cilantro

Citrus Dressing

3 tablespoons vegetable oil

3 tablespoons lemon juice

4 teaspoons sugar

1½ teaspoons grated orange peel

⅛ teaspoon salt

1 In large bowl, mix broccoli slaw and jicama. Peel oranges with sharp paring knife; cut into ¼-inch slices. Cut each slice into fourths. Add oranges, onion and cilantro to broccoli mixture.

2 In a tightly covered container, prepare dressing by shaking all of the ingredients; pour over salad and toss. Serve immediately, or cover and refrigerate up to 24 hours.

Jicama is a crunchy root vegetable with a sweet, nutty flavor that's popular in Mexican cuisine. It keeps its pretty ivory color, which makes it a natural choice to use in salads like this one.

1 Serving: Calories 80 (Calories from Fat 30); Total Fat 3.5g (Saturated Fat 0g); Cholesterol 0mg; Sodium 35mg; Total Carbohydrate 10g (Dietary Fiber 4g); Protein 2g

Lemon Tea Slush

Cranberry-Mint Iced Tea

Pineapple Limeade

Not-So-"Hard" Lemonade

Raspberry Lemonade

Citrus Spritzers

Italian Fruit Punch

Colada Cooler Punch

Iced Hazlenut Coffee Coolers

Peachy Mimosas

Dreamy Tropical Cream Fizz

Cosmo Slush

Strawberry-Rhubarb Slush

Layered Strawberry Shakes

Key Lime–Banana Smoothies

Creamy Mango Smoothies

Frosty Guava-Peach Sippers

Mangoritas

Frozen Strawberry Margaritas

Raspberry-Apricot Sangria

5

refreshing drinks

Lemon Tea Slush

Prep Time: 20 min ▪ Start to Finish: 24 hrs 40 min ▪ 12 Servings (1 cup each)

5 cups water
2 tea bags green tea
1 cup sugar
1 can (12 oz) frozen lemonade concentrate, thawed
1 cup vodka
1 bottle (1 liter) sparkling water, chilled
Lemon slices, if desired

1 In 2-cup microwavable measuring cup, microwave 1 cup of the water on High until boiling. Add tea bags to boiling water; let steep 10 minutes. Remove tea bags; cool tea.

2 Meanwhile, in 2-quart saucepan, heat remaining 4 cups water to boiling. Stir in sugar until dissolved. Remove from heat; cool 20 minutes.

3 In 3-quart plastic container, mix tea, sugar water, lemonade concentrate and vodka. Cover and freeze at least 24 hours.

4 To serve, place ⅔ cup slush in each glass and fill with ⅓ cup sparkling water; stir. Garnish with lemon slices.

Store the slush in a covered container in the freezer for up to 1 month.

1 Serving: Calories 120 (Calories from Fat 0); Total Fat 0g (Saturated Fat 0g); Cholesterol 0mg; Sodium 0mg; Total Carbohydrate 30g (Dietary Fiber 0g); Protein 0g

Cranberry-Mint Iced Tea

Prep Time: 15 min ▪ Start to Finish: 15 min ▪ 6 Servings (1 cup each)

6 cups cranberry juice cocktail (not unsweetened cranberry juice)
4 tea bags black tea
10 mint leaves (1 inch each)
2 tablespoons sugar

1 Heat cranberry juice cocktail to boiling in 2-quart saucepan. Pour over tea bags and mint in 2-quart glass measuring cup or heatproof pitcher. Let steep 5 to 10 minutes.

2 Strain tea mixture. Stir in sugar. Serve tea over ice. Add more sugar if desired.

To keep tea from becoming cloudy, heat the liquid and steep the tea in nonreactive utensils, such as glass or stainless steel.

1 Serving: Calories 160 (Calories from Fat 0); Total Fat 0g (Saturated Fat 0g); Cholesterol 0mg; Sodium 5mg; Total Carbohydrate 41g (Dietary Fiber 0g); Protein 0g

Pineapple Limeade

Prep Time: 10 min ▪ Start to Finish: 10 min ▪ 16 Servings (about 1 cup each)

1 cup sugar
6 cups pineapple juice, chilled
1 cup lime juice
2 liters sparkling water, chilled
Lime slices, if desired

1 In large glass or plastic pitcher, mix sugar and juices. Pour half of mixture into another large pitcher.

2 Just before serving, stir 1 liter sparkling water into each pitcher. Serve over ice. Garnish with lime slices.

1 Serving: Calories 110 (Calories from Fat 0); Total Fat 0g (Saturated Fat 0g); Cholesterol 0mg; Sodium 0mg; Total Carbohydrate 26g (Dietary Fiber 0g); Protein 0g

Not-So-"Hard" Lemonade

Prep Time: 15 min ■ Start to Finish: 2 hrs 15 min ■ 6 Servings (²⁄₃ cup each)

3 orange slices, each cut in half
3 lemon slices, each cut in half
3 small strawberries, cut lengthwise in half
6 green grapes
5 bottles (11.2 oz each) lemon malt beverage, chilled
⅓ cup grenadine syrup

1 Remove any seeds from orange and lemon slices.

2 In ungreased 15×10×1-inch pan, place orange slices, lemon slices, strawberry halves and grapes in single layer. Freeze at least 2 hours until fruit is frozen.

3 When ready to serve, pour malt beverage into each of 6 tall glasses. Drizzle 1 tablespoon grenadine syrup into each glass. Place orange slice, lemon slice, strawberry half and 1 grape into each glass.

Frozen chunks of fresh fruit make colorful and tasty "ice cubes" for any summertime beverage.

1 Serving: Calories 120 (Calories from Fat 0); Total Fat 0g (Saturated Fat 0g); Cholesterol 0mg; Sodium 35mg; Total Carbohydrate 29g (Dietary Fiber 2g); Protein 1g

Raspberry Lemonade

Prep Time: 20 min ■ Start to Finish: 2 hrs 20 min ■ 6 Servings (about 1 cup each)

Raspberry Lemonade
¾ cup sugar
4 cups water
1 cup fresh lemon juice (about 4 lemons)
1 box (10 oz) frozen raspberries in syrup, thawed

Raspberry Ice Cubes
Reserved raspberries
¾ cup water

1 In 1-quart saucepan, mix sugar and ½ cup of the water. Cook over medium heat, stirring once, until sugar is dissolved. Cool to room temperature.

2 In 2-quart nonmetal pitcher, mix cooled sugar syrup, lemon juice and the remaining 3½ cups water. Place raspberries in strainer over small bowl to drain (do not press berries through strainer). Reserve berries for raspberry ice cubes. Stir raspberry liquid into lemon mixture; refrigerate.

3 Make raspberry ice cubes by spooning raspberries evenly into 12 sections of ice-cube tray. Divide water evenly among sections with raspberries. Freeze about 2 hours or until firm.

4 Serve lemonade over ice cubes.

1 Serving: Calories 160 (Calories from Fat 0); Total Fat 0g (Saturated Fat 0g); Cholesterol 0mg; Sodium 10mg; Total Carbohydrate 40g (Dietary Fiber 2g); Protein 0g

Citrus Spritzers

Prep Time: 10 min ▪ Start to Finish: 10 min ▪ 8 Servings (about ¾ cup each)

2 cups cold water
1 can (6 oz) frozen orange juice concentrate, thawed
¾ cup frozen (thawed) grapefruit juice concentrate (from 12-oz can)
1 bottle (1 liter) sparkling water, chilled
Orange slices, if desired
Fresh mint leaves, if desired

1 In large pitcher, mix cold water, orange juice concentrate, grapefruit juice concentrate and sparkling water.

2 Serve spritzers over ice. Garnish each serving with orange slice and mint leaf.

Make garnish "kabobs" by threading thin slices of lime, lemon or orange on decorative toothpicks.

1 Serving: Calories 70 (Calories from Fat 0); Total Fat 0g (Saturated Fat 0g); Cholesterol 0mg; Sodium 0mg; Total Carbohydrate 17g (Dietary Fiber 0g); Protein 1g

Italian Fruit Punch

Prep Time: 15 min ▪ Start to Finish: 10 hrs ▪ 28 Servings (½ cup each)

Ice Ring
1 can (12 oz) frozen lemonade concentrate, thawed
4 cans water
2 cups (about 12 large) frozen strawberries
2 lemons, cut into ¼-inch slices, slices cut in half

Punch
1 can (12 oz) frozen lemonade concentrate, thawed
1 can (12 oz) frozen limeade concentrate, thawed
3 cups cold water
4 cups lemon-lime carbonated beverage, chilled
1 bottle (1 liter) club soda, chilled

1 In pitcher, mix 1 can lemonade concentrate and 4 cans water. Pour 2 cups of the lemonade into 12-cup fluted tube cake pan. Freeze in coldest section of freezer about 45 minutes or until thin coating of ice forms on surface. Crack ice crust with small, sharp knife to expose liquid underneath. Working quickly, place strawberries and lemon slices in liquid, making sure each piece is partially submerged. Return pan to freezer about 1 hour or until lemonade is frozen solid. Remove from freezer and add remaining lemonade. Freeze at least 8 hours or overnight.

2 In 2-quart pitcher, mix 1 can lemonade concentrate, the limeade concentrate and 3 cups water. Refrigerate until ready to use.

3 Just before serving, pour limeade mixture, lemon-lime beverage and club soda into punch bowl. Dip pan with ice ring very quickly into warm water, then turn upside down to release ice ring. Float ring in punch bowl.

1 Serving: Calories 90 (Calories from Fat 0); Total Fat 0g (Saturated Fat 0g); Cholesterol 0mg; Sodium 15mg; Total Carbohydrate 23g (Dietary Fiber 0g); Protein 0g

Colada Cooler Punch

Prep Time: 10 min ▪ Start to Finish: 10 min ▪ 24 Servings (1 cup each)

2 cans (12 oz each) frozen piña colada concentrate, thawed
2 cans (12 oz each) frozen white grape juice concentrate, thawed
6 cups cold water
12 cups (about 3 liters) lemon-lime carbonated beverage
Lemon and lime slices

1 In large glass or plastic container, mix piña colada and juice concentrates. Stir in water.

2 Just before serving, pour into punch bowl. Add lemon-lime beverage and lemon and lime slices. Serve over ice.

Make grape ice cubes by putting 1 or 2 grapes in each section of an ice-cube tray. Cover with water and freeze.

1 Serving: Calories 120 (Calories from Fat 0); Total Fat 0g (Saturated Fat 0g); Cholesterol 0mg; Sodium 15mg; Total Carbohydrate 30g (Dietary Fiber 0g); Protein 0g

Iced Hazelnut Coffee Coolers

Prep Time: 10 min ▪ Start to Finish: 3 hrs 10 min ▪ 12 Servings (1½ cups each)

⅔ cup instant coffee granules or crystals
¾ cup hazelnut-flavored liquid nondairy creamer
1 cup sugar
1 cup water
¼ teaspoon ground cinnamon
8 cups milk
48 water ice cubes

1 In medium bowl, stir coffee, creamer, sugar, water and cinnamon until coffee is dissolved.

2 Pour coffee mixture into 2 ice-cube trays. Freeze at least 3 hours until hardened. Transfer frozen coffee cubes to plastic storage container or freezer bag.

3 For each serving, place 2 coffee cubes, ⅔ cup milk and 4 water ice cubes in blender. Cover and blend on high speed about 20 seconds or until blended and slightly slushy. Pour into glass.

For an extra special touch, top this coffee cooler with a dollop of whipped cream, a dash of ground cinnamon and some hazelnuts (filberts).

1 Serving: Calories 170 (Calories from Fat 40); Total Fat 4.5g (Saturated Fat 2g); Cholesterol 15mg; Sodium 80mg; Total Carbohydrate 28g (Dietary Fiber 0g); Protein 6g

Peachy Mimosas

Prep Time: 5 min ▪ Start to Finish: 5 min ▪ 12 Servings (2/3 cup each)

2 cups orange juice, chilled
2 cups peach nectar, chilled
1 bottle (750 ml) regular or nonalcoholic dry champagne or sparkling wine, chilled

1 In 1½-quart pitcher, mix orange juice and peach nectar.

2 Pour champagne into glasses until half full. Fill glasses with juice mixture.

1 Serving: Calories 100 (Calories from Fat 0); Total Fat 0g (Saturated Fat 0g); Cholesterol 0mg; Sodium 10mg; Total Carbohydrate 11g (Dietary Fiber 0g); Protein 0g

Dreamy Tropical Cream Fizz

Prep Time: 10 min ▪ Start to Finish: 1 hr 10 min ▪ 6 Servings (1 cup each)

¼ cup shredded coconut
2 cups tropical juice blend
½ cup sugar
¼ cup lime juice
12 to 14 ice cubes
1 ½ cups club soda
1 pint coconut ice cream, coconut sorbet or vanilla ice cream

1 Place coconut in food processor or blender. Cover and process until coconut is in small pieces. Place coconut in shallow dish. Dip rims of six 12-ounce stemmed glasses into water, then dip into coconut to coat. Chill glasses in freezer at least 1 hour before serving.

2 Place tropical juice blend, sugar, lime juice and ice cubes in blender. Cover and blend on high speed about 45 seconds or until smooth. Pour mixture into glasses.

3 Pour ¼ cup club soda into juice mixture in each glass. Add 1 large scoop ice cream to each glass. Garnish with remaining coconut if desired.

1 Serving: Calories 230 (Calories from Fat 60); Total Fat 7g (Saturated Fat 4.5g); Cholesterol 20mg; Sodium 50mg; Total Carbohydrate 41g (Dietary Fiber 0g); Protein 2g

Cosmo Slush

Prep Time: 10 min ▪ Start to Finish: 8 hrs 10 min ▪ 14 Servings (½ cup each)

6 oz frozen (thawed) limeade concentrate (from 12-oz can)
3 tablespoons powdered sugar
2 cups citrus-flavored vodka or orange juice
1 cup orange-flavored liqueur or orange juice
4 cups 100% cranberry juice blend

1 In blender, place limeade concentrate and powdered sugar. Cover and blend on high speed until well mixed. Add vodka and orange liqueur. Cover and blend until well mixed.

2 In 13×9-inch glass baking dish, stir limeade mixture and cranberry juice until well mixed.

3 Cover and freeze at least 8 hours until slushy. Stir before serving.

For vibrant flavor and color, make this slush with 100% cranberry juice, not cranberry juice cocktail.

1 Serving: Calories 90 (Calories from Fat 0); Total Fat 0g (Saturated Fat 0g); Cholesterol 0mg; Sodium 0mg; Total Carbohydrate 23g (Dietary Fiber 0g); Protein 0g

Strawberry-Rhubarb Slush

Prep Time: 20 min ▪ Start to Finish: 8 hrs 20 min ▪ 16 Servings (1 cup each)

1 bag (16 oz) frozen rhubarb or 3 cups chopped fresh rhubarb
1 cup sugar
2 packages (10 oz each) frozen sweetened strawberries, slightly thawed
1½ cups vodka
1 can (12 oz) lemon-lime carbonated beverage
1 bottle (2 liters) lemon-lime carbonated beverage, chilled
Fresh strawberries, if desired

1 In 3-quart saucepan, heat rhubarb and sugar to boiling over medium heat, stirring occasionally. Cook 8 to 10 minutes, stirring occasionally, until rhubarb is very tender. Stir in strawberries.

2 Spoon into blender half of the strawberry mixture. Cover and blend on high speed until smooth. Pour into large nonmetal container. Cover and blend remaining strawberry mixture; add to container. Stir in vodka and 12-ounce can of lemon-lime beverage. Freeze at least 8 hours until frozen and slushy.

3 For each serving, stir together ½ cup frozen mixture and ½ cup chilled lemon-lime beverage in tall glass until slushy. Garnish with strawberry.

Turn this recipe into a slushy punch for your next party. Spoon the slush mixture into a large punch bowl, then stir in the carbonated beverage. This is a handy and refreshing beverage when serving a large number of guests.

1 Serving: Calories 170 (Calories from Fat 0); Total Fat 0g (Saturated Fat 0g); Cholesterol 0mg; Sodium 20mg; Total Carbohydrate 41g (Dietary Fiber 1g); Protein 0g

Layered Strawberry Shakes

Prep Time: 20 min ▪ Start to Finish: 20 min ▪ 6 Servings (about ¾ cup each)

1 container (16 oz) fresh strawberries, coarsely chopped
4 cups vanilla ice cream
¾ cup milk

1 In blender, place strawberries. Cover and blend on high speed about 1 minute, stopping blender occasionally to stir, until smooth. Remove from blender. Rinse blender.

2 In blender, place ice cream and milk. Cover and blend on high speed about 2 minutes, stopping blender occasionally to stir, until smooth and creamy.

3 When ready to serve, in each of six 10- to 12-ounce glasses, layer ¼ cup blended ice cream, ⅓ cup strawberry puree and another ¼ cup blended ice cream.

Make these shakes the centerpiece of a kids' party along with peanut butter and jelly sandwiches, grape clusters and sugar wafer cookies.

1 Serving: Calories 230 (Calories from Fat 100): Total Fat 11g (Saturated Fat 7g): Cholesterol 45mg: Sodium 90mg: Total Carbohydrate 29g (Dietary Fiber 2g): Protein 5g

Key Lime–Banana Smoothies

Prep Time: 10 min ■ Start to Finish: 10 min ■ 2 Servings (1 cup each)

1 container (6 oz) Key lime pie low-fat yogurt

1 ripe banana, sliced

½ cup milk

1 tablespoon lime juice

¼ teaspoon dry lemon-lime-flavored soft drink mix (from 0.13-oz package)

1 cup vanilla frozen yogurt

1 In blender, place all ingredients except frozen yogurt. Cover and blend on high speed until smooth.

2 Add frozen yogurt. Cover and blend until smooth.

For the best banana flavor, choose bananas that have flecks of brown on the skin. Bananas that are too green will not be as sweet or flavorful.

1 Serving: Calories 340 (Calories from Fat 40); Total Fat 4.5g (Saturated Fat 2.5g); Cholesterol 15mg; Sodium 160mg; Total Carbohydrate 64g (Dietary Fiber 2g); Protein 12g

Creamy Mango Smoothies

Prep Time: 10 min ▪ Start to Finish: 10 min ▪ 6 Servings (1 cup each)

2 mangoes, peeled, chopped (2 cups)
2 cups mango sorbet
2 containers (6 oz each) French vanilla yogurt
1½ cups milk

1 In blender, place all ingredients. Cover and blend on high speed until smooth.

For the best flavor, choose ripe mangoes. The skins should be yellow with blushes of red.

1 Serving: Calories 220 (Calories from Fat 20); Total Fat 2g (Saturated Fat 1g); Cholesterol 5mg; Sodium 75mg; Total Carbohydrate 46g (Dietary Fiber 2g); Protein 5g

Frosty Guava-Peach Sippers

Prep Time: 10 min ▪ Start to Finish: 10 min ▪ 4 Servings (1 cup each)

1 can (10 oz) frozen fuzzy navel drink mix
1 cup guava juice or guava blend juice
¼ cup dark rum or guava juice
2 cups cracked ice

1 In blender, place all ingredients except ice. Cover and blend on high speed until well mixed.

2 Add ice. Cover and blend until smooth and slushy.

Fuzzy navel drinks combine the summer-fresh flavors of peach and orange. You can find the drink mix near the other frozen juices and beverages at the supermarket.

1 Serving: Calories 40 (Calories from Fat 0); Total Fat 0g (Saturated Fat 0g); Cholesterol 0mg; Sodium 0mg; Total Carbohydrate 10g (Dietary Fiber 0g); Protein 0g

Mangoritas

Prep Time: 10 min ▪ Start to Finish: 10 min ▪ 4 Servings (1 cup each)

1 can (10 oz) frozen margarita drink mix
1 cup mango nectar
½ cup tequila or mango nectar
2 cups cracked ice

1 In blender, place all ingredients except ice. Cover and blend on high speed until well mixed.

2 Add ice. Cover and blend until smooth and slushy.

The rims of margarita glasses are typically coated with lime juice and dipped in coarse salt. For these sweeter "mangoritas," coat the rims with lime juice and dip in coarse sugar.

1 Serving: Calories 210 (Calories from Fat 0); Total Fat 0g (Saturated Fat 0g); Cholesterol 0mg; Sodium 0mg; Total Carbohydrate 53g (Dietary Fiber 0g); Protein 0g

Frozen Strawberry Margaritas

Prep Time: 10 min   ▪   Start to Finish: 24 hrs 10 min   ▪   10 Servings

½ can (12 oz) frozen limeade concentrate, thawed
1 box (10 oz) frozen strawberries in syrup, thawed, undrained
3 cups water
¾ cup tequila or orange juice
1 bottle (1 liter) lemon-lime carbonated beverage, chilled

1 In blender, place limeade concentrate and strawberries. Cover; blend until smooth. Stir in water and tequila. Pour into 2-quart plastic container. Cover; freeze 24 hours or until slushy.

2 If orange juice was used, let stand at room temperature 2 hours before serving. To serve, place ⅔ cup slush in each glass and fill with ⅓ cup lemon-lime beverage; stir.

1 Serving: Calories 140 (Calories from Fat 0); Total Fat 0g (Saturated Fat 0g); Cholesterol 0mg; Sodium 15mg; Total Carbohydrate 26g (Dietary Fiber 0g); Protein 0g

Raspberry-Apricot Sangria

Prep Time: 15 min ■ Start to Finish: 15 min ■ 9 Servings (1 cup each)

1 package (10 oz) frozen sweetened raspberries, thawed
2 cups apricot nectar
1 bottle (750 ml) white wine or nonalcoholic white wine, chilled
¼ cup apricot brandy, if desired
2 cans (12 oz each) lemon-lime carbonated beverage, chilled
½ pint (1 cup) fresh raspberries
Lemon and/or orange slices, if desired

1 In blender, place thawed raspberries. Cover and blend on high speed until pureed. Press blended raspberries through a strainer into small bowl, using wooden spoon; discard seeds.

2 In 2-quart nonmetal pitcher or container, mix raspberry puree, nectar, wine and brandy. Just before serving, add lemon-lime beverage, fresh raspberries and lemon slices. Serve over ice.

Sangria comes from Spain and was originally made with red wine and fruit juices. White or blush wines offer a lighter version of this summer drink.

1 Serving: Calories 165 (Calories from Fat 0); Total Fat 0g (Saturated Fat 0g); Cholesterol 0mg; Sodium 20mg; Total Carbohydrate 29g (Dietary Fiber 3g); Protein 1g

Helpful Nutrition and Cooking Information

Recommended intake for a daily diet of 2,000 calories as set by the Food and Drug Administration

Total Fat	Less than 65g
Saturated Fat	Less than 20g
Cholesterol	Less than 300mg
Sodium	Less than 2,400mg
Total Carbohydrate	300g
Dietary Fiber	25g

Calculating Nutrition Information

- The first ingredient is used wherever a choice is given (such as $1/3$ cup sour cream or plain yogurt).

- The first ingredient amount is used wherever a range is given (such as 2 to 3 teaspoons).

- The first serving number was used wherever a range is given (such as 4 to 6 servings).

- "If desired" ingredients and recipe variations were not included (such as sprinkle with brown sugar, if desired).

- Only the amount of a marinade or frying oil that is absorbed by the food during preparation was calculated.

Ingredients Used in Recipe Testing and Nutrition Calculations

The following ingredients, based on most commonly purchased ingredients, are used unless indicated otherwise:

- Large eggs, 2% milk, 80%-lean ground beef, canned chicken broth and vegetable oil spread containing at least 65% fat when margarine is used.

- Solid vegetable shortening (not butter, margarine, or nonstick cooking spray) is used to grease pans.

Equipment Used in Recipe Testing

- Cookware and bakeware without nonstick coatings were used, unless otherwise indicated.

- No dark-colored, black or insulated bakeware was used.

- When a pan is specified, a metal pan was used; a baking dish or pie plate means ovenproof glass was used.

- An electric hand mixer was used for mixing when mixer speeds are specified.

Metric Conversion Guide

VOLUME

U.S. Units	Canadian Metric	Australian Metric
¼ teaspoon	1 mL	1 ml
½ teaspoon	2 mL	2 ml
1 teaspoon	5 mL	5 ml
1 tablespoon	15 mL	20 ml
¼ cup	50 mL	60 ml
⅓ cup	75 mL	80 ml
½ cup	125 mL	125 ml
⅔ cup	150 mL	170 ml
¾ cup	175 mL	190 ml
1 cup	250 mL	250 ml
1 quart	1 liter	1 liter
1 ½ quarts	1.5 liters	1.5 liters
2 quarts	2 liters	2 liters
2 ½ quarts	2.5 liters	2.5 liters
3 quarts	3 liters	3 liters
4 quarts	4 liters	4 liters

WEIGHT

U.S. Units	Canadian Metric	Australian Metric
1 ounce	30 grams	30 grams
2 ounces	55 grams	60 grams
3 ounces	85 grams	90 grams
4 ounces (¼ pound)	115 grams	125 grams
8 ounces (½ pound)	225 grams	225 grams
16 ounces (1 pound)	455 grams	500 grams
1 pound	455 grams	½ kilogram

MEASUREMENTS

Inches	Centimeters
1	2.5
2	5.0
3	7.5
4	10.0
5	12.5
6	15.0
7	17.5
8	20.5
9	23.0
10	25.5
11	28.0
12	30.5
13	33.0

TEMPERATURES

Fahrenheit	Celsius
32°	0°
212°	100°
250°	120°
275°	140°
300°	150°
325°	160°
350°	180°
375°	190°
400°	200°
425°	220°
450°	230°
475°	240°
500°	260°

NOTE: The recipes in this cookbook have not been developed or tested using metric measures. When converting recipes to metric, some variations in quality may be noted.

Index

Page numbers in italics indicate illustrations.

Whatever's on the menu, make it easy with *Betty Crocker*

Betty Crocker
chicken
tonight
100 Recipes for the Way You Really Cook

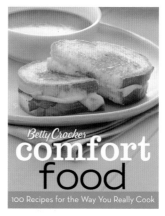

Betty Crocker
comfort
food
100 Recipes for the Way You Really Cook

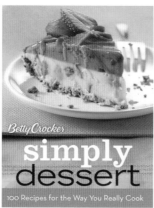

Betty Crocker
simply
dessert
100 Recipes for the Way You Really Cook

Betty Crocker
outdoor
food
100 Recipes for the Way You Really Cook

Betty Crocker
party
food
100 Recipes for the Way You Really Cook

Betty Crocker
quick
fixes
100 Recipes for the Way You Really Cook

IT'S IN THE BAG

KNITTING PROJECTS TO TAKE & MAKE

EDITED BY KARA GOTT WARNER

HOUSE of
WHITE
BIRCHES

PUBLISHERS
SINCE 1947

IT'S IN THE BAG™

EDITOR Kara Gott Warner
ART DIRECTOR Brad Snow
PUBLISHING SERVICES DIRECTOR Brenda Gallmeyer

MANAGING EDITOR Dianne Schmidt
ASSISTANT ART DIRECTOR Nick Pierce
COPY SUPERVISOR Michelle Beck
COPY EDITORS Amanda Ladig, Susanna Tobias
TECHNICAL EDITOR Charlotte Quiggle
TECHNICAL ARTISTS Nicole Gage, Pam Gregory

GRAPHIC ARTS SUPERVISOR Ronda Bechinski
GRAPHIC ARTISTS Jessi Butler, Minette Collins Smith
PRODUCTION ASSISTANTS Marj Morgan, Judy Neuenschwander

PHOTOGRAPHY SUPERVISOR Tammy Christian
PHOTOGRAPHY Scott Campbell, Matthew Owen
PHOTO STYLISTS Martha Coquat, Tammy Steiner

PRINTED IN CHINA
FIRST PRINTING: 2009
LIBRARY OF CONGRESS CONTROL NUMBER: 2008936680
HARDCOVER ISBN: 978-1-59217-247-4
SOFTCOVER ISBN: 978-1-59217-248-1

1 2 3 4 5 6 7 8 9
DRGbooks.com

WELCOME

The concept of this book is one that is near and dear to my heart. As a knitter, it's imperative to have just the right bag, equipped with a fun project and all the important essentials. The "travel-friendly" projects that follow will entice you to pack up your favorite knitting bag (or even buy a new one) and head out the door at a moment's notice. In addition to the range of projects to choose from, we also provide some valuable

travel tips and tricks. Whether you choose to knit with friends, or in solitude, you'll always have your favorite "friend" nearby.

Our designers also share some of their own memorable stories about traveling with their knitting in tow. My story begins back in the time when I commuted by subway each morning to midtown Manhattan. Finding a seat on the subway was virtually impossible during a busy morning commute. Since standing was usually the only option, I was determined to always make the most of it! My yarn was set in such a way that it would flow out of my bag tangle-free, with my instructions positioned in just the right place. When thinking back to the stares of curiosity, I'm sure I provided the subway riders with some much needed entertainment.

I'll never forget the last day of my regular commute downtown, which is a day that I fondly think back to with a smile. I knew then that I would miss this special time each morning dedicated to my knitting. While some may think of being on the subway as a nuisance, I always viewed it as an opportunity. As it became time to get off at my usual stop, a young woman asked me, "How did you do that?" As we proceeded up the steps, I gave her the "quickie" version of how to work a particular stitch. We said good-bye and off we went on our separate ways down the busy city street.

Wishing you memorable knitting adventures!

Kara Gott Warner

Kara Gott Warner

CONTENTS

ACCENT ACCESSORIES

Just as the party starts to die down, spice things up and knit a round or two. In this chapter, you'll love the selection of projects that will be a breeze to make while you travel! Pack that favorite knitting purse, grab some yummy yarn, and let's party!

UPTOWN CHIC SATCHEL

DESIGN BY CECILY GLOWIK MACDONALD

WHAT'S IN THE BAG

Classic Elite Yarns Duchess
   (bulky weight; 40% merino/28%
   viscose/15% nylon/10%
   cashmere/7% angora; 75 yds/
   50g per ball): 4 balls genteel gray #1003
Size 9 (5.5mm) needles or size needed to
   obtain gauge
Stitch markers
Cable needle
2 handles with 12-inch opening (sample
   made with Trendsetter yarns BH-MED/B,
   12-inch length)
Cardboard (optional)

SKILL LEVEL

■■■□ INTERMEDIATE

FINISHED SIZE

12 inches wide x 7 inches tall

GAUGE

16 sts and 20 rows = 4 inches/10cm
in St st.
To save time, take time to check
gauge.

SPECIAL ABBREVIATION

Make Bobble (MB): Knit in front and
back of st, turn; p3, turn, k3, turn; p3,
turn; SK2P.

PATTERN STITCHES

Front/Back Panel pat: See Chart A
Side Panel pat: See Chart B

Slip Stitch Pattern (multiple of 2 sts + 1)
Rows 1 and 3 (WS): Purl.
Row 2 (RS): *K1, sl 1; rep from * to last st,
k1.
Row 4: K1, *k1, sl 1; rep from * to last 2 sts,
k2.
   Rep Rows 1–4 for pat.

FRONT/BACK PIECES

Make 2
Cast on 51 sts.
Row 1 (WS): P17, place marker, work 17 sts
following Chart A, place marker, k17.
   Continue working outer sts in St st and sts
between markers following Chart A until 1 full
rep of chart has been worked, then work Rows
1–9 of Chart A once more.
Next row: Work as for Row 10 of chart except
do not work bobble; purl the st instead.
Next row (WS): P16, p2tog, p15, p2tog, p16—
49 sts.
   Work 4 rows in St st.
   Bind off kwise.

SIDE PIECES
Make 2
Cast on 23 sts.
Work Chart B.
Bind off pwise.

BOTTOM
Cast on 23 sts.
Work even in
Slip Stitch pat until
piece measures 12
inches, ending with
a RS row.
Bind off pwise.

FINISHING
Block pieces.

Sew cast-on edge of 1 front/back piece to
1 long edge of bottom. Rep with other front/
back piece. Sew cast-on edges of side pieces
to short edges of bottom. Sew side seams
leaving 1 inch unsewn at top of all pieces. Slide
bound-off edge of 1 front/back piece through
slit in handle. Wrap around bottom of handle
and sew bound-off edge of front/back piece
to inside of bag; rep for 2nd handle. Fold top 1
inch of side panels to WS and sew to inside of
bag. Weave in ends.

Optional: For a sturdier bottom, cut a piece
of cardboard to measurements slightly smaller
than bottom piece and place inside bag. ■

STITCH KEY
- ☐ K on RS, p on WS
- ⊟ P on RS, k on WS
- ⊠ Ssp
- ⊠ P2tog
- ⊙ MB: Knit in front and back of st, turn; p3, turn; k3, turn; p3, turn; SK2P
- Sl 2 to cn and hold in back, k3, p2 from cn
- Sl 3 to cn and hold in front, p2, k3 from cn
- Sl 1 to cn and hold in back, k1, p1 from cn
- Sl 1 to cn and hold in front, p1, k1 from cn

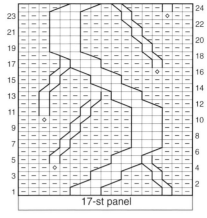

CHART A: FRONT/BACK PANEL

17-st panel

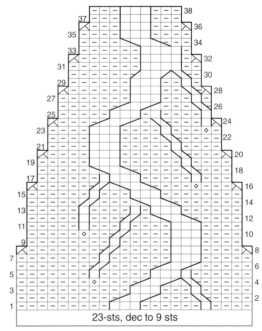

23-sts, dec to 9 sts

CHART B: SIDE PANEL

Tip If you have several projects going at one time, keep a mini "travel filing cabinet." These come in many fun shapes and sizes. You can keep track of your supplies, who you made your project for and where you last left off.

LITTLE MISS HAT & PURSE

DESIGNS BY CHERYL BECKERICH

WHAT'S IN THE BAG

Schaefer Yarn Elaine (bulky
  weight; 99% merino wool/1%
  nylon; 300 yds/8 oz per skein): 1
  skein Peter (A)
Plymouth Galway Worsted (worsted
  weight; 100% wool, 210 yds/100g per
  ball): 1 ball rose #114 (B)
Size 9 (5.5mm) double-point needle (set
  of 4 or 5) and 16-inch circular needles or
  size needed to obtain gauge
Stitch markers, 1 in CC for beg of rnd

5 BULKY

SKILL LEVEL

◼◼◻◻ EASY

SIZES

Bag: 1 size
Hat: Child's small (medium, large) Instructions
are given for smallest size, with larger sizes in
parentheses. When only 1 number is given, it
applies to all sizes.

FINISHED MEASUREMENTS

Bag: 7 inches wide at base; 6 inches wide at
top; 6 inches high
Hat circumference (body): 17 (18, 19) inches

GAUGE

20 sts and 21 rows = 4 inches/10cm in Slip St
Mesh with MC.
14½ sts and 20 rows = 4 inches/10cm in seed st
with MC.
To save time, take time to check gauge.

SPECIAL ABBREVIATIONS

Place marker (pm): Place a marker on the
needle.
Increase 1 (inc 1): Knit in front and back of st.

PATTERN STITCHES

Slip Stitch Mesh (even number of sts)
Rnds 1 and 2: Purl.
Rnd 3: *Sl 1, k1; rep from * around.

Rnd 4: *Sl 1, p1; rep from * around.
Rnd 5: *Yo, k2tog; rep from * around.
Rnd 6: Knit.
  Rep Rnds 1–6 for pat.

Seed Stitch (odd number of sts)
Rnd/Row 1: K1, *p1, k1; rep from * to end.
Rnd/Row 2: Knit the purl sts and purl the knit
sts as they present themselves.
  Rep Rnd/Row 2 for pat.

SPECIAL TECHNIQUE

3-Needle Bind-Off: With RS tog and needles
parallel, using a 3rd needle, knit tog 1 st from
the front needle with 1 from the back. *Knit
tog 1 st from the front and back needles, and sl
the first st over the 2nd to bind off. Rep from *
across, then fasten off last st.

BAG

BASE

With A, cast on 9 sts.
  Work in Seed st until piece measures
7¼ inches.
  Bind off, do not cut yarn.

BODY

Pick up and knit 7 sts along bound-off end, pm,
pick up and knit 28 sts along side, pm, pick up
and knit 7 sts from cast-on end, pm, pick up
and knit 28 sts along rem side, pm for beg of
rnd and join—70 sts.
Set-up rnd: Slipping markers, *work in seed
st to first marker, work in Slip St Mesh to next
marker; rep from * once more.
  Continue in established pats until 2 reps of
Slip St Mesh are complete.
Dec rnd: Continue in established pats, *work
to first marker, p1, p2tog, work in pat to 3 sts
before next marker, p2tog, p1; rep from * once
more—66 sts.
  Work even in established pat for 5 rnds.
  Rep Dec rnd—62 sts.
  Work even for 16 rnds, ending with Rnd 5
of pat.

10

Next rnd: Removing markers, *work in Seed st to marker, k5, bind off 14 sts, knit to next marker; rep from * once more, then work Seed st to first bind-off.

Slip 17 sts at other end to holder—17 sts rem on needle.

HANDLES
Working all sts in established Seed st, bind off 3 sts at beg of next 2 rows; bind off 2 sts at beg of following 2 rows; then bind off 1 st at beg of following 2 rows—5 sts.

Work even until handle measures 6 inches and put sts on holder.

Rep for the other side.

Join the 2 ends of the handle with 3-Needle Bind-Off.

FINISHING
Weave in ends and block.

HAT

BRIM
With circular needles and A, and using long tail method, cast on 90 (96, 100) sts; pm for beg of rnd and join, taking care not to twist sts.

Work 5 rnds in Slip St Mesh.

Dec rnd: Work Rnd 6 of pat and dec 10 sts evenly around—80 (86, 90) sts.

Continue in Slip St Mesh for 5 rnds.

Dec rnd: Work Rnd 6 of pat and dec 20 sts evenly around—60 (66, 70) sts.

BODY
Work [Rnds 1–6 of Slip Stitch Mesh pat] 4 times.

Purl 0 (1, 2) rnds.

Shape crown
Work Rnd 1 of Slip St Mesh.

Dec rnd: Work Rnd 2 of pat and dec 20 sts evenly around—40 (46, 50) sts.

Work Rnds 3–6 of pat.

Dec rnd: Work Rnd 1 of pat and dec 10 (12, 10) sts evenly around—30 (34, 40) sts.

Work Rnds 2-5 of pat.

Dec rnd: [K2tog] around—15 (17, 20) sts.

Dec rnd: [P2tog] around, ending p1 (1, 0)—8 (9, 10) sts.

Cut yarn, leaving a 6-inch tail.

With tapestry needle, thread tail through rem sts, pull tight and secure.

FINISHING
Weave in tails. Block.

FELTED FLOWERS
Make 2

Center
With dpn and B, cast on 6 sts; distribute sts evenly on 3 dpns, pm for beg of rnd and join, taking care not to twist sts.

Rnd 1: Knit.
Rnd 2: Inc 1 in each st around—12 sts.
Rnd 3: Knit.
Rnd 4: *K1, inc 1; rep from * around—18 sts.
Rnd 5: Knit.
Rnd 6: *K2, inc 1; rep from * around—24 sts.
Cut yarn.

Petals
Make 6 on each flower
Distribute sts among the dpns so that you

have 4 sts on 1 dpn and 20 rem sts on hold on 2 dpns to be worked later.

Row 1 (WS): P4.

Inc row: K1, inc 1, work to last 2 sts, inc 1, k1—6 sts.

Continue in St st and rep Inc row [every RS row] twice more—10 sts.

Work 7 rows even.

Next row (RS): K1, ssk, k4, k2tog, k1—8 sts.

Next row (WS): P1, p2tog, p2, ssp, p1—6 sts.

Next row: K1, ssk, k2tog, k1—4 sts.

Next row: P2tog, ssp—2 sts.

Bind off.

Rep for each petal.

SHAPING

With tapestry needle and approx 10 inches of yarn, weave the yarn in and out around the base of the petals to form a bobble in center of flower and place tails in the center of the flower as stuffing for the bobble. Pull tight and secure yarn.

Weave in rem tails.

FELTING

Follow basic felting instructions on page 167 until flowers measure approx 5½ inches across.

ASSEMBLY

Sew flowers to bag and hat, being careful to catch only the back of the petals and center of flowers so that yarn doesn't show on the RS. ∎

Tip Place a copy of your pattern in a page protector. Use a dry erase marker to remember your place. When you're done, just wipe it clean.

KATHMANDU CRAVAT

DESIGN BY JOËLLE MEIER RIOUX FOR CLASSIC ELITE YARNS

WHAT'S IN THE BAG

Classic Elite Yarns Fresco (sport weight; 60% wool/30% baby alpaca/10% angora; 164 yds/50g per hank): 1 hank each purple haze #5379 (A) and cinder #5303 (B)
Size 7 (4.5mm) needles or size needed to obtain gauge

2 FINE

SKILL LEVEL
■□□□ BEGINNER

FINISHED SIZE
Approx 4 x 30 inches

GAUGE
33 sts and 26 rows = 4 inches/10cm in Biased Rib.
To save time, take time to check gauge.

SPECIAL ABBREVIATIONS
Make 1 (M1): Insert LH needle from front to back under the running thread between the last st worked and next st on RH needle; knit into the back of resulting loop.
Make 1 purlwise (M1P): Insert LH needle from front to back under the running thread between the last st worked and next st on RH needle; purl into the back of resulting loop.

PATTERN STITCHES
K3, P3 Rib (multiple of 6 sts +3)
Row 1 (RS): K3, *p3, k3; rep from * across.
Row 2: Knit the knit sts and purl the purl sts as they face you.
  Rep Row 2 for pat.

Biased Rib (multiple of 6 sts + 3)
Rows 1, 5 and 9 (RS): K3, M1P, knit the knit sts and purl the purl sts as they face you to last 4 sts, k2tog, k2.
Rows 2, 3, 4, 6, 7, 8, 10, 11, 12, 14, 15, 16, 18, 19, 20, 22, 23 and 24: K3, knit the knit sts and purl the purl sts as they face you to last 3 sts, k3.

Rows 13, 17 and 21: K3, M1, knit the knit sts and purl the purl sts as they face you to last 4 sts, k2tog, k2.
  Rep Rows 1–24 for pat.

Stripe Sequence
*Work 33 rows with A, then 33 rows with B; rep from * twice more.

PATTERN NOTE
First and last 3 stitches are worked in garter stitch (knit every row) throughout.

SCARF
With A, cast on 33 sts.
Row 1 (RS): Beg Stripe Sequence; k3, work K3, P3 Rib to last 3 sts, k3.
  Maintaining first and last 3 sts in garter st throughout, work even for 5 rows in established rib, ending with a WS row.
Next row (RS): Continue Stripe sequence and change to Biased Rib.
  Work even until Stripe Sequence is complete, ending with Row 24 of Biased Rib.
  Bind off in pat.

FINISHING
Weave in all ends. Block to finished measurements. ■

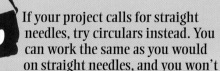
If your project calls for straight needles, try circulars instead. You can work the same as you would on straight needles, and you won't have to fumble around to find the straight needle that fell into the "black hole" of your knitting bag ever again!

DAY AT THE MET MITERED WRAP

DESIGN BY SARA LUCAS

WHAT'S IN THE BAG

Plymouth Boku (worsted weight; 95% wool/5% silk; 99 yds/50g per ball): 2 balls blue-green variegated #10 (A)

Berroco Comfort (worsted weight; 50% nylon/50% acrylic; 210 yds/100g per ball): 1 ball each dried plum #9780 (B), barley #9703 (C) and limone #9706 (D)

Size 8 (5mm) needles or size needed to obtain gauge

SKILL LEVEL

INTERMEDIATE

FINISHED MEASUREMENTS

Approx 18 x 56 inches

GAUGE

18 sts and 36 rows = 4 inches/10cm in garter st. To save time, take time to check gauge.

SPECIAL ABBREVIATION

Centered Double Decrease (S2KP2): Slip 2 sts kwise, k1, pass 2 slipped sts over.

PATTERN STITCHES

Color Sequence

Work 3 rows A, 2 rows B, 2 rows A,

2 rows C, 2 rows A, 2 rows D, 8 rows A, work B to end.

Mitered Square

With A, cast on or pick up and knit a total of 30 sts.

Row 1 (WS): K14, k2tog, k14—29 sts.
Row 2 (RS): K13, S2KP2, k13—27 sts.
Row 3 and all WS rows: Knit.
Row 4: K12, S2KP2, k12—25 sts.
Row 6: K11, S2KP2, k11—23 sts.

Continue in this manner, working garter st with centered double dec at center st every RS row until 3 sts rem.

Next row (WS): Work S2KP2 and fasten off.

Mitered Rectangle

With A, cast on or pick up and knit a total of 60 sts.

Row 1 (WS): K14, k2tog, k28, k2tog, k14—58 sts.
Row 2 (RS): K13, S2KP2, k26, S2KP2, k13—54 sts
Row 3 and all other WS rows: Knit.
Row 4: K12, S2KP2, k24, S2KP2, k12—50 sts.

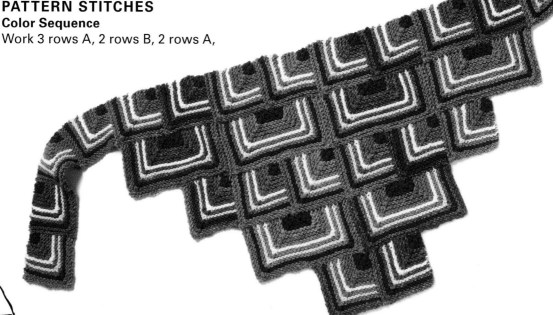

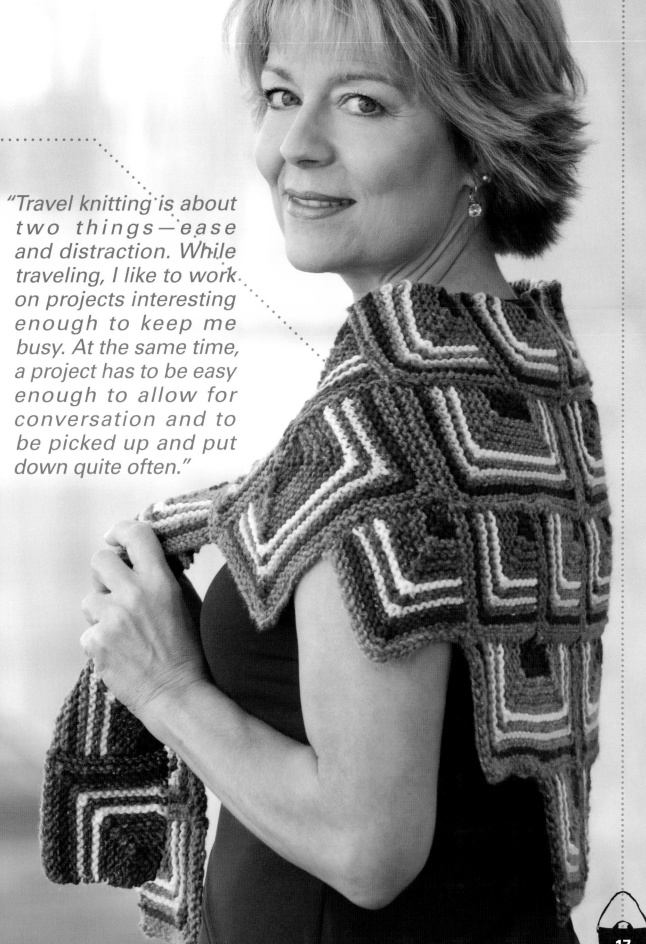

"Travel knitting is about two things—ease and distraction. While traveling, I like to work on projects interesting enough to keep me busy. At the same time, a project has to be easy enough to allow for conversation and to be picked up and put down quite often."

Row 6: K11, S2KP2, k22, S2KP2, k11—46 sts.

Continue in this manner, working garter st with centered double dec every RS row until 2 sts rem.

Next row (WS): K2tog and fasten off.

PATTERN NOTES

Wrap is worked from bottom up with mitered squares and rectangles (see Placement Diagram for order).

Use knit-on method when casting on.

When picking up stitches pick up 1 stitch per stitch or garter ridge.

Use color A to begin each square or rectangle, then follow Color Sequence.

The beginning sides (cast-on or pick-up) of squares are Side A and Side B; the beginning sides of rectangles are Sides A, B, and C (see Diagram).

Weave in ends as you work to avoid excess finishing.

WRAP

Square 1: With A, cast on 30 sts. Work Mitered Square following Color Sequence.

Square 2: With A, pick up and knit 15 sts along Side C of Square 1, then cast on 15 sts—30 sts. Work Mitered Square.

Rectangle 3: Cast on 30 sts, pick up and knit 15 sts along Side D of Square 1, then cast on 15 sts—60 sts. Work Mitered Rectangle.

Rectangle 4: Pick up and knit 15 sts along Side C of Rectangle 3, then 15 sts along Side D of Square 2, cast on 30 sts—60 sts. Work Mitered Rectangle.

Square 5: Cast on 30 sts. Work Mitered Square.

Square 6: Pick up and knit 15 sts along Side C of Square 5, and 15 sts along Side D of Rectangle 3—30 sts. Work Mitered Square.

Continue in this manner, working each square or rectangle in order following Diagram, casting on or picking up as appropriate.

FINISHING

Weave in all rem ends and block. ■

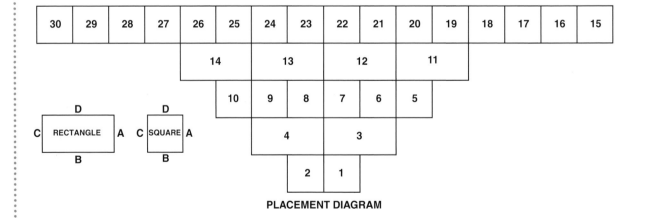

PLACEMENT DIAGRAM

COUNTRY ROADS SCARF

DESIGN BY KYLEANN WILLIAMS

WHAT'S IN THE BAG

Crystal Palace Merino 5 (worsted weight; 100% superwash wool; 110 yds/50g per ball): 3 balls each fall herbs #9809 (A) and nougat #5216 (B)

Size 10 (6mm) needles or size needed to obtain gauge

SKILL LEVEL

 EASY

FINISHED SIZE

Approx 10 x 66 inches (blocked)

GAUGE

17 sts and 23 rows = 4 inches/10cm in St st.
To save time, take time to check gauge.

SPECIAL ABBREVIATION

Make 1 (M1): Insert LH needle from front to back under the running thread between the last st worked and next st on RH needle; knit into the back of resulting loop.

PATTERN NOTES

This scarf is worked in entrelac. "Steps" are spelled out, rather than "Rows;" most steps are worked across and then back, i.e. 2 rows in most steps.

The body of the scarf is made in stockinette stitch; the sides and ends are made in seed stitch to eliminate curling and minimize blocking.

Always work the stitches in the row following the pick-up row through the back loop; this will twist the base of the picked-up stitch, keeping that loop from being too loose.

SCARF

Foundation Triangles

Make 3

With A, very loosely cast on 21 sts, using a larger needle if necessary.

Step 1: K1, p1, turn; p1, k1, turn.
Step 2: K1, p1, k1, turn; k1, p1, k1, turn.
Step 3: [K1, p1] twice, turn; [p1, k1] twice, turn.
Step 4: K1, [p1, k1] twice, turn; k1, [p1, k1] twice, turn.
Step 5: [K1, p1] 3 times, turn; [p1, k1] 3 times, turn.
Step 6: K1, [p1, k1] 3 times, do not turn—7 sts worked.

Rep [Steps 1–6] twice more over the last 14 sts.

Cut A, leaving a 5-inch tail.

FIRST TIER

Left Side Triangle

Step 1 (WS): Join B; k1, p1, turn; p1, M1, p1, turn.
Step 2: P1, k1, p2tog, turn; p1, k1, M1, k1, turn.
Step 3: K1, p1, k1, p2tog, turn; p1, k1, p1, M1, p1, turn.
Step 4: [P1, k1] twice, p2tog; turn [p1, k1] twice, M1, k1, turn.
Step 5: [K1, p1] twice, k1, p2tog, turn; [p1, k1] twice, p1, M1, p1, turn.
Step 6: [P1, k1] 3 times, p2tog; do not turn.

Right Slanting Rectangle
Step 1 (WS): Pick up and purl 7 sts along the selvedge edge of triangle or rectangle of tier below, turn.
Step 2: K7, turn; p6, p2tog, turn.
Rep [Step 2] 6 more times; do not turn after last p2tog—rectangle complete.
Work another Right Slanting Rectangle over the next 7 sts.

Right Side Triangle
Step 1 (WS): Pick up and purl 7 sts along the selvedge edge of the next triangle or rectangle, turn.
Step 2: [K1, p1] 3 times, k1 turn; [k1, p1] 2 twice, k1, k2tog, turn.
Step 3: [P1, k1] 3 times, turn; [k1, p1] twice, k2tog, turn.
Step 4: [K1, p1] twice, k1, turn; k1, p1, k1, k2tog, turn.
Step 5: [P1, k1] twice, turn; k1, p1, k2tog, turn.
Step 6: K1, p1, k1, turn; k1, k2tog, turn.
Step 7: P1, k1, turn; k2tog, turn—1 st rem.
Cut B, leaving a 5-inch tail.

2ND TIER
Left Slanting Rectangle
Step 1 (RS): With A, pick up and knit 6 sts along edge of triangle just completed, turn—7 sts, including last st from right side triangle.
Step 2: P7, turn; k6, ssk.
Rep [Step 2] 6 more times.
Make 2 more Left Slanting Rectangles, picking up 7 sts along the edges of the Right Slanting Rectangles in the tier below.
Cut A, leaving a 5-inch tail.

> *"Circular needles really come in handy when knitting on a plane. You're not a true knitter if you've never dropped a straight needle, and watched it roll all the way to the cockpit"!*

Work 25 more reps of first and 2nd tiers, ending with first tier.

ENDING TRIANGLES
Make 3
Step 1: With A, pick up and knit 6 sts along side of triangle just completed, turn—7 sts, including last st from Right Side Triangle.
Step 2: K1, [p1, k1] 3 times, turn; [k1, p1] 3 times, ssk, turn.
Step 3: [K1, p1] twice, k1, p2tog, turn; p1, [k1, p1] twice, ssk, turn.
Step 4: [K1, p1] twice, k2tog, turn; [k1, p1] twice, ssk, turn.
Step 5: K1, p1, k1, p2tog, turn; p1, k1, p1, ssk, turn.
Step 6: K1, p1, k2tog, turn; k1, p1, ssk, turn.
Step 7: K1, p2tog, turn, p1, ssk, turn.
Step 8: K2tog, turn; ssk, do not turn.
Rep [Steps 1–8] twice more, picking up sts along sides of rectangles of previous tier.
Fasten off.

FINISHING
Weave in ends. Wet-block the scarf and let dry thoroughly. ∎

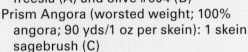

SIMPLY STRIPES SCARF

DESIGN BY LAURA BRYANT FOR PRISM YARN

WHAT'S IN THE BAG

Prism Lotus (worsted weight; 58% wool/27% bamboo/15% silk; 105 yds/2 oz per skein): 1 skein each freesia (A) and olive #604 (B)

Prism Angora (worsted weight; 100% angora; 90 yds/1 oz per skein): 1 skein sagebrush (C)

Size 10 (6mm) 29-inch circular needle or size needed to obtain gauge

Size 13 (9mm) 29-inch circular needle

Cardboard, 8-inches wide

4 MEDIUM

SKILL LEVEL
■□□□ BEGINNER

FINISHED SIZE
Approx 6 x 57 inches, not including fringe

GAUGE
14 sts and 28 rows = 4 inches/10cm in garter stitch with smaller needle. To save time, take time to check gauge.

PATTERN NOTES
This scarf is knit sideways and is self-fringing.

Leave an 8-inch tail when attaching or cutting each yarn; when turning between first and 2nd row of each color, wrap yarn around an 8-inch piece of cardboard, then continue with 2nd row.

Tip "Fringe as you work" is the perfect solution for working with multiple yarns. When you finish a row, cut the yarn and turn it into fringe. You can be resourceful and use your paperback book to conveniently measure it too!

SCARF

With A and larger needle, cast on 200 sts.

With smaller needle, work in garter stitch, leaving 8-inch lengths for fringe at each end of row *(see Pattern Notes)*, in the following sequence: 2 rows A, 2 rows B, 2 rows C.

Work for 6 inches (or desired width), finishing with A or B.

Bind off with larger needle.

Make an overhand knot at edge of fabric with every 2–3 strands of yarn.

Cut fringe evenly. ■

CITY GIRL SCARF

DESIGN BY JACQUELINE W. HOYLE

WHAT'S IN THE BAG

Schaefer Yarn Judith (DK weight; 100% prime alpaca; 330 yds/4oz per skein): 1 skein Renata Tebaldi

Size 10 (6mm) needles or size needed to obtain gauge

SKILL LEVEL

 EASY

FINISHED SIZE

Approx 4 x 68 inches, not including fringes

GAUGE

17 sts and 32 rows = 4 inches/10cm in Lacy pat. To save time, take time to check gauge.

PATTERN STITCH

Lacy Pattern (any number of sts)
Row 1: K1, *[yo] twice, k1; rep from * to end.

Row 2: K1, *drop both yo's, k1; rep from * to end.
Rows 3–10: Knit.
Rep Rows 1–10 for pat.

PATTERN NOTE

When casting on at the beginning of a row to start a fringe, turn work and use cable cast-on method, then turn work again and work stitches following instructions.

SCARF

Cast on 18 sts.
Knit 6 rows.

First Fringe Section

Rows 1 and 2 (side fringes): Cast on 18 sts, turn; k18, turn; p18, turn; bind off the 18 cast on sts, then k18 rem sts.
Row 3: K1, *yo, k1; rep from * to end.
Row 4: K1, *drop yo, k1; rep from * to end.
Rows 5 and 6: Knit.
Rows 7 and 8: Rep Rows 1 and 2.
Rows 9–11: Knit.
Rep [Rows 1–11] 8 times.

Main Section

Work Lacy pat until scarf is desired length minus the length of fringe section.

Second Fringe section

Work Rows 3–11 of first fringe section, then work [Rows 1–11] 8 times, and [Rows 1 and 2] once.
Knit 6 rows.
Bind off loosely.
Weave in all ends. ∎

Tip Place your yarn into a resealable plastic bag. Cut a small hole in the bottom corner and pull the end of the yarn through the opening.

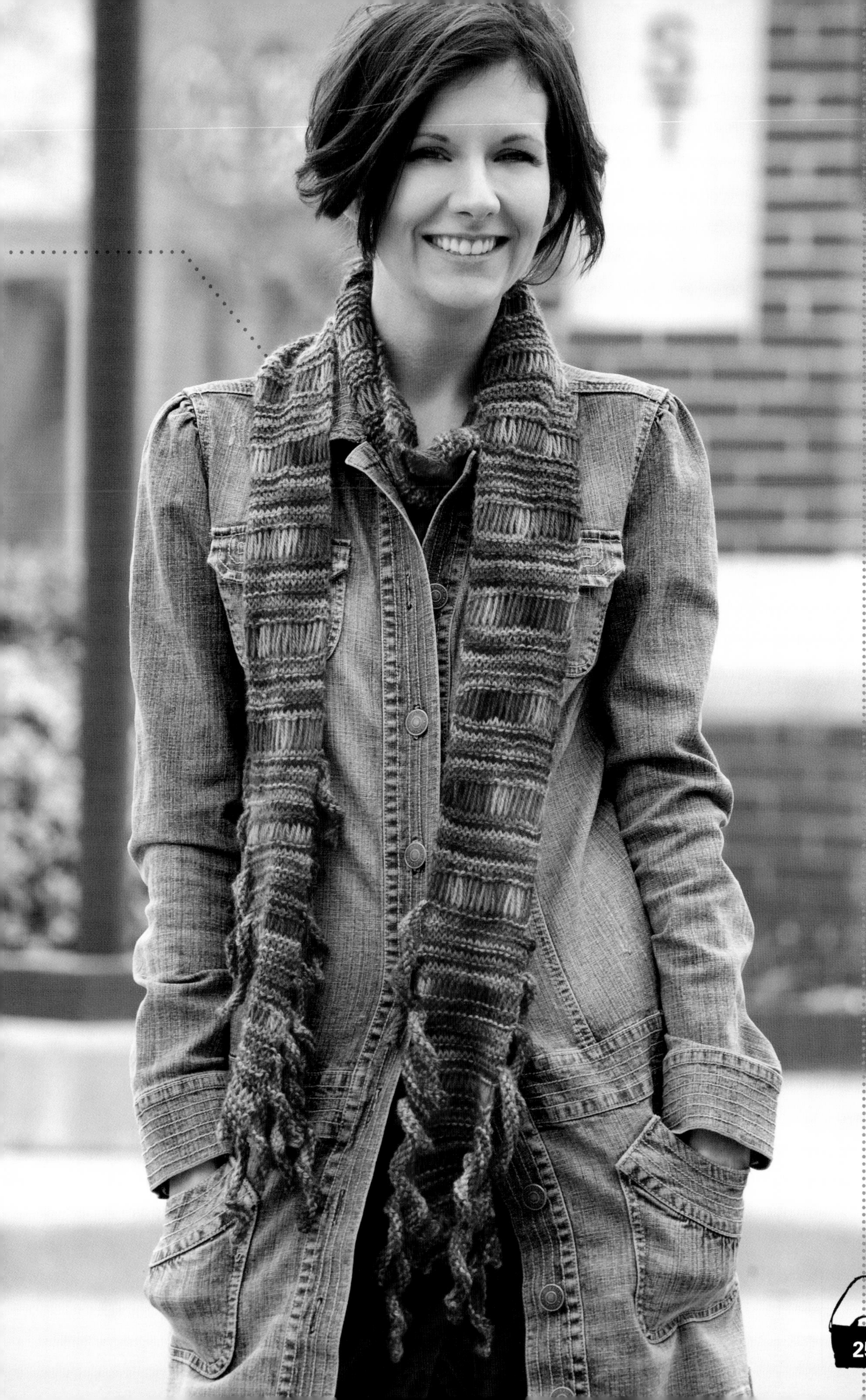

KALEIDOSCOPE MARKET BAG

DESIGN BY CELESTE PINHEIRO

WHAT'S IN THE BAG

Plymouth Galway Worsted
(worsted weight; 100% wool;
210 yds/100g per ball): 1 ball each
dark brown #66 (A), mulberry
#117 (B), lime #127 (C), orange #91 (D),
pink #141 (E), turquoise #149 (F), light
purple #89 (G) and gold #60 (H)
Size 8 (5mm) straight and 24-inch circular
needles or size needed to obtain gauge
Open stitch marker
½ yd of fabric (optional for lining)

SKILL LEVEL

■■■☐ INTERMEDIATE

FINISHED MEASUREMENTS

Length: 14 inches
Width: 13½ inches

GAUGE

18 sts and 23 rows=4 inches in St st.
To save time, take time to check gauge.

PATTERN NOTES

Bag is worked from bottom up.

The mitered squares are worked in 2 color sequences: A and B.

The instructions for Square A are given first; instructions for Square B are in parentheses.

Place center stitch marker in the fabric, not on the needle; the center stitch will become obvious after you've worked several decrease rows but if necessary

move marker up as you work.

Weave in ends as you work to eliminate tedious finishing.

Refer to Figure 1 for labeled points and sides.

Refer to Figure 2 for placement of Squares A and B when working bag.

BAG

SQUARE A (B)

With B (G) cast on 39 sts and mark center st.
Knit 1 WS row.

Row 1 (RS): Knit to 1 st before center st, sk2p, knit to end—37 sts.

Continuing to work sk2p dec over center 3 sts every RS row and purling all sts on WS rows through Row 28, work as follows:

Row 2: Purl.
Row 3: Knit—35 sts.
Row 4: Purl.
Row 5: Knit—33 sts.
Row 6: Change to A (A) and knit.
Row 7: Knit—31 sts.
Row 8: Purl.
Row 9: Knit—29 sts.
Row 10: Change to C (H) and knit.
Row 11: Knit—27 sts.
Row 12: Purl.
Row 13: Knit—25 sts.
Row 14: Change to D (E) and knit.
Row 15: Knit—23 sts.
Row 16: Purl.
Row 17: Knit—21 sts.
Row 18: Change to E (F) and knit.
Row 19: Knit—19 sts.
Row 20: Purl.
Row 21: Knit—17 sts.
Row 22: Change to A (A) and knit.
Row 23: Knit—15 sts.
Row 24: Purl.

Row 25: Knit—13 sts.
Row 26: Change to F (D) and knit.
Row 27: Knit—11 sts.
Row 28: Purl.
Row 29: Knit—9 sts.
Row 30: P3, p3tog-tbl, p3—7 sts.
Row 31: Knit—5 sts.
Row 32: P1, p3tog-tbl, p1—3 sts
Row 33: Sk2p—1 st.
   Fasten off.

BOTTOM
Make 2 Square A's.
Put points C of squares together; with color B, pick up and knit 20 sts along side D–C of first square, then pick up and knit 19 sts along side C–B of 2nd square.
   Knit 1 row.
   Continue working Rows 1–33 of Square A.
   Rep on other side of original squares.
   You now have a large square made from 4 Square A's.

First Layer of Squares
With color G, pick up and knit 20 sts along side A–D of 1 square of bottom, then pick up and knit 19 sts along side B–A of adjoining square.
   Knit 1 row.
   Work Rows 1–33 of Square B.
   Rep around, making 3 more Square B's.

2nd Layer of Squares
With color B, pick up and knit 20 sts along side A–D of 1 square of first layer, then pick up and knit 19 sts along side B–A of adjoining square.
   Knit 1 row.
   Work Rows 1–33 of Square A.
   Rep around, making 3 more Square A's.

3rd Layer of Squares
Work as for first layer of squares.

FINISHING
Top border
With RS facing and color A, pick up and knit 18 sts along side B–A, then 18 sts along side A–D of first square in 3rd layer.
   Rep along tops of rem squares on 3rd layer; place marker for beg of rnd and join—144 sts.
   [Purl 1 rnd, knit 1 rnd] 4 times, purl 1 rnd. Bind off very loosely kwise.
   Weave in all ends. Block to finished measurements.

Tip To avoid the tangled mess of using several different color yarns, place one skein of each color inside a small drawstring bag. Pull out only the color you need. When you're done, snip off the yarn at the opening of the bag, leaving just an inch hanging out so you can see the color for later use.

STRAPS
Make 2
Cut 3 strands 30-inches long from each color except A.
   Holding all strands tog, make an overhand knot near 1 end, leaving tails as fringe.
   Divide strands into 3 mixed-color groups and braid.
   Make an overhand knot in end, leaving tails as fringe.
   Sew one knotted end and approx 1 inch of strap to one point of top border; sew other end to adjacent point.
   Rep for other strap.

Lining (optional)
Fold fabric with RS together. Lay completed tote on top and trace around outside of bag. Sew ¼-inch seam, attach to bag around top opening. ■

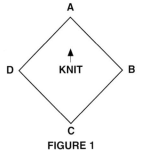

FIGURE 1

FIGURE 2

HARLEQUIN SOCKS

DESIGN BY KATHRYN BECKERDITE

WHAT'S IN THE BAG

Plymouth Yarn Happy Feet
 (sock weight; 90% superwash
 merino wool/10% nylon; 192
 yds/50g per skein): 3 skeins
 grape/garnet #5
Size 1 (2.25mm) double-point needles (set
 of 5) or size needed to obtain gauge
Size C/2 (2.75mm) crochet hook
Stitch marker

SKILL LEVEL

■■■☐ INTERMEDIATE

SIZES

Woman's small (woman's large, man's small,
man's large) to fit woman's shoe sizes 6-7
(woman's 8–9, man's 8–9, man's 10–11)
Instructions are given for the smallest size,
with larger sizes in parentheses. When only
1 number is given, it applies to all sizes.

FINISHED MEASUREMENTS

Circumference: 8 (8¼, 8⅝, 8¾) inches
Foot length: 9 (9⅜, 9⅞, 10¼) inches

GAUGE

32 sts and 44 rnds =
4 inches/10cm in St st.
To save time, take time
to check gauge.

SPECIAL ABBREVIATIONS

Wrap and Turn (W&T):
Bring yarn to RS of
work between needles,
slip next st pwise to
RH needle, bring yarn
around this st to WS,
slip st back to LH needle,
turn work to begin
working back in the
other direction.

Work wrapped sts and wraps tog (WW): *On RS:* Knit to wrapped st, slip the wrapped st pwise from LH needle to RH needle. Use tip of LH needle to pick up wrap(s) and place it/them on RH needle. Slip wrap(s) and st back to LH needle and knit them tog.

 On WS: Purl to wrapped st, slip the wrapped st kwise from LH needle to RH needle. Use tip of LH to pick up wrap(s) and place it/them on RH needle. Slip wrap(s) and st back to LH needle and purl them tog.

Make 1 (M1): Insert LH needle from front to back under the running thread between the last st worked and next st on LH needle. With RH needle, knit into the back of this loop.

PATTERN STITCH

Diamond Panel
(multiple of 15 sts over 26 rnds)
Rnds 1 and 2: P7, k1, p7.
Rnds 3 and 4: P6, k1, p1, k1, p6.
Rnds 5 and 6: P5, (k1, p1) twice, k1, p5.
Rnds 7 and 8: P4, (k1, p1) 3 times, k1, p4.
Rnds 9 and 10: P3, (k1, p1, k1, p3) twice.
Rnds 11 and 12: P2, k1, p1, k1, p5, k1, p1, k1, p2.
Rnds 13 and 14: P1, k1, p1, k1, p7, k1, p1, k1, p1.
Rnds 15 and 16: Rep Rnds 11 and 12.
Rnds 17 and 18: Rep Rnds 9 and 10.
Rnds 19 and 20: Rep Rnds 7 and 8.
Rnds 21 and 22: Rep Rnds 5 and 6.
Rnds 23 and 24: Rep Rnds 3 and 4.
Rnds 25 and 26: Rep Rnds 1 and 2.
 Rep Rnds 1–26 for pat.

SPECIAL TECHNIQUES

Provisional Cast-On: With crochet hook and waste yarn, make a chain several sts longer than desired cast on. With knitting

needle and project yarn, pick up indicated number of sts in the "bumps" on back of chain. When indicated in pat, "unzip" the crochet chain to free live sts.

Sewn Bind-Off: Cut yarn, leaving a 1-yd tail. Using a tapestry needle, *thread the yarn pwise through the first 2 sts on the needle. Pull through, leaving the sts on the needle. Thread the yarn kwise through the first st on the needle, pull through. Drop the first st off the needle. Rep from * around.

PATTERN NOTES

This sock is worked on 4 double-point needles from the toe up, with short-row toe and heel shaping and ending with a Sewn Bind-Off.

A chart for the Diamond Panel is included for those preferring to work from charts.

SOCK

SHORT-ROW TOE

Using provisional method, cast on 32 (34, 36, 38) sts.

Row 1 (WS): Purl.
Row 2: Knit to last st, W&T.
Row 3: Purl to last st, W&T.
Row 4: Knit to st before last wrapped st, W&T.
Row 5: Purl to st before last wrapped st, W&T.

Rep Rows 4 and 5 until 12 (12, 14, 14) sts rem unwrapped.

Row 6: Knit to the first wrapped st, WW, W&T.
Row 7: Purl to the first wrapped st, WW, W&T.
Row 8: Knit to the first double-wrapped st, WW, W&T.
Row 9: Purl to the first double-wrapped st, WW, W&T.

Rep Rows 8 and 9 until one double-wrapped st rem at each end of work.

Row 10: Knit to double-wrapped st, knit double-wrapped st, do not turn; place marker for beg of rnd.

Unzip Provisional Cast-On and distribute newly live (instep) sts and sole sts evenly divided on 4 dpns—64 (68, 72, 76) total sts with 16 (17, 18, 19) sts on each needle.

FOOT

Rnd 1: Knit.
Rnd 2 (inc instep sts): K7 (8, 7, 8), [M1, k3] 6 (6, 7, 7) times, M1, knit to end—71 (75, 80, 84) sts.
Rnd 3: K5 (6, 5, 6), [p1, k1] 14 (14, 16, 16) times, p1, knit to end.

Rep Rnd 3 until piece measures approx 7¼ (7¾, 8, 8½) inches from beg.

SHORT-ROW HEEL

Turn work.

Leaving instep sts unworked, work heel as for toe over 32 (34, 36, 38) sole sts.

LEG

Rnd 1 (inc heel sts): Work instep sts in established pat; work heel sts as follows: k8, [M1, k3] 5 (5, 6, 6) times, k3, p7 (8, 7, 8)—76 (80, 86, 90) sts.
Rnd 2: *P8 (9, 8, 9), [k1, p1] 11 (11, 13, 13) times, k1, p7 (8, 7, 8); rep from * around.
Rnd 3: Work in established pat to last 7 (8, 7, 8) sts, place marker for new beg of rnd. Redistribute sts as desired.
Rnd 4: *P0 (1, 0, 1), work Diamond Panel over next 15 sts, p0 (1, 0, 1), [k1, p1] 11 (11, 13, 13) times, k1; rep from * around.

Continue in established pat and work Diamond Panel 3 times total.
Last 2 rnds: *P15 (17, 15, 17), [k1, p1] 11 (11, 13, 13) times; rep from * once.

Bind off using Sewn Bind-Off.

FINISHING

Weave in ends. Block. ■

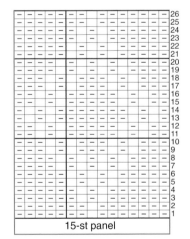

| | | | | | | | | | | |26 |
| | | | | | | | | | | |25 |

DIAMOND PANEL

15-st panel

STITCH KEY
☐ Knit
⊟ Purl

 Tip Socks couldn't be easier to take on the go. If your pattern calls for double-point needles, try a 12 inch circular needle instead. You can neatly store away your project, without those needles poking out at you!

TRAVELING LACE BEADED SHAWL

DESIGN BY CHRISTINE L. WALTER

WHAT'S IN THE BAG

Berroco Ultra Alpaca (worsted
weight; 50% alpaca/50% wool;
215 yds/100g per hank): 3 hank
lavender mix #6283

38 Mill Hill Pebble Beads size 3/0 in
midnight rainbow #05086

Size 10½ (6.5mm) circular needle or size
needed to obtain gauge

One blunt tapestry needle small enough to
fit through beads

SKILL LEVEL
■■■□ INTERMEDIATE

FINISHED SIZE
Approx 20 x 62 inches

GAUGE
12 sts and 17 rows = 4 inches/10cm in Traveling
Lace pat (after blocking).
To save time, take time to check gauge.

SPECIAL ABBREVIATION
Bring Up Bead (BUB): Slide a bead up against
the st just worked.

PATTERN STITCH
Traveling Lace Pat (multiple of 10 sts + 1)
Row 1 (RS): K1, *yo, k8, k2tog; rep from *
across.
Row 2 and all WS rows: Purl.
Row 3: K1, *k1, yo, k7, k2tog; rep from * across.
Row 5: K1, *k2, yo, k6, k2tog; rep from * across.
Row 7: K1, *k3, yo, k5, k2tog; rep from * across.
Row 9: K1, *k4, yo, k4, k2tog; rep from * across.
Row 11: K1, *k5, yo, k3, k2tog; rep from * across.
Row 13: K1, *k6, yo, k2, k2tog; rep from * across.
Row 15: K1, *k7, yo, k1, k2tog; rep from * across.
Row 17: K1, *k8, yo, k2tog; rep from * across.
Row 19: *Ssk, k8, yo; rep from * to last st, k1.
Row 21: *Ssk, k7, yo, k1; rep from * to last st, k1.
Row 23: *Ssk, k6, yo, k2; rep from * to last st, k1.
Row 25: *Ssk, k5, yo, k3; rep from * to last st, k1.

Row 27: *Ssk, k4, yo, k4; rep from * to last st, k1.
Row 29: *Ssk, k3, yo, k5; rep from * to last st, k1.
Row 31: *Ssk, k2, yo, k6; rep from * to last st, k1.
Row 33: *Ssk, k1, yo, k7; rep from * to last st, k1.
Row 35: *Ssk, yo, k8; rep from * to last st, k1.
Row 36: Purl.
Rep Rows 1–36 for pat.

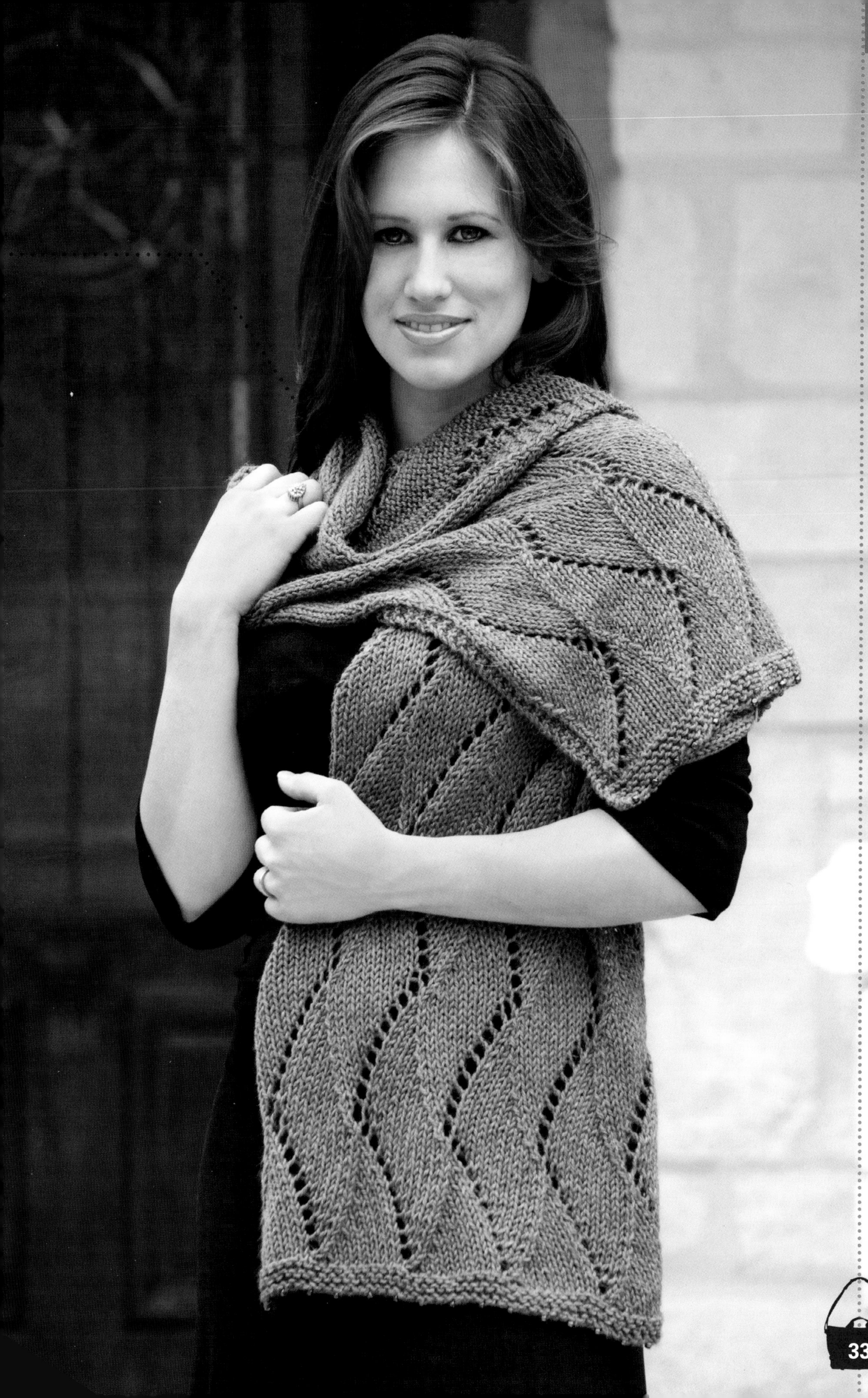

PATTERN NOTES

Purchase extra beads because some beads may have bad center holes.

A chart is provided for those preferring to work from charts.

SHAWL

Measure off approx 50 inches of yarn, make a slip knot and place on needle.

String 19 beads on the 50-inch tail.

Beaded cast-on row: Using Long-Tail Cast-On method, BUB, [cast on 3 sts, BUB] 18 times, cast on 1 st—56 sts.

Knit 7 rows, increasing 1 st on last row—57 sts.

Row 1 (RS): K3, work Row 1 of Traveling Lace pat, k3.

Row 2: K3, purl to last 3 sts, k3.

Continue working first and last 3 sts in garter st and working Traveling Lace pat between

In social settings, avoid patterns that require excessive counting of rows or stitches. Instead, find easy projects with no shaping and simple stitch patterns.

markers as established.

Work 8 complete reps of Traveling Lace pat.

Knit 7 rows, decreasing 1 st on first row—56 sts.

Cut yarn, leaving a 50-inch tail.

With RS facing, working from left to right, using small tapestry needle and keeping the working yarn above, thread a bead onto the yarn and BUB; *go into the 2nd st from the front, then into the first st from the back; pull the yarn through both sts; slip the first st off the needle; rep from * twice more omitting the bead and keeping the tension fairly loose. Continue binding off in this manner, introducing a bead every 3rd maneuver until 19 beads have been placed and all sts have been bound off.

FINISHING

Weave in ends. Block to finished measurements. ■

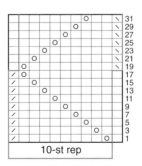

STITCH KEY

☐ K on RS

⊡ Yo

⧄ K2tog

⧅ Ssk

Note: This 32-row chart shows RS rows only. Purl all WS rows.

10-st rep

TRAVELING LACE

GOSSAMER CAPELET

DESIGN BY LAURA BRYANT FOR PRISM YARN

WHAT'S IN THE BAG

Prism Gossamer (lace weight; 80% kid mohair/20% nylon; 935 yds/100g per skein): 1 skein gelato

Size 8 (5mm) needles or size needed to obtain gauge

Stitch markers

1 large button

1 small button

SKILL LEVEL

 INTERMEDIATE

SIZE

One size fits most

FINISHED MEASUREMENTS

Circumference: As desired by knitter
Length: Approx 22 inches

GAUGE

18 sts and 28 rows = 4 inches/10cm in garter st with 2 strands held together.

To save time, take time to check gauge.

PATTERN NOTES

This capelet is worked sideways in garter stitch, with very loose stitches worked with multiple wraps at one side (the bottom as worn) and regular knit stitches at the other side (the neck as worn); all extra wraps from previous rows are dropped as new stitches are formed.

It is critical that cast on and bind off be very loose.

Two strands of yarn are held together throughout.

CAPELET

Cast on 11 sts, place marker; cast on 22 sts, place marker; cast on 33 sts, place marker—66 sts.

Set-up row (RS): [K1, wrapping yarn around needle 3 times; drop next 2 sts from needle] 11 times; [k1, wrapping yarn around needle twice; drop next st from needle] 11 times; k11—33 sts.

Row 1: K11; k11, wrapping yarn around needle twice and dropping extra yo's from previous row; k11, wrapping yarn around needle 3 times and dropping yo's from previous row–33 sts.

Row 2: K11, wrapping yarn around needle 3 times and dropping yo's; k11, wrapping yarn around needle twice and dropping extra yo's; k11.

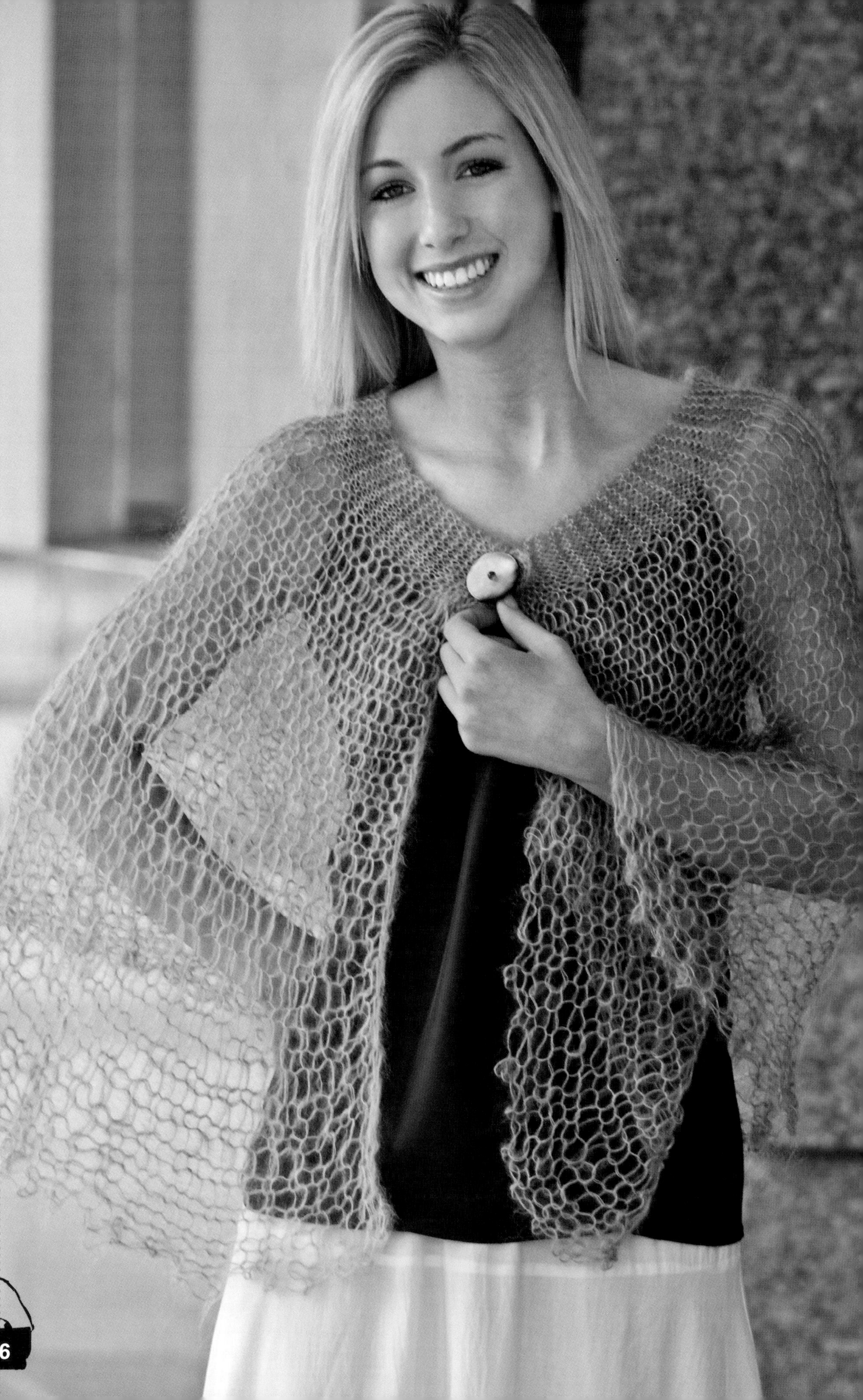

"While visiting India, I ventured out on a harrowing bus tour from Delhi to Jaipur. We wound our way up the two-lane road barely missing goats, carts and children. However, I was oblivious—engaged with a P.D. James mystery on tape and engrossed in an entrelac coat. Taking notice of my interest in knitting, our tour guide made certain that we saw local textile businesses in each city where we stayed. We visited a rug manufacturer, an embroidery studio, a crafts museum, and we had a private tour of a hand weaving studio. It's amazing the worlds that knitting can open."

Rep Rows 1 and 2, dropping extra yo's from needle on each row until short edge (neckline) measures approx 26 inches when laid flat and pulled straight.

Try capelet on and work more rows if desired for additional width, ending with Row 2.

Next row (RS): Make buttonhole in center of first 11 sts (size will depend on size of your large button), work to end of row.

Work 4 rows in established pat.

Removing all markers, bind off as follows: Dropping yo's from previous row as you knit, [k1; yo, pass st over yo; yo, pass st over yo] 11 times; [k1, pass st over previous st, yo, pass st over yo] 11 times; bind off rem sts.

FINISHING

Block as necessary.

Sew larger button to left front, sewing through capelet and then through 2nd, smaller button on the inside (to provide support). ∎

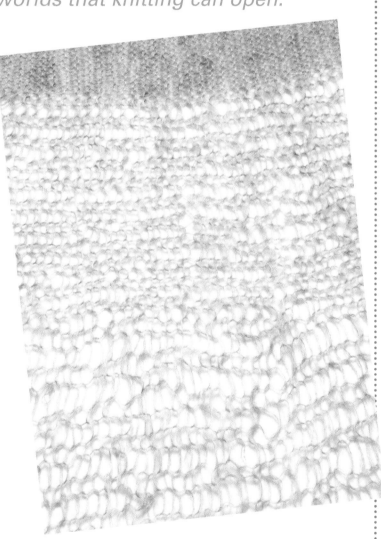

WANDERING WEARABLES

You'll enjoy our refreshing selection of garments with clever and easy stitch designs, making it a breeze to bring your project along on that morning hike. Take a break, enjoy the scenery and knit a few rows!

DUAL TEXTURE TUNIC

DESIGN BY MELISSA LEAPMAN

WHAT'S IN THE BAG

Ornaghi Filati United (worsted weight; 55% bamboo/45% cotton; 92 yds/50g per ball): 10 (11, 12, 12, 13) balls earth #518

Size 6 (4mm) needles or size needed to obtain gauge

SKILL LEVEL

■■☐☐ EASY

SIZES

Woman's small (medium, large, extra-large, 2X-large) Instructions are given for smallest size, with larger sizes in parentheses. When only 1 number is given, it applies to all sizes.

FINISHED MEASUREMENTS

Chest: 32 (36, 40, 43, 47) inches
Length: 30 (31, 32, 33, 34) inches

GAUGE

20 sts and 25 rows = 4 inches/10cm in St st.
22 sts and 30 rows = 4 inches/10cm in Double Seed st.
To save time, take time to check gauge.

PATTERN STITCH

Double Seed St
(even number of sts)
Row 1 (RS): *K1, p1; rep from * across.
Row 2: Rep Row 1.
Rows 3 and 4: *P1, k1; rep from * across.
Rep Rows 1–4 for pat.

PATTERN NOTE

Work all shaping decreases 1 stitch

from the edge, working the edge stitch in Stockinette stitch. On right side rows, work slip, slip, knit decrease at beginning of rows and knit 2 together decrease at end of rows; on wrong side rows, work purl 2 together decrease at beginning of rows and slip, slip, purl decrease at end of rows.

BACK

Cast on 95 (105, 115, 125, 135) sts.

Work even in St st until piece measures approx 18½ (19¼, 20, 20¾, 21½) inches allowing lower edge to curl, ending with a RS row.

Empire Waist

Next Row (WS): Purl, dec 7 (5, 5, 7, 5) sts evenly across row—88 (100, 110, 118, 130) sts.

Work even in Double Seed st until piece measures 22 (22½, 23, 23½, 24) inches, ending with a WS row.

Shape armholes

Bind off 5 (6, 7, 7, 8) sts at beg of next 2 rows, then bind off 2 (2, 3, 3, 4) sts at beg of following 2 rows—74 (84, 90, 98, 106) sts.

Dec 1 st each side [every row] 0 (0, 2, 6, 10) times, [every other row] 1 (8, 8, 7, 6) time(s), then [every 4th row] 3 (0, 0, 0, 0) times—66 (68, 70, 72, 74) sts.

Work even in established pat until armholes measure approx 6½ (7, 7½, 8, 8½) inches, ending with a WS row.

Shape neck

Next Row (RS): Work across first 15 (16, 17, 18, 19) sts; join 2nd ball of yarn and bind off center 36 sts, work to end of row. Working both sides at once with

39

Work even until piece measures same as back to shoulders.

Shape shoulders
Work same as for back.

FINISHING
Block pieces to finished measurements. Sew right shoulder seam.

Neckband
With RS facing, pick up and knit 163 sts along neckline.

Work 7 rows in St st.

Bind off loosely, allowing neckband to roll to RS.

Sew left shoulder seam, including side of neckband.

Armbands
With RS facing, pick up and knit 90 (98, 106, 114, 122) sts along armhole.

Work as for neckband.

Sew side seams, including side of armbands. Weave in all ends. ■

separate balls of yarn, dec 1 st at each neck edge once—14 (15, 16, 17, 18) sts each side.

Work even until armholes measure approx 7 (7½, 8, 8½, 9) inches, ending with a WS row.

Shape shoulders
Bind off 4 (4, 4, 4, 5) sts at beg (armhole edge) of next 6 rows, then bind off 2 (3, 4, 5, 3) sts at beg of following 2 rows.

FRONT
Work as for back until armholes measure approx 1½ (2, 2½, 3, 3½) inches, ending with a WS row.

Shape neck
Continue armhole shaping same as for back and at the same time, shape neck as follows:

Next row (RS): Join 2nd ball of yarn and bind off center 16 sts, then work to end of row.

Working both sides at once with separate balls of yarn, bind off at each neck edge as follows: 4 sts once, 3 sts once, 2 sts once.

Dec 1 st at each neck edge [every row] twice—14 (15, 16, 17, 18) sts each side.

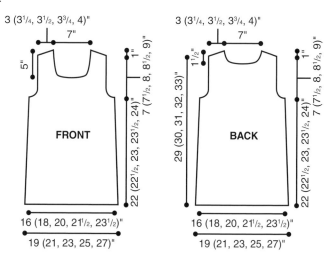

FRONT

3 (3¼, 3½, 3¾, 4)"

7"

5"

22 (22½, 23, 23½, 24)"

1"

7 (7½, 8, 8½, 9)"

16 (18, 20, 21½, 23½)"

19 (21, 23, 25, 27)"

BACK

3 (3¼, 3½, 3¾, 4)"

7"

1½"

1"

29 (30, 31, 32, 33)"

22 (22½, 23, 23½, 24)"

7 (7½, 8, 8½, 9)"

16 (18, 20, 21½, 23½)"

19 (21, 23, 25, 27)"

Tip Fill a compact-sized make-up bag with various-size circular needles, notions, travel scissors, tapestry needles and stitch holders. This bag can easily be moved from one knitting bag to another so you're never without your supplies.

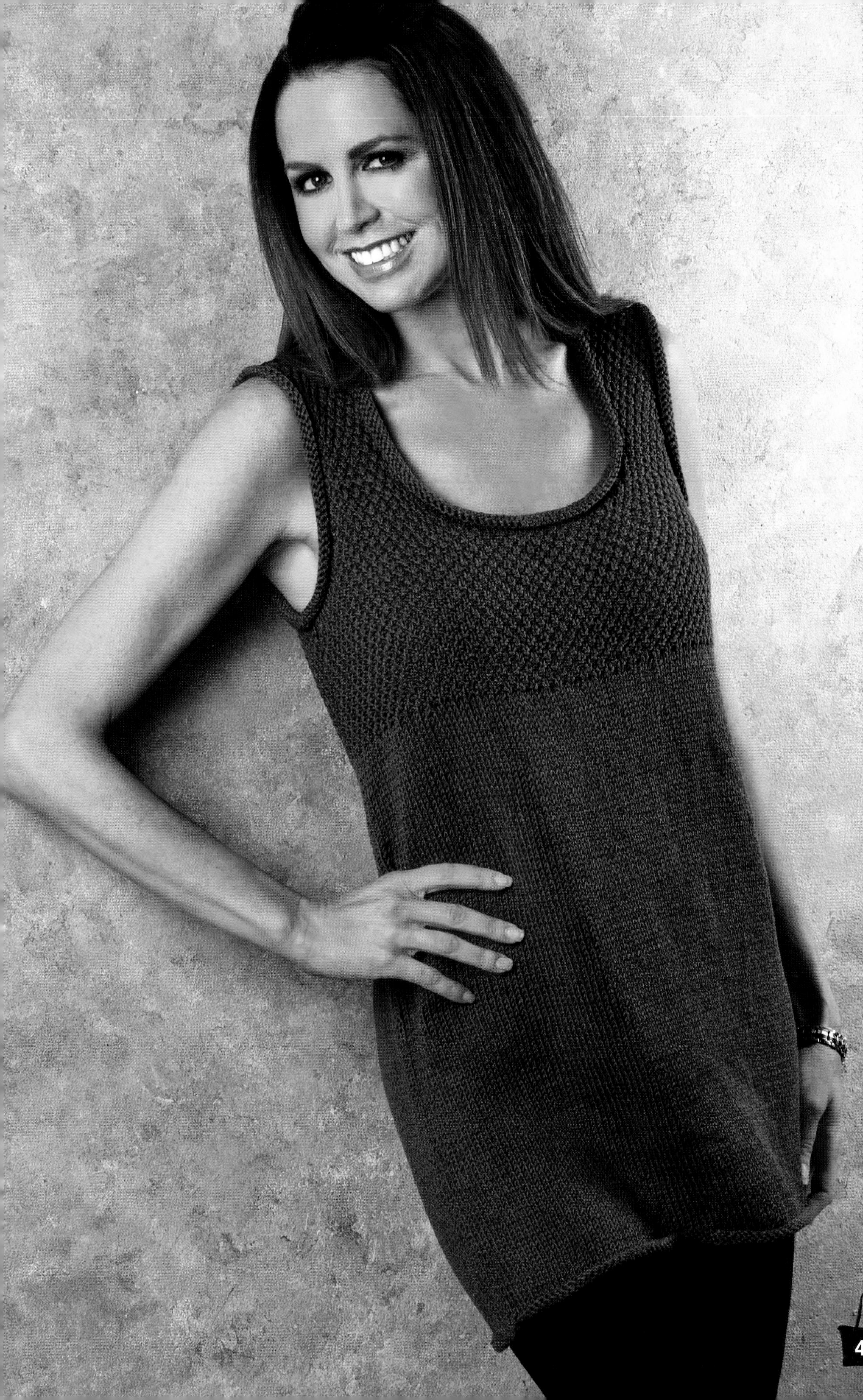

EUROPEAN TOUR SET

DESIGNS BY KATE ATHERLEY

WHAT'S IN THE BAG

Knit One Crochet Too Soxx
   Appeal (fingering weight; 96%
   superwash merino wool/3%
   nylon/1% elastic; 208 yds/50g
   per ball): 4 (4, 5, 6, 7) balls lavender
   cream #9122
Size 4 (3.5mm) 16- and 24-inch circular
   needles or size needed to obtain gauge
Stitch markers

(1) SUPER FINE

SKILL LEVEL

■■■☐ INTERMEDIATE

VEST

VEST SIZES
Woman's extra-small (small, medium, large,
extra-large) Instructions are given for smallest
size, with larger sizes in parentheses. When
only 1 number is given, it applies to all sizes.

FINISHED MEASUREMENTS
Chest: 30 (34, 38, 42, 46) inches
Length to shoulder: 19¼ (20¾, 21¾, 22¾, 24)
inches

GAUGE
28 sts and 44
rnds = 4 inches/
10cm in St st.
To save time,
take time to check
gauge.

SPECIAL ABBREVIATIONS
Slip, slip, slip, knit (sssk): Slip next 3
sts 1 at a time kwise,
then knit the 3 slipped
sts tog—a left-leaning
double dec.

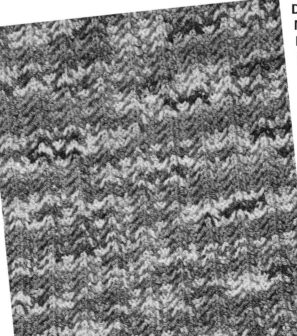

Wrap and Turn (W&T): Bring yarn to RS of
work between needles, slip next st pwise to RH
needle, bring yarn around this st to WS, slip st
back to LH needle, turn work to begin working
back in the other direction.

SPECIAL TECHNIQUE
3-Needle Bind-Off: With RS tog and needles
parallel, using a 3rd needle, knit tog a st from
the front needle with 1 from the back. *Knit tog
a st from the front and back needles, and slip
the first st over the 2nd to bind off. Rep from *
across, then fasten off last st.

PATTERN NOTE
Neck and armhole shaping occurs at different
rates for different sizes; where the letters "xx"
appear instead of stitch count numbers, it
means that these sizes are not being worked
on these rows.

BODY
Using the longer circular needle, cast on
212 (240, 268, 296, 324) sts; place marker to
indicate beg of rnd and join, taking care not to
twist sts.
   Work K3, P1 Rib for 1½ (1½, 1¾, 2, 2¼) inches.
   Change to St st and work even until piece
measures 12 (13, 13½, 14, 14½) inches.

Divide for front & back
   Next rnd: Bind off 1 st,
   k104 (118, 132, 146, 160)
   including st rem from
   bind off, bind off 2 sts,
   k104 (118, 132, 146, 160)
   including st rem from
   bind off, bind off 1 st.

BACK
   Row 1 (RS): With
   shorter circular needle,
   pick up and knit 1 st
   in first bound-off st,
   p1, k1, p1, sssk, knit
   to last 6 sts, k3tog,

"Once, on flight across the Atlantic, I was knitting a cabled sweater made on circular needles. When taking breaks, I tend to tuck my needles in the neckline of my top. When it came time to land, I packed away my project, deplaned, proceeded through customs, picked up my luggage, and took a taxi to the hotel. Not until getting ready to shower and change did I realize that the big green cable needle was still tucked neatly into my V-neck t-shirt!"

p1, k1, p1; pick up and knit 1 st in first of the 2 bound-off sts—102 (116, 130, 144, 158) back sts. Leave rem 104 (118, 132, 146, 160) sts on longer circular needle to hold for front.
Row 2 and all WS rows: Sl 1, k1, p1, k1, purl to last 4 sts, k1, p1, k1, p1.

Shape Armholes
For sizes S, M, L, XL only
Dec row (RS): Sl 1, p1, k1, p1, sssk, knit to last 7 sts, k3tog, p1, k1, p1, k1—xx (112, 126, 140, 154) sts.

Rep Dec row [every other row] 0 (0 1, 1, 1) time more—xx (112, 122, 136, 150) sts.
For all sizes
Dec row (RS): Sl 1, p1, k1, p1, ssk, knit to last 6 sts, k2tog, p1, k1, p1, k1—100 (110, 120, 134, 148) sts

Rep Dec row [every other row] 8 (8, 9, 11, 13) more times—84 (94, 102, 112, 122) sts.

Maintaining first and last 4 sts in established rib, work even until armhole measures 6¾ (7¼, 7¾, 8¼, 9) inches, ending with a WS row.

Back Neck
Row 1 (RS): Work 20 (25, 28, 32, 34) sts in established pat, place marker, [p1, k1] 11 (11, 11, 12, 13) times, M1, [k1, p1] 11 (11, 12, 12, 14) times, place marker, work in established pat to end of row—85 (95, 103, 113, 123) sts.
Row 2: Slipping markers, work in pat to marker, work in established rib to next marker, work in pat to end of row.

Work even for 4 rows.

Shape Shoulders
Row 1 (RS): Work in pat to last 7 (9, 10, 11, 12) sts, W&T.
Row 2: Work in pat to last 7 (9, 10, 11, 12) sts, W&T.
Row 3: Work in pat to last 14 (17, 19, 22, 23) sts, W&T.

Row 4: Work in pat to last 14 (17, 19, 22, 23) sts, W&T.
Row 5: Work in pat to last 20 (25, 28, 32, 34) sts, W&T.
Row 6: Bind off 45 (45, 47, 49, 55) rib sts in pat, turn.

Cut yarn.

Slip back shoulder sts to longer needle and front sts to shorter needle.

DIVIDE FOR LEFT & RIGHT FRONTS
With RS facing, rejoin yarn to front sts.
Next rnd: Pick up and knit 1 st in bound-off st at beg of row, p1, k1, p1, sssk, k45 (52, 59, 66, 72), bind off 2 sts, k45 (52, 59, 66, 73) including st rem from bind off, k3tog, p1, k1, p1, pick up and knit 1 st in bound-off st at end of row; slip left front sts to the longer circular needle to hold for later—50 (57, 64, 71, 78) right front sts.

RIGHT FRONT
Shape Armholes and V-Neck
Row 1 (WS): Sl 1, k1, p1, k1, purl to last 3 sts, k1, p1, k1.
Row 2 (XS only): Pick up 1 st in 2nd bound-off st, p1, k1, p1, knit to last 6 sts, k2tog, p1, k1, p1, k1—50 sts.
Row 2 (S, M, L, XL only): Pick up 1 st in 2nd bound-off st, p1, k1, p1, knit to last 7 sts, k3tog, p1, k1, p1, k1—xx (56, 63, 70, 77) sts.
Row 3 and all WS rows: Sl 1, k1, p1, k1, purl to last 4 sts, k1, p1, k1, p1.
Row 4 (XS and S only): Sl 1, p1, k1, p1, ssk, knit to last 6 sts, k2tog, p1, k1, p1, k1—48 (54, xx, xx, xx) sts.
Row 4 (M, L, XL only): Sl 1, p1, k1, p1, ssk, knit to last 7 sts, k3tog, p1, k1, p1, k1—xx (xx, 60, 67, 74) sts.
Row 5: Sl 1, p1, k1, p1, knit to last 6 sts, k2tog, p1, k1, p1, k1—47 (53, 59, 66, 73) sts.

Continue in pat as established, dec 1 inside

armhole ribbing [every RS row] 6 (7, 9, 11, 13) times and dec 1 inside neck ribbing [every other RS row] 17 (17, 18, 19, 22) times—24 (29, 32, 36, 38) sts.

Work even, maintaining rib on first and last 4 sts of the rows, until front measures same as back to shoulder shaping, ending with a WS row.

Shape Shoulders

Row 1 (RS): Work in pat to last 7 (9, 10, 11, 12) sts, W&T.

Rows 2, 4, 6: Work even.

Row 3: Work in pat to last 14 (17, 19, 22, 23) sts, W&T.

Row 5: Work in pat to last 20 (25, 28, 32, 34) sts, W&T.

Slip right front sts to the longer circular needle.

Left Front

Slip 50 (57, 64, 71, 78) left front sts from the longer needle to shorter needle.

With WS facing, rejoin yarn.

Shape Armholes and V-Neck

Row 1 (WS): Sl 1, k1, p1, k1, purl to last 3 sts, k1, p1, k1.

Row 2 (XS only): K1, p1, k1, p1, ssk, knit to last 3 sts, p1, k1, p1, pick up 1 st in bound-off st —50 sts.

Row 2 (S, M, L, XL only): K1, p1, k1, p1, sssk, knit to last 4 sts, p1, k1, p1, k1, pick up 1 st in bound-off st—xx (56, 63, 70, 77) sts.

Row 3 and all WS rows: Sl 1, k1, p1, k1, purl to last 4 sts, k1, p1, k1, p1.

Row 4 (XS and S only): Sl 1, p1, k1, p1, ssk, knit to last 6 sts, k2tog, p1, k1, p1, k1—48 (54, xx, xx, xx) sts.

Row 4 (M, L, XL only): Sl 1, p1, k1, p1, sssk, knit

to last 7 sts, k2tog, p1, k1, p1, k1—xx (xx, 58, 67, 74) sts.

Row 5: Sl 1, p1, k1, p1, ssk, knit to last 4 sts, p1, k1, p1, k1—47 (53, 59, 66, 73) sts.

Continue in pat as established, dec 1 inside armhole ribbing [every RS row] 6 (7, 9, 11, 13) times and dec 1 inside neck ribbing [every other RS row] 17 (17, 18, 19, 22) times—24 (29, 32, 36, 38) sts.

Work even, maintaining rib on first and last 4 sts of the rows, until front measures same as back to shoulder shaping, ending with a WS row.

Shape Shoulders

Row 1 (WS): Work in pat to last 7 (9, 10, 11, 12) sts, W&T.

Rows 2, 4, 6 (RS): Work even.

Row 3 (WS): Work in pat to last 14 (17, 19, 22, 23) sts, W&T.

Row 5 (WS): Work in pat to last 20 (25, 28, 32, 34) sts, W&T.

FINISHING

Slip sts for right shoulder back to shorter needle.

Join front and back shoulder sts using 3-Needle Bind-Off.

Weave in ends.

Block to finished measurements.

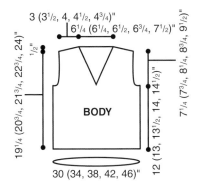

3 (3¹/₂, 4, 4¹/₂, 4³/₄)"

6¹/₄ (6¹/₄, 6¹/₂, 6³/₄, 7¹/₂)"

¹/₂"

19¹/₄ (20³/₄, 21³/₄, 22³/₄, 24)"

7¹/₄ (7³/₄, 8¹/₄, 8³/₄, 9¹/₂)"

12 (13, 13¹/₂, 14, 14¹/₂)"

BODY

30 (34, 38, 42, 46)"

SOCKS

WHAT'S IN THE BAG

Knit One Crochet Too Soxx
   Appeal (fingering weight; 96%
   superwash merino wool/3%
   nylon/1% elastic; 208 yds/50g
   per ball): 1 (2, 2) balls lavender cream
   #9122
Size 1 (2.5mm) double-point needles (set
   of 4 or 5) or size needed to obtain gauge
Stitch marker

SOCKS SIZES

Woman's small (medium, large) to fit shoe
sizes 5-7 (7-9, 10+) Instructions are given for
smallest size, with larger sizes in parentheses.
When only 1 number is given, it applies to all
sizes.

FINISHED MEASUREMENTS

Circumference: 7¼ (7¾, 8¼) inches
Foot length: 8 (8½, 9) inches

GAUGE

32 sts and 48 rnds = 4 inches/10cm in St st.
To save time, take time to check gauge.

SPECIAL ABBREVIATION

N1, N2, N3: Needle 1, Needle 2, Needle 3

PATTERN NOTE

Due to the elastic in the yarn, the fabric has a
lot of vertical stretch. The finished sock foot
will seem shorter than you would normally
work in a non-stretch yarn.

INSTRUCTIONS

Cast on 58 (62, 66) sts; distribute evenly on
3 dpn; place marker for beg of rnd and join,
being careful not to twist sts.
   Work in K1, P1 Rib for 1 inch.

Heel flap

Row 1 (RS): K29 (31, 33) heel sts and turn,
leaving rem 29 (31, 33) instep sts on hold on
single dpn.
   Work heel sts in St st for 21 (23, 23) rows,
ending with a WS row.

Turn heel

Row 1 (RS): K19 (21, 22), ssk, turn.
Row 2: Sl 1, p9 (11, 11), p2tog, turn.
Row 3: Sl 1, k9 (11, 11), ssk, turn.
   Rep Rows 2 and 3 until all sts have been
worked, ending with a WS row—11 (13, 13) sts
rem.

Gusset

Rnd 1: With N1, k11 (13, 13) heel sts, then pick
up and knit 15 (16, 16) along heel flap; with N2,
knit across 29 (31, 33) instep sts; with N3, pick
up and knit 15 (16, 16) sts along heel flap, then
k6 (7, 7) sts heel sts, place marker for beg of
rnd—70 (76, 78) sts with 20 (22, 22) sts on N1,
29 (31, 33) sts on N2 and 21 (23, 23) sts on N3.
Rnd 2: Knit around, working all picked up
sts tbl.
Rnd 3 (dec): N1: Knit to last 3 sts, k2tog, k1; N2:
knit; N3: k1, ssk, knit to end—68 (74, 76) sts.
Rnd 4: Knit.
   Rep [Rnds 3 and 4] 5 (6, 5) times—58 (62, 66)
sts with 14 (15, 16) sts on N1, 29 (31, 33) sts on
N2 and 15 (16, 17) sts on N3.

Foot

Work even in St st until foot measures 6 (6½, 7)
inches from back of heel.

Toe

Dec rnd: N1: Knit to last 3 sts, k2tog, k1; N2: k1,
ssk, knit to last 3 sts, k2tog, k1; N3: k1, ssk, knit

to end—54 (58, 62) sts.

Work Dec rnd [every 3rd rnd] 3 times—42 (46, 50) sts.

Work Dec rnd [every other rnd] 3 times—30 (34, 38) sts.

Work Dec rnd [every rnd] 5 (6, 7) times—10 sts.

Cut yarn and using the crochet hook or yarn needle, pull through remaining sts to close. Weave in ends.

FINISHING

Soak socks in lukewarm water for a few minutes, roll in a towel to wring out and then put them on. Take them off again, and leave them to air dry. This blocks the socks to ensure a good fit.

SCARF

WHAT'S IN THE BAG

Knit One Crochet Too Soxx
Appeal (fingering weight; 96% superwash merino wool/3% nylon/1% elastic; 208 yds/50g per ball): 4 balls lavender cream #9122

1 SUPER FINE

Size 4 (3.5mm) 24-inch circular needle or size needed to obtain gauge

SCARF FINISHED SIZE
Approx 16 x 48 inches

GAUGE
26 sts and 36 rows = 4 inches/10cm in lace rib pattern using larger needles.
To save time, take time to check gauge.

PATTERN STITCH
Lace Rib (multiple of 6 sts + 2)
Row 1: K1, *yo, SK2P, yo, k1, p1, k1; rep from * to last st, k1.
Rep Row 1 for pat.

PATTERN NOTE
To make scarf wider, cast on more stitches in multiples of 6.

INSTRUCTIONS
Cast on 104 sts.
Work even in Lace Rib pat for approx 48

inches or until you've just about run out of yarn.

To bind off, lift the sts 1 by 1 over each other, without working them.

Weave in ends and block. ∎

CASUAL COTTON T-SHIRT

DESIGN BY AVA LYNNE GREEN

WHAT'S IN THE BAG

Rowan Wool Cotton (DK weight; 50% merino wool/50% cotton; 123 yds/50g per ball): 6 (7, 8, 9, 10) balls pumpkins #962

Size 5 (3.75mm) needles or size needed to obtain gauge

SKILL LEVEL

■■■□ INTERMEDIATE

SIZES

Woman's extra-small (small, medium, large, extra-large) Instructions are given for smallest size, with larger sizes in parentheses. When only 1 number is given, it applies to all sizes.

FINISHED MEASUREMENTS

Chest: 32 (36, 40, 44, 48) inches
Length to shoulder: 21 (22, 23, 24, 24) inches

GAUGE

20 sts and 27 rows = 4 inches/10cm in St st.
To save time, take time to check gauge.

SPECIAL ABBREVIATION

Make 1 (M1): Insert LH needle from front to back under the running thread between the last st worked and next st on RH needle; knit into the back of resulting loop.

PATTERN STITCH

Seed Stitch
Row 1 (RS): *K1, p1; rep from * to end.
Row 2: Knit the purl sts and purl the knit sts as they present themselves.
Rep Row 2 for pat.

FRONT

Cast on 60 (70, 80, 90, 100) sts.
Rows 1 (RS)–3: Work in Seed st.
Row 4 (inc row): Work 3 sts in Seed st, M1, purl to the last 3 sts, M1, work 3 sts in Seed st—62 (72, 82, 92, 102) sts.
Row 5: Work 3 sts in Seed st, knit to the last 3 sts, work 3 sts in Seed st.
Rep [Rows 4 and 5] 9 times—80 (90, 100, 110, 120) sts.
Discontinue Seed st border and work even in St st until piece measures 13 (14, 14, 15, 15) inches, ending with a WS row.

Shape armhole
Row 1 (RS): K1, M1, knit to last st, M1, k1—82 (92, 102, 112, 122) sts.
Row 2: Purl.
Rows 3–6: Rep [Rows 1 and 2] twice—86 (96, 106, 116, 126) sts.
Work even in St st until armholes measure 5 (5, 6, 6, 6) inches, ending with a WS row.

Shape front neck
Row 1 (RS): K34 (37, 42, 46, 50), join a 2nd ball

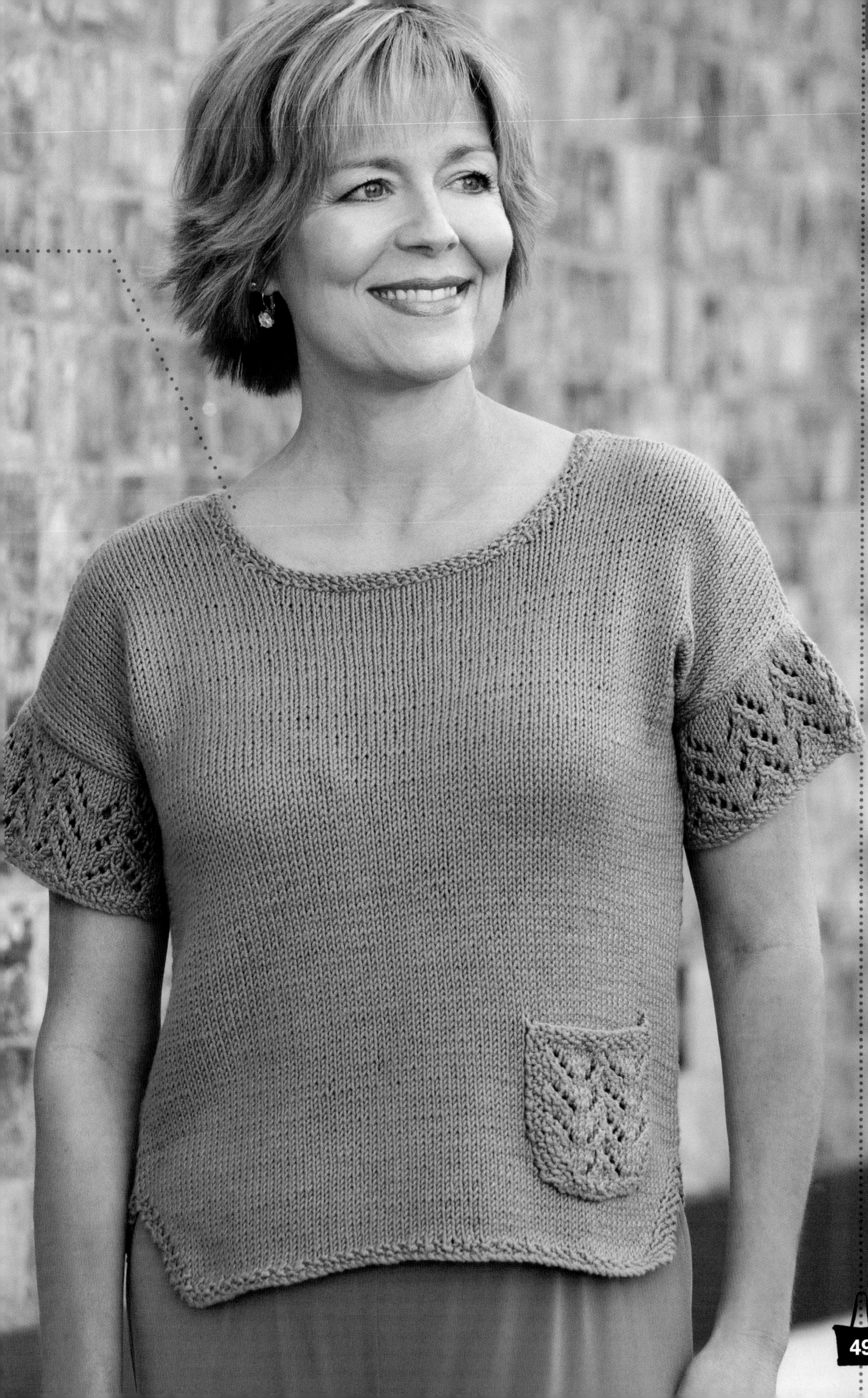

"*Getting stranded at an airport for 5 hours due to bad weather was an ironic stroke of good luck! I found a cozy corner, pulled out my knitting and made great progress on a 3-color, top-down raglan sweater design. To this day, I think of it fondly as my airport sweater.*"

of yarn and bind off center 18 (22, 22, 24, 26) sts, knit to end.

Row 2: Working both sides at once with separate balls of yarn, purl across.

Row 3 (dec row): Knit to 3 sts before neck, k2tog, k1; k1, ssk, knit to end—33 (36, 41, 45, 49) sts each side.

Rep [Rows 2 and 3] 3 (3, 5, 6, 7) times—30 (33, 36, 39, 42) sts each side.

Work even until armholes measure 8 (8, 9, 9, 9) inches.

Bind off 10 (11, 12, 13, 14) sts at beg (armhole edge) of next 6 rows.

BACK

Cast on 60 (70, 80, 90, 100) sts.

Work as for front until armholes measure 6 (6, 7, 7, 7) inches, ending with a WS row.

Shape back neck

Row 1 (RS): K32 (35, 40, 44, 47), join a 2nd ball of yarn and bind off center 22 (26, 26, 28, 32) sts, knit to end.

Row 2: Working both sides at once with separate balls of yarn, purl across.

Row 3 (dec row): Knit to 3 sts before neck, k2tog, k1; k1, ssk, knit to end—31 (34, 39, 43, 46) sts each side.

Rep [Rows 2 and 3] 1 (1, 3, 4, 4) times—30 (33, 36, 39, 42) sts each shoulder.

Work even until piece measures same as front to shoulders.

Bind off 10 (11, 12, 13, 14) sts at beg (armhole edge) of next 6 rows.

SLEEVE

Cast on 64 (64, 72, 72, 72) sts.

Rows 1 (RS)–3: Work in Seed St.

Rows 4, 6, 8 and 10: Work 3 sts in Seed st, purl to last 3 sts, work 3 sts in Seed st.

Row 5: Work 3 sts in Seed st, M1, *k2, yo, ssk, k2, k2tog, yo; rep from * to last 5 sts, k2, M1, work 3 sts in Seed st—66 (66, 74, 74, 74) sts.

Row 7: Work 3 sts in Seed st, M1, k4, *yo, ssk, k2tog, yo, k4; rep from * to last 3 sts, M1, work 3 sts in Seed st—68 (68, 76, 76, 76) sts.

Row 9: Work 3 sts in Seed st, M1, k6, *yo, ssk, k6; rep from * to last 3 sts, M1, work 3 sts in Seed st—70 (70, 78, 78, 78) sts.

Row 11: K4, k2tog, yo, *k2, yo, ssk, k2, k2tog, yo; rep from * to last 8 sts, k2, yo, ssk, k4.

Row 12 and all rem WS rows: Purl.

Row 13: K3, k2tog, yo, *k4, yo, ssk, k2tog, yo; rep from * to last 9 sts, k4, yo, ssk, k3.

Row 15: K2, k2tog, yo, k6, *yo, ssk, k6; rep from * to last 4 sts, yo, ssk, k2.

Rows 17–22: Rep Rows 11-16.

Row 23: Knit.

Row 24: Purl.

Bind off.

POCKET

Cast on 16 sts.

Rows 1 (RS)–3: Work in Seed st.

Row 4 and all WS rows: Work 3 sts in Seed st, purl to last 3 sts, work 3 sts in Seed st.

Row 5: Work 3 sts in Seed st, M1, k2, yo, ssk, k2, k2tog, yo, k2, M1, work 3 sts in Seed st—18 sts.

Row 7: Work 3 sts in Seed st, M1, k4, yo, ssk, k2tog, M1, k4, work 3 sts in Seed st—20 sts.

Row 9: Work 3 sts in Seed st, M1, k6, yo, ssk, k6, M1, work 3 sts in Seed st—22 sts.

Row 11: Work 3 sts in Seed st, k1, k2tog, yo, k2, yo, ssk, k2, k2tog, yo, k2, yo, ssk, k1, work 3 sts in Seed st.

Row 13: Work 3 sts in Seed st, k2tog, yo, k4, yo, ssk, k2tog, yo, k4, yo, ssk, work 3 sts in Seed st.

Row 15: Work 2 sts in Seed st, k2tog, yo, k6, yo, ssk, k6, yo, ssk, work 2 sts in Seed st.

Rows 17–28: Rep [Rows 11-16] twice.

Rows 29–31: Work in Seed st.

FINISHING

Weave in all ends. Block all pieces to finished measurements. Sew 1 shoulder seam.

NECK EDGING

With RS facing, pick up and knit 67 (75, 75, 79, 83) sts along neck edge.

Work 3 rows in Seed st.

Bind off.

ASSEMBLY

Sew 2nd shoulder seam, including neck edging. Sew on sleeves between shoulder and last inc row on body. Sew side seams between top of curve and sleeves.

Sew pocket to the lower left front with the bottom edge 2 inches from the cast-on edge and the outside of the pocket 2 inches from the side seam. ■

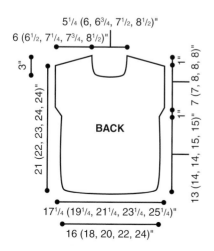

BACK

POCKET

SLEEVE

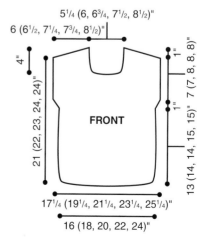

FRONT

SLEEK & STYLISH SLEEVELESS TOP

DESIGN BY CECILY GLOWIK MACDONALD

WHAT'S IN THE BAG

NaturallyCaron.com Spa (DK weight; 75% microdenier acrylic/25% bamboo; 251 yds/85g per ball): 3 (3, 3, 4, 4) balls of green sheen #0004

Size 5 (3.75mm) needles or size needed to obtain gauge

SKILL LEVEL

■■□□ EASY

SIZES

Woman's small (medium, large, extra-large, 2X-large) Instructions are given for smallest size, with larger sizes in parentheses. When only 1 number is given, it applies to all sizes.

FINISHED MEASUREMENTS

Chest: 32 (36, 40, 44, 48) inches
Length: 18 inches

GAUGE

24 sts and 36 rows = 4 inches/10cm in Diagonal st.
To save time, take time to check gauge.

PATTERN STITCH

Diagonal Stitch
(multiple of 6 sts)
Row 1 (RS): *K5, p1; rep from * to end.
Row 2: P1, *k1, p5; rep from * to last 5 sts, k1, p4.
Row 3: K3, *p1, k5; rep from * to last 3 sts, p1, k2.
Row 4: P3, *k1, p5; rep from * to last 3 sts, k1, p2.

Row 5: K1, *p1, k5; rep from * to last 5 sts, p1, k4.
Row 6: *P5, k1; rep from * to end.
Rep Rows 1–6 for pat.

FRONT

Cast on 96 (108, 120, 132, 144) sts.
Work in garter st for ¾ inch, ending with a WS row.
Work in Diagonal St until piece measures 4 inches, ending with a WS row.
Work K3, P3 Rib until piece measures 7 inches, ending with a WS row.
Work in Diagonal St until piece measures 11 (10, 10, 9, 9) inches or desired length to armhole.

Armhole

Slipping the first st of every row pwise, continue in established pat until piece measures 16 inches, ending with a WS row.
Discontinue slipping

the first st; work K3, P3 Rib until piece measures 18 inches, ending with a WS row.
  Bind off all sts in rib.

BACK
Work as for front, but work P3, K3 Rib at top 2 inches.

FINISHING
Block pieces to finished measurements, allowing waist ribbing to pull in naturally.
  Starting at bottom, sew side seams for 11 (10, 10, 9, 9) inches, leaving rem 7 (8, 8, 9, 9) inches open for armholes. Beg at each shoulder edge, sew 3 (4, 5, 6, 7)-inch shoulder seams. Weave in ends. ■

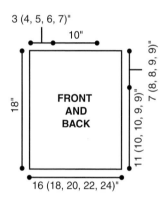

3 (4, 5, 6, 7)"

10"

18"

FRONT AND BACK

11 (10, 10, 9, 9)"

7 (8, 8, 9, 9)"

16 (18, 20, 22, 24)"

Tip Here's a great way to organize multiple projects in your knitting bag: place various projects in separate plastic containers with lids. When you're ready to work, just remove the top, and knit away! This keeps your projects and yarn neatly contained and avoids wasting precious time untangling yarn.

TAKE IT ON THE ROAD TANK

DESIGN BY DIANE ZANGL

WHAT'S IN THE BAG

Mission Falls 1824 Cotton
  (worsted weight; 100% cotton;
  85 yds/50g per ball): 6 (7, 8, 9)
  balls vintage #775
Size 6 (4mm) needles or size needed to
  obtain gauge
Size G/6 (4mm) crochet hook
Stitch holders
Stitch markers

SKILL LEVEL

 EASY

SIZES

Woman's small (medium, large, extra-
large) Instructions are given for smallest
size, with larger sizes in parentheses.
When only 1 number is given, it applies to
all sizes.

FINISHED MEASUREMENTS

Chest: 34 (36, 40, 47) inches
Length: 20 (20½, 22, 22½) inches

GAUGE

18 sts and 25 rows = 4 inches/10cm in K1,
P3 Rib.
To save time, take time to check gauge.

PATTERN STITCHES

K1, P1 Rib (odd number of sts)
Row 1 (RS): K1, *p1, k1; rep from * across.
Row 2: P1, *k1, p1; rep from * across.
  Rep Rows 1 and 2 for pat.

K1, P3 Rib (multiple of 4 sts + 1)
Row 1 (WS): P1, *k3, p1; rep from * across.
Row 2 (RS): K1, *p3, k1; rep from * across.
  Rep Rows 1 and 2 for pat.

BACK

Cast on 77 (81, 89, 101) sts.

Work in K1, P3 Rib until piece measures
13 (13, 14, 14) inches, ending with a WS row.

Shape underarm

Bind off 4 (4, 5, 7) sts at beg of next 2 rows—
69 (73, 79, 87) sts.
Dec row (RS): Ssk, work in pat to last 2 sts,
k2tog—67 (71, 77, 85) sts.
  Continue in established pat and rep Dec row
[every RS row] 3 (3, 4, 6) times—61 (65, 69,
73) sts.
  Work even until armhole measures 3 (3½,
4, 4½) inches, ending with a WS row.

Shape neck

Mark center 19 (23, 23, 23) sts.

Next row (RS): Work in K1, P1 Rib to first marker, join 2nd ball of yarn and bind off marked sts, work in K1, P1 Rib to end—21 (21, 23, 25) sts each side.

Working both sides at once with separate balls of yarn in established K1, P1 Rib, bind off 3 sts at each neck edge once, then 2 sts once—16 (16, 18, 20) sts each side.

Dec 1 st at each neck edge every RS row 3 (3, 3, 5) times—13 (13, 15, 15) sts each side.

Straps

Work even in established rib until armholes measure 7 (7½, 8, 8½) inches.

Bind off all sts.

FRONT

Work same as for back.

FINISHING

Weave in all ends. Block to finished measurements. Sew shoulder and side seams.

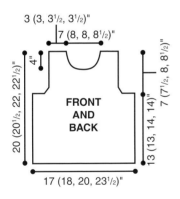

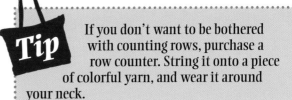

If you don't want to be bothered with counting rows, purchase a row counter. String it onto a piece of colorful yarn, and wear it around your neck.

EDGINGS

Beg at underarm, work 1 row sc around entire armhole, keeping work flat; join with slip st and fasten off.

Rep for 2nd armhole.

Beg at shoulder seam, work 1 row sc around neckline.

Beg at side seam, work 1 row sc around lower edge. ∎

"IT'S A WRAP" CABLED SHRUG

DESIGN BY COLLEEN SMITHERMAN

WHAT'S IN THE BAG

Nashua Creative Focus Worsted (worsted weight; 75% wool/25% alpaca; 220 yds/100g per ball): 4 (4, 5) skeins blue moor heather #CFW.0791
Size 7 (4.5 mm) needles or size needed to obtain gauge
Stitch markers
Stitch holder
Cable needle

SKILL LEVEL

■■■□ INTERMEDIATE

SIZES

Woman's small (medium, large) Instructions are given for smallest size, with larger sizes in parentheses. When only 1 number is given, it applies to all sizes.

FINISHED MEASUREMENTS

Chest: 38 (42, 46) inches
Length to shoulder: 14½ (15¼, 15½) inches

GAUGE

19 sts and 25 rows = 4 inches/10cm in St st.
To save time, take time to check gauge.

SPECIAL ABBREVIATIONS

Cable 4 Back (C4B): Sl 2 to cn and hold in back, k2, k2 from cn.
Cable 4 Front (C4F): Sl 2 to cn and hold in front, k2, k2 from cn.
Make 1 (M1): Insert LH needle from front to back under the running thread between the last st worked and next st on RH needle; knit into the back of resulting loop.

PATTERN STITCH

Braided Cable (10-st panel)
Row 1 (RS): P2, k6, p2.
Row 2 and all WS rows: K2, p6, k2.
Row 3: P2, k2, C4B, p2.

Row 5: Rep Row 1.
Row 7: P2, C4F, k2, p2.
Row 8: Rep Row 2.
Rep Rows 1–8 for pat.

PATTERN NOTES

A chart of the cable pattern is provided for those preferring to work from charts.

Each front has a cable border; this border is continued around the back neck by sewing separate cable piece to back neck after back is knit.

BACK

Cast on 90 (100, 110) sts.
Set up rib (RS): K2 (1, 2), work in P2, K2 Rib to last 4 (3, 4) sts, p2, k2 (1, 2).

Continue in established rib until piece measures 2 inches, ending with a WS row.

Beg working in St st and work even until back measures 6½ (6¾, 6¾) inches, ending with a WS row.

Shape armhole
Bind off 6 (7, 10) sts at beg of next 2 rows—78 (86, 90) sts.

Work even until armhole measures 6¾ (7¼, 7½) inches, ending with a WS row.

Shape back neck & shoulders
Next row (RS): K20 (24, 25), join 2nd ball of yarn and bind off center 38 (38, 40) sts, knit to end of row.

Working both sides of neck with separate balls of yarn, bind off 4 sts at each neck edge once, then 2 sts once, then 1 st once; at the same time, when armhole measures 8 (8½, 8¾) inches, bind off 6 (8, 9) sts once, then 7 (9, 9) sts once at each shoulder edge.

LEFT FRONT
Cast on 45 (50, 55) sts.
Set up rib and cable pat (RS): K1 (2, 3), *p2, k2; rep from * 7 (8, 9) times, place marker, work Braided Cable over next 10 sts, place marker, k1, sl 1 wyif.
Row 2: P2, work Braided Cable between markers, work established rib pat to end.

Rep Rows 1 and 2 until piece measures 2 inches, ending with a WS row.

Shape neck & armhole
Row 1 (RS): Knit to marker, work Braided Cable between markers, k1, sl 1 wyif.
Row 2: P2, work Braided Cable between markers, purl to end of row.
Dec row: Knit to 2 sts before first marker, k2tog, work Braided Cable, k1, sl 1 wyif.

Continue in established pat and rep Dec row [every 6 rows] 13 (13, 14) times and *at the same time*, when the front measures 6½ (6¾, 6¾) inches, ending with a WS row, shape armhole as follows:
Next row (RS): Bind off 6 (7, 10) sts, work to end of row.

Working in established pat, continue dec at front neck, then work even until armhole

measures 8 (8½, 8¾) inches, ending with a WS row.

Shape shoulder
At shoulder edge, bind off [6 (7, 8) sts] 3 times, then [7 (8, 6) sts] once.

RIGHT FRONT
Cast on 45 (50, 55) sts.
Set up rib and cable pat (RS): Sl 1, k1, place marker, work Braided Cable over next 10 sts, place marker, *k2, p2; rep from * 7 (8, 9) times, k1 (2, 3).
Row 2: Work established rib to marker, work Braided Cable pat between markers, p2.

Rep Rows 1 and 2 until piece measures 2 inches, ending with a WS row.

Shape center front & armholes
Row 1 (RS): Sl 1, k1, work Braided Cable between markers, knit to end of row.
Row 2: Purl to marker, work Braided Cable between markers, p2.
Dec row (RS): Sl 1, k1, work Braided Cable, ssk, knit to end of row.

Continue in established pat and rep Dec row [every 6 rows] 13 (13, 14) times and *at the same time,* when the front measures 6½ (6¾, 6¾) inches, ending with a RS row, shape armhole as follows:

Next row (WS): Bind off 6 (7, 10) sts, work to end of row.

Working in established pat, continue dec at front neck, then work even until armhole measures 8 (8½, 8¾) inches, ending with a RS row.

Shape shoulders
At shoulder edge, bind off [6 (7, 8) sts] 3 times, then [7 (8, 6) sts] once.

SLEEVES
Cast on 38 (46, 46) sts.

Set up rib and cable pat (RS): K2, [p2, k2] 3 (4, 4) times, place marker, work Braided Cable across next 10 sts, place marker, k2, [p2, k2] 3 (4, 4) times.

Continue in established pat, working Braided Cable between markers, until sleeve measures 2 inches, ending with a WS row.

Next row (RS): K14 (18, 18), work Braided Cable between markers, knit to end of row.

Working St st on either side of Braided Cable, work even until piece measures 3½ (3, 2½) inches, ending with a WS row.

Inc row (RS): K2, M1, work in pat to last 2 sts, M1, k2—40 (48, 48) sts.

Continue in pat and rep Inc row [every 5 (6, 6) rows] 19 (17, 18) times—76 (80, 82) sts.

Work even until sleeve measures 19½ (19¾, 20) inches, ending with a WS row.

Shape sleeve cap
Next 8 (12, 12) rows: Bind off 8 (6, 6) sts at beg of each row—12 (8, 10) sts.

Bind off rem sts.

Back neck cable
Cast on 14 sts.
Row 1 (RS): Sl 1, k1, work Braided Cable over next 10 sts, k2.
Row 2: P2, work Braided Cable, p2.

Rep Rows 1 and 2, allowing band to gently curl, until longer edge measures approx 13 (14, 14) inches. Place sts on holder.

FRONT TIES
Make 2
Cast on 10 sts.

Work in K2, P2 Rib until tie measures 9 inches.

FINISHING
Block all pieces to finished measurements. Sew long edge of back neck cable to back neck edge, easing in back neck fabric as necessary. If cable is too long, unravel extra rows, then bind off. Sew shoulder seems. Sew in sleeves. Sew sleeve and side seams. Sew ties to lower center fronts. Weave in all ends. ■

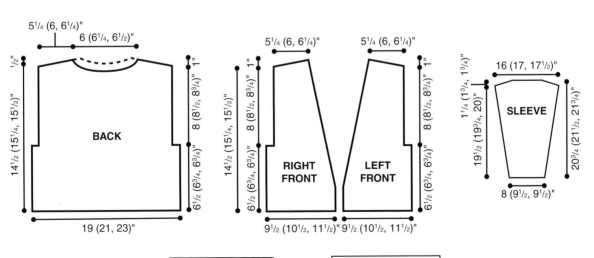

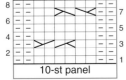

BRAIDED CABLE

10-st panel

STITCH KEY
- ▭ P on RS, k on WS
- ▢ K on RS, p on WS
- ⬦ C4B
- ⬦ C4F

OUTBACK BASKET WEAVE PULLOVER

DESIGN BY MELISSA LEAPMAN

WHAT'S IN THE BAG

Schachenmayr Ecologico
(worsted weight; 100% wool;
83 yds/50g per ball): 15 (16, 17,
18, 19, 20) balls medium gray #84
Size 8 (5mm) needles
Size 9 (5.5mm) needles or size needed to
obtain gauge

4 MEDIUM

SKILL LEVEL

■■■□ INTERMEDIATE

SIZES

Man's small (medium, large, extra-large,
2X-large, 3X-large) Instructions are given for
smallest size, with larger sizes
in parentheses. When only 1
number is given, it applies to
all sizes.

FINISHED MEASUREMENTS

Chest: 45½ (48½, 51½, 54½, 57½,
60½) inches
Length: 26 (26½, 27, 27, 27½, 27½)
inches

GAUGE

16 sts and 26 rows = 4 inches/10cm
in Basket Weave pat with larger
needles.
To save time, take time to check
gauge.

PATTERN STITCHES

K3, P3 Rib (multiple of 6 sts + 3)
Row 1 (RS): K3, *p3, k3; rep from *
to end.
Row 2: P3, *k3, p3; rep from * to end.
   Rep Rows 1 and 2 for pat.

Basket Weave (multiple of 6 sts + 3)
Rows 1 and 3 (RS): P3, *k3, p3; rep
from * to end.

Rows 2 and 4: K3, *p3, k3; rep from * to end.
Rows 5 and 7: K3, *p3, k3; rep from * to end.
Rows 6 and 8: P3, *k3, p3; rep from * to end.
   Rep Rows 1–8 for pat.

Neckband Rib (multiple of 6 sts + 2)
Row 1 (RS): K1, *k3, p3; rep from * to last
st, k1.
Row 2: P1, *k3, p3; rep from * to last st, p1.
   Rep Rows 1 and 2 for pat.

PATTERN NOTE

For ease in finishing, one selvedge stitch has
been added to each side; these stitches are not
reflected in final measurements.

BACK

With smaller needles, cast on 93 (99, 105, 111, 117, 123) sts.

Work in K3, P3 Rib for 3 inches, ending with a WS row.

Change to larger needles and work even in Basket Weave pat until piece measures approx 15½ inches, ending with a WS row.

Shape armholes

Bind off 9 (12, 15, 15, 18, 18) sts at beg of next 2 rows—75 (75, 75, 81, 81, 87) sts.

Work even in established pat until armholes measure approx 9½ (10, 10½, 10½, 11, 11) inches, ending with a WS row.

Shape shoulders

Bind off 7 (7, 7, 8, 8, 9) sts at beg of next 4 rows, then bind off 8 (8, 8, 9, 9, 10) sts at beg of following 2 rows— 31 sts.

Bind off.

FRONT

Work same as back until armholes measure 7¼ (7¾, 8¼, 8½, 8¾, 8¾) inches, ending with a WS row.

Shape neck

Work across first 30 (30, 30, 33, 33, 36) sts, join 2nd ball of yarn and bind off center 15 sts, work to end row.

Working both sides at once with separate balls of yarn, bind off 3 sts at each neck edge once, then 2 sts at each neck edge once—25 (25, 25, 28, 28, 31) sts each side.

Dec 1 st each neck edge [every row] twice, then dec 1 st each neck edge [every other row] once—22 (22, 22, 25, 25, 28) sts each side.

Work even until piece measures same as back to shoulders.

Tip What did we do before sticky notes? These nifty creations are our saving grace when it comes to knitting. Keep your place on your pattern by moving the sticky note down as you work— you'll never forget where you left off! Keep extra pads available in the glove compartment of your car and in your knitting bag.

Shape shoulders

Work same as for back.

SLEEVE

With smaller needles, cast on 39 (39, 39, 39, 45, 45) sts.

Work in K3, P3 Rib for 1½ inches, ending with a WS row.

Change to larger needles, beg Basket Weave pat, inc 1 st each side [every 4 rows] 1 (8, 16, 16, 14, 17) times, then [every 6 rows] 18 (13, 7, 7, 8, 5) times, working new sts into pat as they accumulate—77 (81, 85, 85, 89, 89) sts.

Work even until piece measures approx 21 (21½, 21½, 21½, 22, 21) inches, ending with a WS row.

Bind off.

FINISHING

Block pieces to finished measurements.
Sew right shoulder seam.

NECKBAND

With RS facing and using smaller needles, pick up and knit 86 sts around neckline.

Work even in Neckband Rib Pat until band measures approx 2½ inches.

Bind off in rib.

ASSEMBLY

Sew left shoulder seam, including side of neckband. Fold neckband in half to WS and loosely whipstitch into place. Set in sleeves. Sew side seams. Weave in all ends. ■

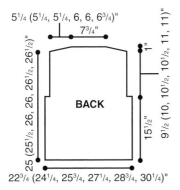

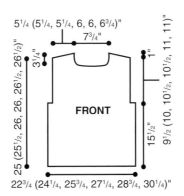

FOR THE
LITTLE ONES

If you're searching for the perfect gift for next weekend's shower, you're in the right place! When it comes to knitting for those little cuties in your life, we've made it easier than ever to pack up your knitting bag for your excursions. With easy-to-memorize stitch combinations, you'll never lose your place again!

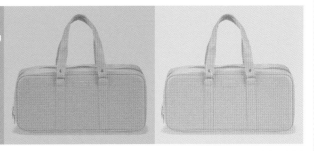

ROUNDABOUT RUFFLED TOP

DESIGN BY LOIS S. YOUNG

WHAT'S IN THE BAG

Reynolds Saucy (worsted weight; 100% cotton; 185 yds/100g per ball): 2 (3, 3, 4) balls coral reef #4545 (MC); 1 ball each persimmon #125 (A) and light yellow #133 (B)

 **4 MEDIUM**

Size 5 (3.75mm) straight and 16-inch circular needles or size needed to obtain gauge
Stitch markers, 1 in CC for beg of rnd
Stitch holders

SKILL LEVEL
■■■□ INTERMEDIATE

SIZES
Child's 2–4 (4–6, 6–8, 8–10)
Instructions are given for smallest size with larger sizes in parentheses. When only 1 number is given, it applies to all sizes.

FINISHED MEASUREMENTS
Chest: 24 (26, 28, 30) inches
Length to shoulder: 13 (14¼, 17¼, 19¼) inches

GAUGE
20 sts and 28 rows = 4 inches/10cm in St st.
To save time, take time to check gauge.

SPECIAL ABBREVIATIONS
Place marker (pm): Place a marker on needle to separate sections.
Centered Double Decrease (S2KP2): Slip 2 sts kwise, k1, pass slipped sts over.

BACK
With A, cast on 64 (70, 74, 80) sts.

Knit 1 row.
Change to MC and knit 6 rows.
Work in St st until back measures 7½ (8¼, 10¼, 11¾) inches, ending with a WS row.

Shape armholes
Bind off 4 (4, 4, 5) sts at beg of next 2 rows, and 3 sts at beg of the following 2 rows—50 (56, 60, 64) sts.
Dec row (RS): K1, ssk, knit to last 3 sts, k2tog, k1—48 (54, 58, 62) sts.
Rep Dec row [every RS row] 0 (0, 0, 1) time more—48 (54, 58, 60) sts.
Work even until armhole measures 2½ (3, 3½, 4) inches, ending with a WS row.

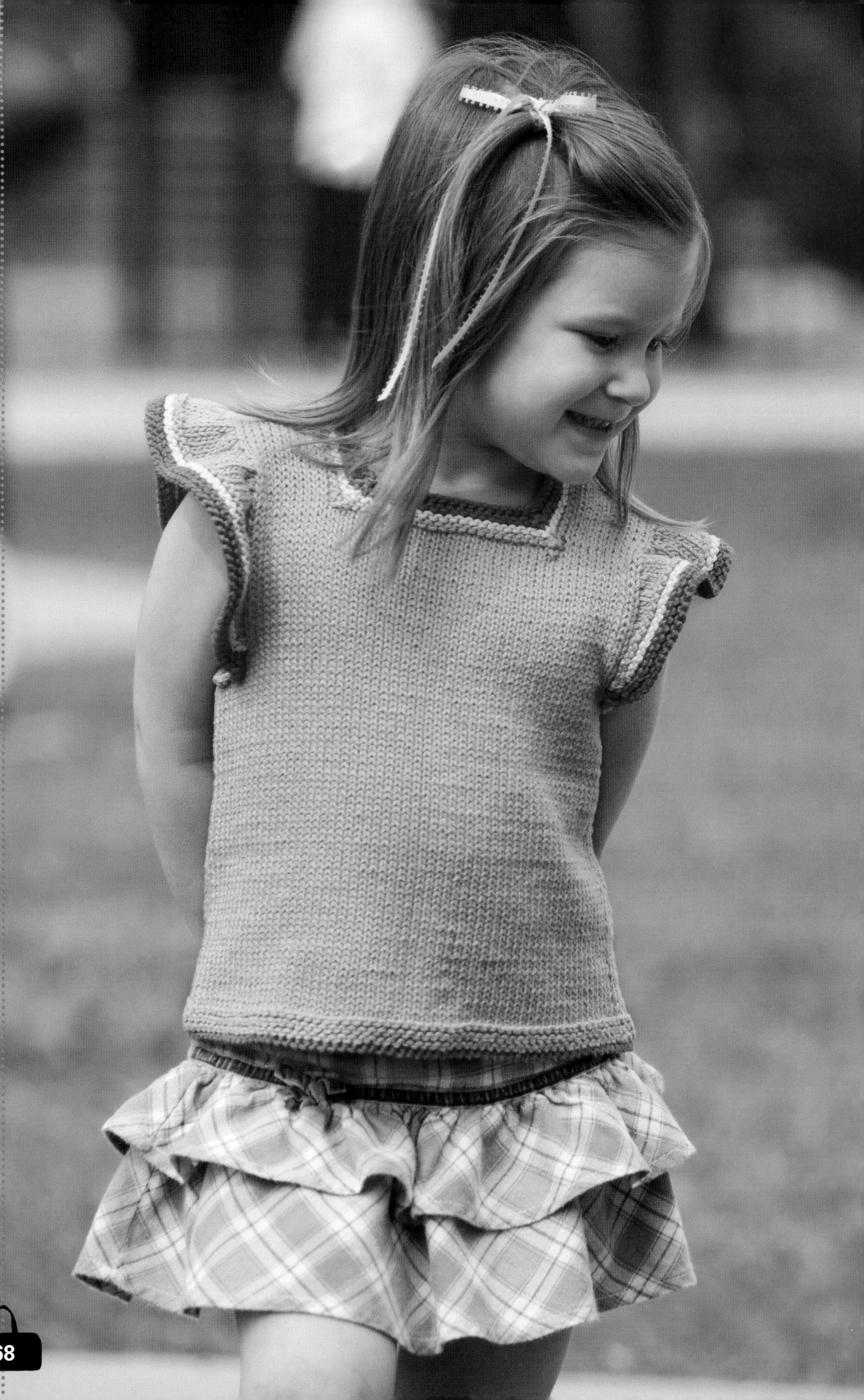

Divide for neck

Next row (RS): K12 (14, 15, 16) sts for left shoulder, join 2nd ball of yarn and k24 (26, 28, 28) sts and put on holder for neck, k12 (14, 15, 16) sts for right shoulder.

Working both sides at once, work even until armholes measure 5 ½ inches, ending with a WS row.

Shape shoulders

Bind off 6 (7, 8, 8) sts at armhole edges at beg of next 2 rows and 6 (7, 7, 8) sts at beg of following 2 rows.

FRONT

Work same as for back.

ASSEMBLY

Sew shoulder and side seams.

NECK BORDER

With RS facing, using circular needle and MC, beg at right shoulder, pick up and knit 16 (16, 18, 18) sts evenly spaced along right yoke; pm, k24 (26, 28, 28) sts from back neck holder; pm, pick up and knit 32 (32, 36, 36) sts along left yoke; pm, k24 (26, 28, 28) sts from front neck holder; pm, pick up and knit 16 (16, 18, 18) sts along right yoke; place beg of rnd marker—112 (116, 128, 128) sts.

Rnds 1, 3, 5: Purl with color used on previous rnd.

Rnd 2 (dec): With B, *knit to 1 st before marker, sl 1, remove marker, return slipped st to LH needle, replace marker on RH needle, S2KP2, knit to 2 sts before marker, slip both sts, remove marker, S2KP2, replace marker; rep

from * once more, knit to end—104 (108, 120, 120) sts.

Rnds 4 and 6: With A, work as for Rnd 2—88 (92, 104, 104) sts.

Rnd 7: Bind off pwise.

UNDERARM BORDER

With RS facing, using circular needle and MC, pick up and knit 16 (16, 16, 18) sts along bottom of armhole. Turn and bind off kwise.

RUFFLE

Count up 22 (26, 32, 36) rows from underarm and mark positions on front and back.

With RS facing, using circular needle and MC, beg at first marker, pick up and knit around upper armhole at rate of 3 sts for every 2 rows as follows: *pick up and knit 1 st, yo, pick up and knit 1 st; rep from *, ending at 2nd marker—approx 51 (59, 71, 79) sts.

Work back and forth in St st and at end of each row, [pick up and knit (on RS)/purl (on WS) 6 more sts along armhole] 6 (6, 8, 12) times, [(RS) pick up and knit or (WS) purl 4 more sts along armhole] 2 (4, 4, 0) times—approx 95 (111, 135, 151) sts; exact st count is not critical.

Knit next WS row.

Change to B and knit 2 rows.

Change to A and knit 3 rows.

Bind off kwise on WS.

FINISHING

Sew ends of ruffle to underarm.

Weave in ends. Block to finished measurements. ■

Tip No stitch marker? No problem! Using a contrasting-color yarn, make a slip knot as if to cast on one stitch. Cut about a ½ inch below the knot, and voilà—a stitch marker!

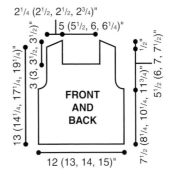

2¼ (2½, 2½, 2¾)"

5 (5½, 6, 6¼)"

3 (3, 3½, 3½)"

13 (14¼, 17¼, 19¼)"

½"

5½ (6, 7, 7½)"

FRONT AND BACK

7½ (8½, 10½, 11¾)"

12 (13, 14, 15)"

LITTLE PRINCESS DRESS UP SET

DESIGNS BY LOIS S. YOUNG

WHAT'S IN THE BAG

Berroco Plush (bulky weight; 100% nylon; 90 yds/50g per skein): 1 (1, 2) skeins raspberry strawberry #1926 (MC)

Berroco Touché (worsted weight; 50% cotton/50% rayon; 89 yds/50g per hank): 1 hank sachet #7931 (CC)

Size 10 (6mm) 24- or 29-inch circular needle or size needed to obtain gauge

SKILL LEVEL
■■□□ EASY

SIZES
Child's 2 (4–6, 8) Instructions are given for smallest size with larger sizes in parentheses. When only 1 number is given, it applies to all sizes.

"MINK" STOLE

FINISHED MEASUREMENTS
Length: 32 (36, 40) inches
Width: 4 (5, 6) inches

GAUGE
12 sts and 24 rows = 4 inches/10cm in garter st with MC. To save time, take time to check gauge.

STOLE
With MC, cast on 106 (120, 134) sts.
Knit 5 (6, 7) rows.
With CC, knit 1 row, purl 1 row.
With MC, knit 4 (6, 8) rows.

Rep [last 6 (8, 10) rows] 3 more times.
With MC, knit 1 row.
With MC, bind off kwise on WS.

CROWN

WHAT'S IN THE BAG

Berroco Touché (worsted weight; 50% cotton/50% rayon; 89 yds/50g per hank): 1 hank sachet #7931 (CC)

Berroco Lumina (worsted weight; 54% cotton/36% acrylic/10% polyester; 95 yds/25g per hank): 1 hank lip gloss #1607 (CC)

Size 7 (4.5mm) straight and double-pointed (set of 2) needles or size needed to obtain gauge

FINISHED MEASUREMENTS
Circumference (will stretch when worn): 16½ (18, 20½) inches
Height: 3½ (4, 4½) inches

GAUGE
20 sts and 40 rows = 4 inches/10cm in garter stitch with MC. To save time, take time to check gauge.

SPECIAL ABBREVIATION
Make 1 (M1): Insert LH needle from front to back under the running thread between the last st worked and next st on RH needle; knit into the back of resulting loop.

SPECIAL TECHNIQUES

Attached I-cord: Without turning, slide sts to other end of needle. K2, ssk, pick up and knit 1 st from edge.

Unattached I-cord Row: Without turning, slide sts to other end of needle, k3.

PATTERN NOTE

Top and bottom of point will occur on different-side rows on different sizes. When changing from one to another, always work increases and decreases at point edge of crown.

CROWN

With MC, cast on 11 (13, 15) sts.
Mark beg of RS row.

Bottom to top of point

RS rows: Knit to last st, M1, k1—1 st inc.
WS rows: K1, M1, knit to end—1 st inc.
Work RS and WS rows until there are 19 (23, 27) sts in row.
Knit 1 row.

Top to bottom of point

RS rows: Knit to last 3 sts, k2tog, k1—1 st dec.
WS rows: K1, ssk, knit to end of row—1 st dec.
Work RS and WS rows until there are 11 (13, 15) sts in row.
Knit 1 row.
1 point complete.
Make 5 more points in same manner.
Bind off.
Sew ends of crown tog.

BOTTOM I-CORD BORDER

With dpns and CC, cast on 3 sts.
With RS facing, pick up and knit 1 st from bottom of crown.
Work Attached I-cord around bottom of crown at rate of 1 row per ridge of garter st.
When border is complete, bind off.
Sew ends of I-cord tog.

POINT I-CORD BORDER

Beg border several ridges up from bottom of one point.
Work as for bottom border, working attached I-cord up point at rate of 1 row per ridge, ending 1 row before point.
Turning the point: Work 2 rows Attached I-cord in next st; work 1 row Attached I-cord in point, but omit the "pick up and knit 1 st"; work 1 row Unattached I-cord; work 1 row Unattached I-cord, but pick up and knit 1 st in point st; work 2 rows Attached I-cord in next st (point completed).

Work Attached I-cord down point to bottom st between points; skip this st and begin next point's border.

Continue around points.

Bind off when border is complete, sew ends of I-cord tog.

BALLET LENGTH SKIRT

WHAT'S IN THE BAG

Plymouth Eros (worsted weight; 100% nylon; 165 yds/50g per ball): 2 (2, 3) balls red/pink #2010 (MC)

Plymouth Encore DK (DK weight; 75% acrylic/25% wool; 150 yds/50g per ball): 1 ball fuchsia #1385 (CC)

Size 5 (3.75mm) needles
Size 9 (5.5mm) double-point needles (set of 2)
Size 11 (6mm) 24 or 29-inch circular needle or size needed to obtain gauge
Stitch marker

FINISHED MEASUREMENTS

Length: 12 (14, 17) inches
Waist: 21 (23, 25) inches, before gathering with tie

GAUGE

13 sts and 16 rows = 4 inches/10cm in St st.
To save time, take time to check gauge.

WAISTBAND

Using smaller needles and CC, cast on 8 sts.
Knit 2 rows.
Row 1 (eyelet row, RS): K2, k2tog, [yo] twice, ssk, k2.
Row 2: K3, [k1, p1] in double-yo, k3.
Rows 3 and 5: Knit.
Rows 4 and 6: K2, p4, k2.
Rep [Rows 1–6] 21 (23, 25) times.
Knit 2 rows.
Bind off kwise on WS.

SKIRT

With RS facing, using larger needle and MC, pick up and knit along edge at rate of 3 sts for every 4 rows (approx 134, 143, 152 sts); place marker for beg of rnd.

Knit all rnds until skirt measures 11 (13, 16) inches.

With MC and CC held tog, knit 1 rnd, purl 1 rnd, knit 1 rnd.

Bind off loosely pwise.

Weave in ends. Block.

WAISTBAND TIE

Using dpns and 1 strand each MC and CC held tog, cast on 4 sts; do not turn.
I-cord row: Slide sts to other end of needle, k4, do not turn.
Rep I-cord row until tie measures 32 (36, 40) inches.
Bind off.
Weave in ends.
Thread tie through holes on waistband. Tack tie to waistband in center of skirt to prevent it from being pulled out. ■

BODACIOUS BOBBLE HAT

DESIGN BY IRINA POLUDNENKO

WHAT'S IN THE BAG

Tahki Stacy Charles Torino
(worsted weight; 100% merino
wool; 94 yds/50g per ball):
1 ball each lime green #119 (A),
fuchsia #120 (B) and dark lavender
#129 (C)

 4 MEDIUM

Size 8 (5mm) double-pointed (set of 5) and
16-inch circular needles or size needed
to obtain gauge
Size F/5 (3.75mm) crochet hook
Stitch markers (1 in CC for beg of rnd)

SKILL LEVEL
■■□□ EASY

SIZES
Child's small (medium, large)

FINISHED MEASUREMENT
Circumference: 16 (17¾, 19½) inches

GAUGE
18 sts and 32 rnds = 4 inches/10cm in pat st.
To save time, take time to check gauge.

PATTERN STITCH
Stripe pat (any number of sts)
Rnd 1: With A, knit.
Rnd 2: With A, purl.
Rnds 3 and 4: With B, knit.
Rnds 5 and 6: Rep Rnds 1 and 2.
Rnds 7 and 8: With C, knit.
Rep Rnds 1–8 for Stripe pat.

PATTERN NOTES
When working Stripe pattern, carry colors not
in use up inside of hat.

Change to double-pointed needles when
stitches no longer fit comfortably on circular
needle.

HAT
With A, cast on 72 (80, 88) sts; place marker for

beg of rnd and join, taking care not to twist sts.
Beg with Rnd 2, work [Rnds 1–8 of Stripe pat]
5 (6, 7) times, then work Rnds 1 and 2 once
more.

Next rnd: Continuing in Stripe pat, *k9 (10, 11),
place marker; rep from * around.
Dec rnd: Knit to 2 sts before marker, k2tog; rep
from * around—64 (72, 80) sts.

Continue in Stripe pat and rep Dec rnd
[every 4th rnd] 7 (8, 9) times—8 sts rem.

Work 14 more rnds in Stripe pat.

With A, bind off.

Weave in all ends.

BOBBLE TASSELS
Make 8
With B, cast on 3 sts.
Row 1: K1, [k1, yo, k1, yo, k1] in next st, k1—7 sts.
Row 2: Purl.
Row 3: Knit.
Row 4: Purl.
Row 5: K1, ssk, k1, k2tog, k1—5 sts.
Row 6: K1, p3tog, k1—3 sts.
Row 7: K3tog and put resulting st on crochet
hook.

Cut yarn, leaving a 5-inch tail.

With crochet hook and A, beg with the last st
of bobble, chain 20 sts, attach with slip st to a
bound-off st on hat, turn; work a slip st in each
chain st, cut yarn and fasten off.

Using 5-inch tail and tapestry needle, draw
through edge sts to form bobble.

Weave all ends inside bobble.

Make 7 more bobble tassels with 3 bobbles
in B and 4 bobbles in C; work all tassel cords in
A and attach each one to next bound-off st on
top of hat. Make tassel cords different lengths
as desired. ∎

Tip Always have your scissors handy by
tying them onto a pretty piece of
ribbon. You can attach them to your
yarn bag or wear them around your neck.

LACY A-LINE BABY DRESS

DESIGN BY SHIRLEY MACNULTY

WHAT'S IN THE BAG

Rowan Cashsoft Baby DK
 (DK weight; 57% extra
 fine merino/33% acrylic
 microfiber/10% cashmere; 142
 yds/50g per ball): 4 balls bloom #00815

3 LIGHT

Size 6 (4mm) straight and 16-inch circular
 needles or size needed to obtain gauge
1 [½-inch] button to match yarn
Small amount sewing thread to match
 button color
Sewing needle

SKILL LEVEL

■■■□ INTERMEDIATE

SIZES

Infant's 6–9 (9–12, 12–18) months Instructions
are given for the smallest size; with larger sizes
in parentheses. When only 1 number is given,
it applies to all sizes.

FINISHED MEASUREMENTS

Chest: 18½ (20½, 22½) inches
Length to shoulders: 12¾ (13½, 14¾) inches

GAUGE

23 sts and 32 rows = 4 inches/10cm in Lacy pat.
To save time, take time to check gauge.

SPECIAL ABBREVIATION

Make 1 (M1): Insert LH needle from front to
back under the running thread between the
last st worked and next st on RH needle; knit
into the back of resulting loop.

PATTERN STITCH

Lace Pat for Back/Front [multiple of 14 (16, 18)
sts +13]
Row 1 (RS): K4, *k2tog, yo, k1, yo, ssk, k9 (11,
13); rep from * to last 9 sts, k2tog, yo, k1, yo,
ssk, k4.
Row 2: and all WS rows: Purl.
Row 3: K3, *k2tog, yo, k3, yo, ssk, k7 (9, 11);

rep from * to last 10 sts, k2tog, yo, k3, ssk, k3.
Row 5: K4, *yo, ssk, yo, k3tog, yo, k9 (11, 13); rep
from * to last 9 sts, yo, ssk, yo, k3tog, yo, k4.
Row 7: K5, *yo, sk2p, yo, k11 (13, 15); rep from
* to last 8 sts, yo, sk2p, yo, k5
Row 9: K11 (12, 13), *k2tog, yo, k1, yo, ssk, k9
(11, 13); rep from * to last 2 (1, 0) sts, k2 (1, 0).
Row 11: K10 (11, 12), *k2tog, yo, k3, yo, ssk, k7
(9, 11); rep from * to last 3 (2, 1) sts, k3 (2, 1).
Row 13: K11 (12, 13), *yo, ssk, yo, k3tog, yo, k9
(11, 13); rep from * to last 2 (1, 0) sts, k2 (1, 0).
Row 15: K12 (13, 14), *yo, sk2p, yo, k11 (13, 15);
rep from * to last 15 (16, 17) sts, sk2p, yo, k12
(13, 14).
Row 16: Purl.
 Rep Rows 1–16 for pat.

Lace Pat for Sleeves

*Note: The number of knit sts at beg and end of
rows will inc twice as the sleeve inc are made.*
Row 1 (RS): K3 (4, 3), [k2tog, yo, k1, yo, ssk, k9
(9, 11)] twice, k2tog, yo, k1, ssk, k3 (4, 3).
Row 2 and all WS rows: Purl.
Row 3: K2 (3, 2), [k2tog, yo, k3, yo, ssk, k7 (7, 9)]
twice, k2tog, yo, k3, yo, ssk, k2 (3, 2).
Row 5: K3 (4, 3), [yo, ssk, yo, k3tog, yo, k9 (9,
11)] twice, yo, ssk, yo, k3tog, yo, k3 (4, 3).
Row 7: K4 (5, 4), [yo, sk2p, yo, k11 (11, 13)]
twice, yo, sk2p, yo, k4 (5, 4).
Row 9: K1, M1, k9 (10, 10), k2tog, yo, k1, yo,
ssk, k9 (9, 11), k2tog, yo, k1, yo, ssk, k9 (10, 10),
M1, k1.

 *Note: The M1 inc is worked on just this first
round of the sleeve pat rep and is shown here.
The 2nd M1 inc is worked on Row 1 of the first
rep. To keep in pat after the incs, the number of
knit sts at the beg and end of the rows is also
increased.*
Row 11: K10 (11, 11), k2tog, yo, k3, yo, ssk, k7
(7, 9), k2tog, yo, k3, yo, ssk, k10 (11, 11).
Row 13: K11 (12, 12), yo, ssk, yo, k3tog, yo, k9
(9, 11), yo, ssk, yo, k3tog, yo, k11 (12, 12).
Row 15: K12 (13, 13), yo, sk2p, yo, k11 (11, 13),
yo sk2p, yo, k12 (13, 13).
Row 16: Purl.
 Rep Rows 1–16 for pat, increasing again on
the first Row 1 rep.

PATTERN NOTES

A chart is provided for the Lace pattern (front/back) for those preferring to work from charts.

When decreasing or increasing, be sure that if you work a pattern stitch yarn over that you also work a corresponding pattern stitch decrease, and if you work a pattern stitch decrease that you have a corresponding pattern stitch yarn over or your stitch count will not come out even. Do not confuse decrease shaping stitches with pattern stitches.

The back neck is split and closed with a button.

The garter stitch bottom edge is a slightly wider gauge than the pattern stitch; when blocking, the bottom should be wider than the chest (see schematic).

BACK

Using long-tail method, cast on 55 (61, 67) sts.
Knit 4 rows.
Purl 1 row.
Work even in Lace pat until piece measures 9 (9½, 10) inches or desired length to underarm.

Shape Armholes

Continuing in pat, bind off 3 (4, 4) sts at the beg of the next 2 rows—49 (53, 59) sts.
Dec row (RS): K2, ssk, work in pat to last 3 sts, k2tog, k1—47 (51, 57) sts.
Rep Dec row [every RS row] 2 (2, 3) times more—43 (47, 51) sts.
Work even until armhole measures 2¾ (3, 3¾) inches, ending with a WS row,

RIGHT BACK

Row 1 (RS): Work 21 (23, 25) sts; turn, leaving rem 22 (24, 26) sts on holder.
Row 2: Cast on 3 sts, k3 (the sts just cast-on), purl to end—24 (26, 28) sts.
Next 6 rows: Work 21 (23, 25) sts in established Lace pat and 3 new sts in garter st.

Shape Right Back Shoulder

Bind off 3 (4, 4) sts at beg of next row, then 4 (5, 5) at the beg of the next 2 RS rows. Bind off rem 13 (12, 14) sts.

LEFT BACK

Row 1 (RS): Slip sts back to needle, join yarn and work to end of row.
Row 2: Purl to last st, k1.
Next 7 rows: Rep last 2 rows, ending with Row 1.

Shape Left Back Shoulder

Bind off 3 (4, 4) sts at beg of next row, then 4 (5, 5) sts at the beg of next 2 WS rows.

Note: *At some point in this section, you will work a yo for the Lace pat near the right edge that can be used for the buttonhole.*
Bind off the rem 11 (10, 12) sts.

FRONT

Work front the same as back until piece measures 1 (1, 1¼) inches less than back to shoulders.

Shape Front Neck

Work in pat across 16 (18, 20) sts, join a 2nd ball of yarn and bind off center 11 sts, work in pat to end of row—16 (18, 20) sts each side.

Working both sides at once with separate balls of yarn, bind off 2 sts at each neck edge once, then dec 1 st at each neck edge on RS rows 3 (2, 4) times—11 (14, 14) sts each side.

Work even in pat until front measures same as for back to shoulders, ending with a WS row.

Bind off 3 (4, 4) sts at beg of the next 2 rows, then 4 (5, 5) sts at beg of the next 4 rows.

SLEEVES

With long-tail method, cast on 39 (41, 43) sts.

Tip Make waiting in line worthwhile! Choose a bag that rests comfortably across your chest and shoulder, allowing for easy maneuvering of your project and yarn.

Knit 4 rows.
Purl 1 row.
Work 18 (20, 24) rows in Lace Sleeve pat, inc as indicated in the pat—43 (45, 47) sts.

Sleeve Cap
Bind off 3 (4, 4) sts at beg of the next 2 rows—37 (37, 39) sts.
Dec row (RS): K1, ssk, work in pat to last 3 sts, k2tog, k1—35 (35, 37) sts.
Rep Dec rows [every RS row] 10 (10, 11) times—15 sts.
Bind off.

FINISHING
Sew shoulder seams. Overlap right back neck with left back neck and sew closed at bottom.

NECKLINE
With circular needle, beg at the left neck edge, pick up and knit 11 (10, 12) left back neck sts, 15 (16, 17) left front sts, 11 front sts, 15 (16, 17) right front sts, and 13 (12, 14) right back neck sts—65 (65, 71) sts.
Knit 3 rows. Bind off loosely kwise.

ASSEMBLY
Set in sleeves. Sew side and sleeve seams. Weave in loose ends. Block to finished measurements. Sew button on right back neck edge to correspond to the pattern yo on left neck edge. ■

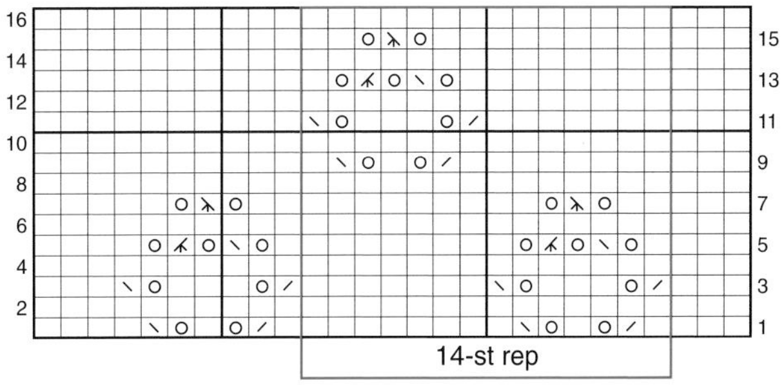
16
14
12
10
8
6
4
2
15
13
11
9
7
5
3
1
14-st rep

LACE PATTERN FRONT/BACK (SIZE 6-9)

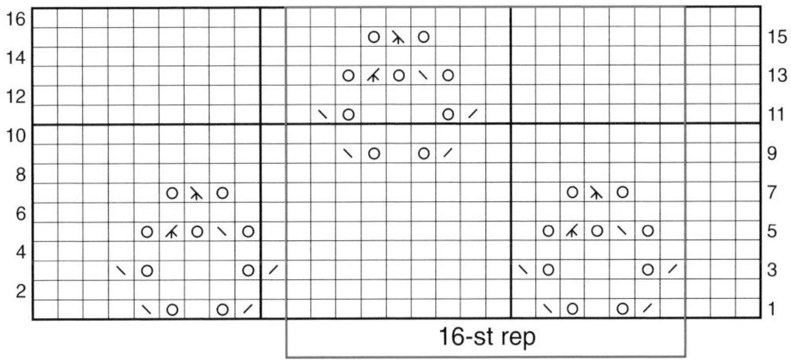
16
14
12
10
8
6
4
2
15
13
11
9
7
5
3
1
16-st rep

LACE PATTERN FRONT/BACK (SIZE 9-12)

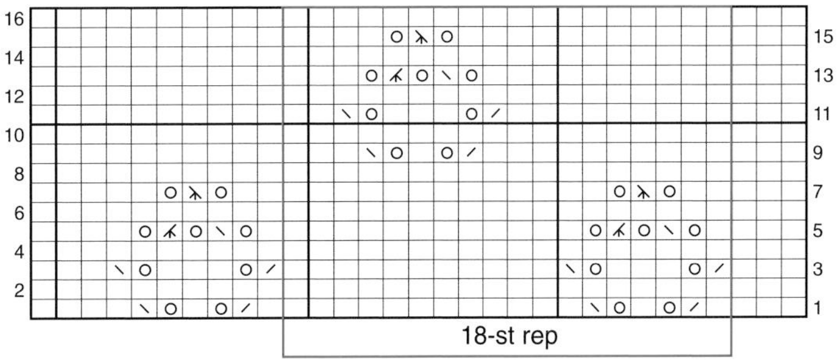
16
14
12
10
8
6
4
2
15
13
11
9
7
5
3
1
18-st rep

LACE PATTERN FRONT/BACK (SIZE 12-18)

STITCH KEY
- □ K on RS, p on WS
- ⁄ K2tog
- O Yo
- ∖ Ssk
- K3tog
- Sk2p

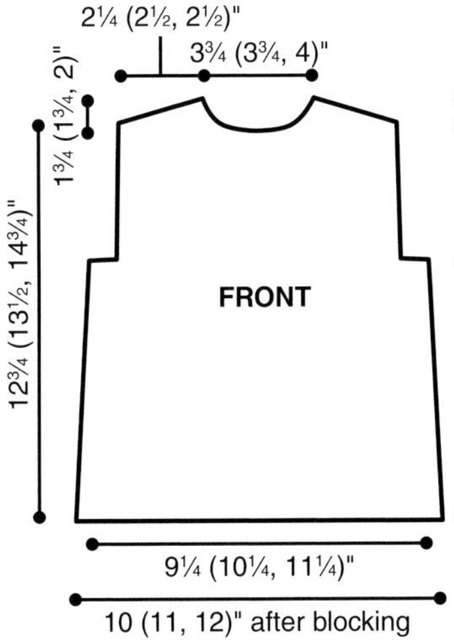
2¼ (2½, 2½)"
3¾ (3¾, 4)"
1¾ (1¾, 2)"
12¾ (13½, 14¾)"
¾"
3¾ (4, 4¾)"
9 (9½, 10)"
FRONT
9¼ (10¼, 11¼)"
10 (11, 12)" after blocking

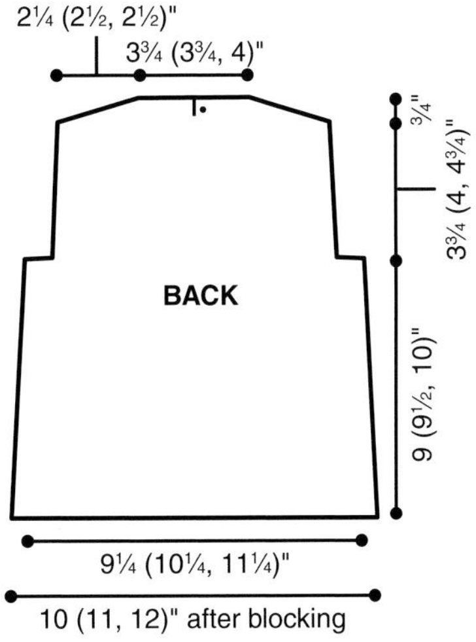
2¼ (2½, 2½)"
3¾ (3¾, 4)"
¾"
3¾ (4, 4¾)"
9 (9½, 10)"
BACK
9¼ (10¼, 11¼)"
10 (11, 12)" after blocking

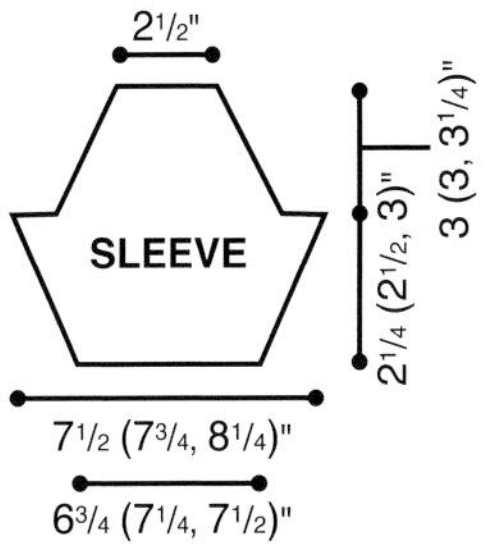
2½"
SLEEVE
2¼ (2½, 3)"
3 (3, 3¼)"
7½ (7¾, 8¼)"
6¾ (7¼, 7½)"

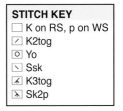

BABY DEAREST

DESIGNS BY KATHARINE HUNT

WHAT'S IN THE BAG

Plymouth Jeannee D.K. (DK
   weight; 51% cotton/49% acrylic;
   136 yds/50g per ball): 3 (4, 4)
   balls pale blue #21 (A) and 4 (5,
   6) balls denim #10 (B)
Size 3 (3.25mm) 16-inch circular needle (hat)
Size 4 (3.5mm) needles (sweater)
Size 5 (3.75mm) double-point and 16-inch
   circular needle or size needed to obtain
   gauge (hat)
Size 6 (4mm) needles or size needed to
   obtain gauge (sweater)
Size G/6 (4mm) crochet hook (optional)
Stitch markers, 1 in CC for beg of rnd
3 (3, 4) [15mm] buttons

SKILL LEVEL

■■■■ EXPERIENCED

SIZES

Sweater: Child's 2 (4, 6) Instructions are
given for smallest size, with larger sizes in
parentheses. When only 1 number is given,
it applies to all sizes.
Hat: Child's small (medium/large)

FINISHED MEASUREMENTS

Chest: 27 (31½, 36) inches
Length to shoulders: 14 (16, 17¾) inches
Hat circumference: 16 (18) inches

GAUGE

Sweater: 22 sts and 39 rows = 4 inches/10cm
in Honeycomb pat st with size 6 needles.
Hat: 24 sts and 41 rnds = 4 inches/10cm in
Honeycomb pat with size 5 needles.
To save time, take time to check gauge.

SPECIAL ABBREVIATIONS

Make Bobble (MB): [K1, p1] 3 times, all into the
next st, then pass last 5 sts over the first st and
off the needle.

Place marker (pm): Place marker on needle
to separate patterns.
Yarn forward (yf): Bring yarn between needles
to front of work.
Yarn back (yb): Bring yarn between needles to
back of work.

PATTERN STITCHES

Honeycomb Pat (worked flat on multiple of 12
sts + 15)
   Sts should only be counted on Rows 1, 6, 7
and 12; if counting on other rows, do not count
the yo's and resulting sts on following rows.
Row 1 (WS): With A, knit.
Row 2 (RS): With B, k6, *[sl 1, yo] twice, sl 1, k9;
rep from *, ending last rep k6.
   *Note: Be sure to keep the 2 yo's carefully
positioned between the 3 slipped sts.*
Row 3: With B, p6, *sl 1, purl the first yo, sl 1,
knit the next yo, sl 1, p9; rep from *, ending last
rep p6.
   *Note: Slip each A slipped st onto RH needle
before working the following yo.*
Row 4: With B, k6, *[sl 1, k1] twice, sl 1, k9; rep
from *, ending last rep k6.
Row 5: With B, p6, *[sl 1, p1] twice, sl 1, p9; rep
from *, ending last rep p6.
Row 6: With A, k5, *k2tog, k3, ssk, k7; rep from
*, ending last rep k5.
Row 7: With A, knit.
Row 8: With B, k1, sl 1, yo, sl 1, *k9, [sl 1, yo]
twice, sl 1; rep from * to last 12 sts, k9, sl 1, yo,
sl 1, k1.
Row 9: With B, [p1, sl 1] twice, *p9, sl 1, purl
the first yo, sl 1, knit the next yo, sl 1; rep from
* to last 13 sts, p9, [sl 1, p1] twice.
Row 10: With B, [k1, sl 1] twice, *k9, [sl 1, k1]
twice, sl 1; rep from * to last 13 sts, k9, [sl 1, k1]
twice.
Row 11: With B, [p1, sl 1] twice, *p9, [sl 1, p1]
twice, sl 1; rep from * to last 13 sts, p9, [sl 1,
p1] twice.
Row 12: With A, k3, *ssk, k7, k2tog, k3; rep
from * to end.
   Rep Rows 1–12 for pat.

Honeycomb Pat (worked in round on multiple of 12 sts)

Sts should only be counted on Rnds 1, 6, 7 and 12; if counting on other rnds, do not count the yo's and resulting sts on following rnds.

Rnd 1: With A, purl.

Rnd 2: With B, *k2, [sl 1, yo] twice, sl 1, k7; rep from * around.

Note: Be sure to keep the 2 yo's carefully positioned between the 3 slipped sts.

Rnd 3: With B, *k2, sl 1, knit the first yo, sl 1, purl the next yo, sl 1, k7; rep from * around.

Note: Slip each A slipped st onto RH needle before working the following yo.

Rnds 4 and 5: With B, *k2, [sl 1, k1] twice, sl 1, k7; rep from * around.

Rnd 6: With A, *k1, k2tog, k3, ssk, k6; rep from * around.

Rnd 7: With A, purl.

Rnd 8: With B, *k8, [sl 1, yo] twice, sl 1, k1; rep from * around.

Rnd 9: With B, *k8, sl 1, knit the first yo, sl 1, purl the next yo, sl 1, k1; rep from * around.

Rnds 10 and 11: With B, *k8, [k1, sl 1] twice, sl 1, k1; rep from * around.

Rnd 12: With A, *k1, *k2tog, k3, ssk, k6; rep from *around.

Rep Rnds 1–12 for pat.

Stripe Pattern

Rnd 1: With A, knit.

Rnd 2: With A, purl.

Rnds 3–6: With B, knit.

Rep Rnds 1–6 for pat.

SPECIAL TECHNIQUE

1-Row 3-St Buttonhole: Work to buttonhole position, yf, slip next st pwise, yb; [slip next st, then pass 2nd st on RH needle over first st and off RH needle] 3 times to bind off 3 sts; slip first st on RH needle back to LH needle; turn. Wyib, cable cast on 4 sts (1 more than bound off) as follows: insert RH needle between the first and 2nd sts on LH needle, draw up a loop, and place it on the LH needle; rep from * 3 times; turn. Wyib, slip first st on LH needle to RH needle and pass the extra cast-on st over it to close the buttonhole. (This 4th st worked and is not part of the 3-St Buttonhole).

PATTERN NOTES

In order to maintain the correct stitch count when shaping armholes, neck and shoulders,

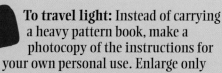

Tip   **To travel light:** Instead of carrying a heavy pattern book, make a photocopy of the instructions for your own personal use. Enlarge only the part you're working on, making it easier to keep track of your progress.

unless shaping on rows with the original number of stitches (i.e., Rows 1, 6, 7 and 12), omit yarn overs immediately following or before the edges that will be affected by the shaping. (Work the yarn overs on the rest of that row as required by the pattern stitch.)

When working Honeycomb pattern, count stitches on Rows 1, 6, 7 and 12; if counting on other rows, do not count the yarn overs or their resulting stitches.

Pattern is written as shown on a boy with button band on left shoulder; if preferred for a girl, reverse it to the right shoulder.

For hat, change to double-point needles when stitches no longer fit comfortably on circular needle.

SWEATER

BACK

With larger needles and A, cast on 75 (87, 99) sts.

Knit 4 rows.

Change to B and work 2 rows St st.

Bobble row (RS): K1 B, *MB with A, k5 B; rep from * to last 2 sts, MB with A, k1 B.

Cut A.

With B, purl 1 row.

With A, knit 3 rows.

Beg Honeycomb pat and work even until piece measures approx 7¾ (9½, 10½) inches, ending with Row 1 or 7 of pat.

Armhole

Bind off 6 sts at the beg of the next 2 rows, omitting yo's at edges if necessary to maintain st count—63 (75, 87) sts.

Work even until armhole measures approx 6¼ (6½, 7) inches, ending Row 1 or 7 of pat.

Shape shoulders

Bind off 9 (8, 9) sts at the beg of the next 2 rows, 8 (7, 9) sts at beg of the following 2 rows, and 0 (7, 9) sts at the beg of the last 2 rows, omitting yo's as necessary at edges—

29 (31, 33) back neck sts.
Bind off.

FRONT

Work as for back until piece measures approx 2½ (2¾, 2¾) inches shorter than back, ending with Row 1 or 7 of pat.

Next row (RS): Work pat across 23 (28, 33) sts and slip to waste yarn or holder, bind off center 17 (19, 21) sts, work established pat to end.

Right front neck and shoulder

Dec 1 st at neck edge on the next 6 rows, omitting yo's as necessary at edge—17 (22, 27) sts.

Work even until front measures same as back to shoulder shaping, ending with a RS row.

Bind off 9 (8, 9) sts at beg of next row, then 8 (7, 9) sts at the beg of the following WS row, then 0 (7, 9) sts at the beg of the last WS row.

Left front neck & buttonhole band shoulder

With WS facing, join yarn at neck edge of left front.

Dec 1 st at neck edge on the next 6 rows, omitting yo's as necessary at edge—17 (22, 27) sts.

Work even until front measures 1 inch short of back to shoulder shaping, ending with a WS row.

Bind off 9 (8, 9) sts at beg of next row, then 8 (7, 9) sts at beg of the following RS row, then 0 (7, 9) sts at beg of the last RS row.

SLEEVES

Note: To keep track of the pattern while inc, place markers as indicated, moving them up on each row. This marks where rep starts and ends, so the sts before and after can be worked in the correct sequence and taken into pattern where possible.

With smaller needles and A, cast on 39 (41, 43) sts.

Knit 4 rows.

Change to B and work 2 rows St st.

Bobble Row (RS): Inc 1 B, k0 (1, 2) B, *MB with A, k5; rep from *, ending MB with A, k0 (1, 2) B, inc 1 B—41 (43, 45) sts.

Cut A.
With B, purl 1 row.
With A, knit 3 rows.

Next row (WS): K1 (2, 3), pm, work Row 1 of Honeycomb pat, pm, k1 (2, 3).

Change to larger needles and inc 1 st at each edge on Pat Row 4, then [every 4 rows] 9 (9, 10) times, 61 (63, 67) sts, [every 6 rows] 2 (2, 3) times, and [every 8 rows] twice, working new sts in pat as possible—69 (71, 77) sts (not counting yo's).

Work even until piece measures 9¼ (10¼, 11½) inches.

Place marker at each end of the row, and work even for 1¼ inches.

Bind off all sts.

ASSEMBLY

Block pieces to finished measurements.
Sew right shoulder seam.

NECKBAND

With B, crochet a row of sc around the neckline (optional).

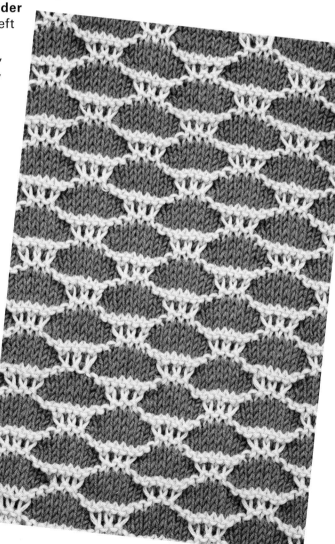

With RS facing, using smaller needles and B, pick up and knit 14 (15, 15) sts along left front neck edge, 17 (19, 21) sts across center front, 21 (22, 22) sts along right front neck edge, and 29 (31, 33) sts across back neck edge—81 (87, 91) sts.

Rows 1 (WS)–3: With B, knit.
Row 4 (RS): With A, knit and dec 4 sts evenly across—77 (83, 87) sts.
Row 5: Purl.
Bobble row: K1 A, *MB with B, k5 A; rep from * to last 4 (4, 2) sts, MB with B, k3 (3, 1) A. Cut B.
Row 7: With A, purl. Cut A.
Row 8: With B, knit.
Row 9: Knit, dec 4 sts evenly across the front—73 (79, 83) sts.
Row 10: Knit.
Bind off kwise on WS.

BUTTON BAND

With RS facing, smaller needles and B, pick up and knit 27 (31, 36) sts evenly along neckband edge and left back shoulder.
Knit 6 rows.
Bind off kwise on WS.

BUTTONHOLE BAND

With RS facing, smaller needles and B, pick up and knit 27 (31, 36) sts along left front shoulder and neckband edge.
Knit 3 rows.
Next row (RS): Working from shoulder edge, k4, *work 1 row 3-St Buttonhole over next 4 sts, k5 (7, 5); rep from * 1 (1, 2) time(s), work buttonhole over next 4 sts, k1.
Knit 2 rows.
Bind off kwise on WS.

FINISHING

Lap the buttonhole band over the button band, and sew the shoulder ends tog. Sew buttons on button band opposite buttonholes. Set in sleeves. Sew side and sleeve seams.

HAT

BODY

With smaller needle and A, cast on 96 (108) sts; pm for beg of rnd and join, taking care not to twist sts.
Work K1, P1 Rib for 1 inch.
Purl 1 rnd, knit 1 rnd, purl 1 rnd.
Change to B and knit 2 rnds.
Bobble Rnd: *K3 B, *MB with A, k2 A; rep from * around.
With B, knit 1 rnd.
With A, knit 1 rnd, purl 1 rnd, knit 1 rnd.
Change to larger needle and work 19 rnds in Honeycomb pat, ending with Rnd 7.
Next rnd: Work Rnd 1 of Stripe pat and inc 4 (2) sts evenly around—100 (110) sts.
Work Stripe pat until piece measures approx 5 ¼ (5 ½) inches, ending with Rnd 2, 4 or 6.
Next rnd: Change to smaller needle and continue established Stripe pat.
Next rnd: Continue established Stripe pat, *work 10 (11) sts, pm; rep from * around.

CROWN

Dec rnd: *Knit to 2 sts before marker, k2tog; rep from * around—90 (100) sts.
Continue in established pat, rep Dec rnd [every other rnd] 8 (9) times—10 sts.
Work 1 more rnd.
Cut yarn, leaving a 6-inch tail.
With tapestry needle, thread tail through rem sts, pull tight and secure to WS.

FINISHING

Weave in ends. Block. ∎

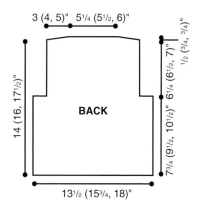

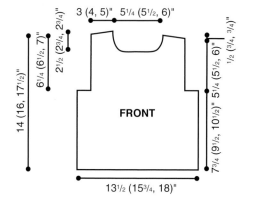

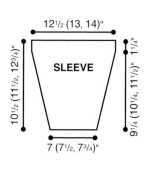

SAUCY STRIPES PULLOVER

DESIGN BY MELISSA LEAPMAN

WHAT'S IN THE BAG

Cascade Yarns Luna (worsted weight; 100% Peruvian cotton; 82 yds/50g per hank): 4 (4, 5, 6) hanks each of teal #734 (A) and blue #721 (B)

Size 7 (4.5mm) needles or size needed to obtain gauge

SKILL LEVEL

■■□□ EASY

SIZES

Child's 2 (4, 6, 8) Instructions are given for smallest size, with larger sizes in parentheses. When only 1 number is given, it applies to all sizes.

FINISHED MEASUREMENTS

Chest: 28 (30, 32, 35) inches
Total length (with lower edge unrolled): 15 (16, 17, 18) inches

GAUGE

18 sts and 26 rows = 4 inches/10cm in St st. To save time, take time to check gauge.

SPECIAL ABBREVIATION

Make 1 (M1): Insert LH needle from front to back under the running thread between the last st worked and next st on RH needle; knit into the back of resulting loop.

PATTERN STITCH

Stripe Pattern

Work 6 rows of A in St st.
    Work 6 rows of B in St st.
    Rep these 12 rows for pat.

PATTERN NOTE

When measuring length, unroll lower edges of knitted fabric.

BACK

With A, cast on 64 (68, 72, 78) sts.
    Work even in Stripe pat until piece measures approx 8½ (9, 9½, 10) inches, ending with a WS row.

Shape armholes

Bind off 4 (5, 6, 7) sts at beg of next 2 rows—56 (58, 60, 64) sts.
    Work even until armhole measures approx 5½ (6, 6½, 7) inches, ending with a WS row.

Shape shoulders

Bind off 5 (5, 5, 6) sts at beg of next 4 rows, then 4 (5, 6, 6) sts at beg of next 2 rows—28 sts.
    Bind off.

FRONT

Work same as for back until armholes measure approx 4½ (5, 5½, 6) inches, ending with a WS row.

Shape neck & shoulders

Next Row (RS): K22 (23, 24, 26) sts; join 2nd ball of yarn and bind off center 12 sts, knit to end of row.

Working both sides at once with separate balls of yarn, bind off at each neck edge 4 sts once then 2 sts once—16 (17, 18, 20) sts each side.

Dec 1 st at each neck edge [every row] twice; *at the same time*, when piece measures same as back to shoulders, shape shoulders same as for back.

SLEEVES

With A, cast on 30 (32, 32, 34) sts.

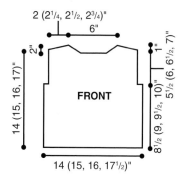

Work 6 rows in Stripe pat.

Inc row (RS): Continuing in Stripe pat, k1, M1, knit to last st, M1, k1—32 (34, 34, 36) sts.

Rep Inc row [every 6th row] 1 (3, 9, 14) time(s), then [every 8th row] 8 (7, 3, 0) times—50 (54, 58, 64) sts.

Work even until piece measures approx 12¾ (13½, 14½, 15½) inches.

Bind off.

FINISHING

Block pieces to finished measurements. Sew right shoulder seam.

NECKBAND

With RS facing and A, pick up and knit 70 sts along neckline.

Work even in St st until for 1½ inches.

Bind off loosely, allowing neckband to roll to RS.

ASSEMBLY

Set in sleeves.

Sew left shoulder seam, including side of neckband.

Sew sleeve and side seams. ■

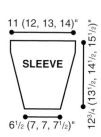

Tip While on a hike, carry along an "easy access" knapsack. Place your yarns in various plastic or drawstring bags. Zip up your bag, leaving a small opening, to "knit while you hike." You won't miss a beat enjoying the fall foliage!

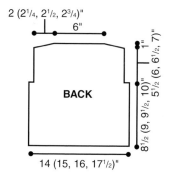

2 (2¼, 2½, 2¾)"
6"
2"
14 (15, 16, 17)"
1"
5½ (6, 6½, 7)"
FRONT
8½ (9, 9½, 10)"
14 (15, 16, 17½)"

2 (2¼, 2½, 2¾)"
6"
1"
5½ (6, 6½, 7)"
BACK
8½ (9, 9½, 10)"
14 (15, 16, 17½)"

11 (12, 13, 14)"
SLEEVE
12¾ (13½, 14½, 15½)
6½ (7, 7, 7½)"

COZY HOODED SLEEPING SACK

DESIGN BY FAINA GOBERSTEIN

WHAT'S IN THE BAG

Nashua Snowbird (worsted weight; 70% wool/30% alpaca; 73 yds/50g per skein): 10 (12, 15) skeins blue # NSB.9155

Size 8 (5mm) 36-inch circular needle

Size 10 (6mm) double-point and 24-inch circular needles or size needed to obtain gauge

Size I/9 (5.5mm) or J/10 (6mm) crochet hook

Stitch marker

Stitch holders

Six [¾-inch] buttons

SKILL LEVEL

 INTERMEDIATE

SIZES

Infant's 0–6 (6–12, 12–18) months Instructions are given for smallest size, with larger sizes in parentheses. When only 1 number is given, it applies to all sizes.

FINISHED MEASUREMENTS

Chest: 24 (32, 40) inches (buttoned)
Length: 26 (28, 30) inches
Sleeve length: 7 (7½, 8) inches

GAUGE

14 sts and 22 rnds/rows = 4 inches/10cm in Seed St Rib with larger needle.
To save time, take time to check gauge.

SPECIAL ABBREVIATIONS

M1L (Make 1 Left): Insert LH needle from front to back under the running thread between the last st worked and next st on LH needle; knit into the back of resulting loop.

M1R (Make 1 Right): Insert LH needle from back to front under the running thread between the last st worked and next st on LH needle. With RH needle, knit into the front of resulting loop.

PATTERN STITCHES

Seed Stitch (odd number of sts)
Rnd/Row 1: K1, *p1, k1; rep from * around/across.
Rnd/Row 2: Knit the purl sts and purl the knit sts as they present themselves.
    Rep Rnd/Row 2 for pat.

Seed Stitch Rib (multiple of 14 sts)
Rnd/Row 1: *Work 7 sts in Seed St, 7 sts in St st; rep from * around.
    Rep Rnd/Row 1 for pat.

SPECIAL TECHNIQUES

Provisional Cast-On: With crochet hook and waste yarn, make a chain several sts longer than desired cast on. With knitting needle and project yarn, pick up indicated number of sts in the "bumps" on back of chain. When indicated in pattern, "unzip" the crochet chain to free live sts.

3-Needle Bind-Off: With RS tog and needles parallel, using a 3rd needle, knit tog 1 st from the front needle with 1 from the back. *Knit tog 1 st each from front and back needles, and sl the first st over the 2nd to bind off; rep from * across, then fasten off last st.

PATTERN NOTE

The sack is worked in the round from bottom up, then split at center front for opening and worked back and forth in rows. The sleeves are knit in the round. The hood extends the central panel on the back.

BODY

With larger circular needle, using provisional method, cast on 83 (111, 139) sts; place marker for beg of rnd and join, taking care not to twist sts.

    Work 10 rnds Seed St.
Next rnd: Change to Seed St Rib and work to last st, k1 in front and back of last st—84 (112, 140) sts.

    Work even in Seed St Rib until piece measures 9 (10, 11) inches.

"I often travel to different countries and never miss an opportunity to visit a yarn shop. I spent one summer in Melbourne, Australia and, while visiting, I found the most amazing little shop. Since it was hard to decide what to buy, the only choice was to purchase as much yarn as I could carry. Upon my arrival in the United States, the customs officials were quite amused, noticing that I had 'smuggled' in two large suitcases of yarn!"

Divide for Front Opening

Next row (RS): Work 46 (60, 74) sts in established pat, turn.

Next row (WS): Bind off 1 st, work to last st, k1-tbl—83 (111, 139) sts.

Next row: Sl 1, work to last st, k1-tbl.

Continue working established pat back and forth, slipping first st and knitting last st tbl on all rows, until piece measures 20 (22, 23) inches, ending with WS row.

Separate for armholes

Row 1 (RS): Sl 1, work 61 (82, 103) sts in established pat, turn; put rem 21 (28, 35) sts on hold for left front.

Row 2: Sl 1, work 39 (53, 67) sts in pat, k1-tbl, turn; put rem 21 (28, 35) sts on hold for right front.

BACK

Work 41 (55, 69) back sts even in established pat, slipping first st and knitting last st tbl on all rows, until armholes measure 6 (6, 7) inches.

Place 11 (14, 18) left shoulder sts, 19 (27, 33) neck sts, 11 (14, 18) right shoulder sts on separate holders.

LEFT FRONT

Slip 21 (28, 35) left front sts from holder to larger needle and with RS facing, join yarn.

Work even in established pat, slipping first st and knitting last st tbl on all rows, until armholes measure 4 (4, 5) inches, ending with RS row.

Shape Neck

Bind off 3 sts at neck edge 3 (4, 5) times, then bind off 1 (2, 2) st(s)—11 (14, 18) sts.

Place sts on holder.

RIGHT FRONT

Slip 21 (28, 35) right front sts from holder to larger needle and with RS facing, join yarn.

Work even in established pat, slipping first st and knitting last st tbl on all rows, until armholes measure 4 (4, 5) inches, ending with WS row.

Shape Neck

Bind off 3 sts at neck edge 3 (4, 5) times, then bind off 1 (2, 2) st(s)—11 (14, 18) sts.

Place sts on holder.

SLEEVE

With dpns, cast on 33 (33, 37) sts; place marker for beg of rnd and join, taking care not to twist sts.

Work 10 rnds in Seed St.

Set-up rnd: K13 (13, 15), pm, work 7 sts Seed St, pm, k13 (13, 15).

Inc rnd: K1, M1L, knit to marker, work 7 sts in Seed St, knit to last st, M1R, k1—35 (35, 39) sts.

Continue in established pat and rep Inc rnd [every 5 rnds] 4 (4, 5) times—43 (43, 49) sts.

Work even until piece measures 7 (7½, 8) inches.

Bind off all sts.

ASSEMBLY

Weave in all ends. Block all pieces.

Join left and right shoulders using 3-Needle Bind-Off.

Unzip Provisional Cast-On, putting first 24 (31, 38) back sts on smaller circular needle, then next 42 (56, 70) front sts larger circular needle, and last 17 (24, 31) back sts on smaller circular needle. With larger dpn, join bottom using 3-Needle Bind-Off and on last st, work 2 front sts tog as you bind off.

Sew sleeves into armholes.

HOOD

With RS facing, join yarn at right front edge. With smaller circular needle, pick up and knit 18 (20, 22) sts along right neck; slip back neck sts from holder to dpn and work 19 (27, 33) sts

Rep Rows 1 and 2 until all side sts are worked in.

Leave rem 23 (23, 27) sts on needle.

BUTTON/BUTTONHOLE BAND

With RS facing and using smaller circular needle, beg at right front of opening, pick up and knit 66 (66, 66) sts along right side of opening, 25 (25, 27) sts along right side of hood, knit 23 (23, 27) top hood sts, pick up and knit 25 (25, 27) sts along left side of hood, 66 (66, 66) sts along left side of opening—205 (205, 213) sts.

Row 1 (RS): Sl 1, *p1, k1; rep from * to last st, k1-tbl.

Row 2: Sl 1, *k1, p1; rep from * to last st, k1-tbl.

Buttonhole row: Sl 1, p1, k1, *yo, k2tog, work 10 sts in established rib; rep from * 4 times, yo, k2tog, work established rib to last st, k1-tbl.

Row 4: Rep Row 2.

Row 5: Rep Row 1.

Bind off all sts in pat.

FINISHING

Position buttonhole band on top of button band and sew them together with the bottom front.

Weave in all ends and block again.

Sew on buttons opposite buttonholes. ∎

---

in established pat; pick up and knit 18 (20, 22) sts along left neck—55 (67, 77) sts.

Rows 1 and 3 (WS): Sl 1, *k1, p1; rep from * to last 2 sts, k1, k1-tbl.

Row 2: Sl 1, *p1, k1; rep from * to last 2 sts, p1, k1-tbl.

Change to larger circular needle.

Set-up row (RS): Sl 1, k23 (29, 34), place marker, work 7 sts in Seed St, place marker, k23 (29, 34), k1-tbl.

Work even in established pat, working side sts in St st, center 5 sts in Seed St, and slipping first st and knitting last st tbl, until hood measures 7 (8, 8) inches from neckline, ending with a WS row.

Turning the hood

Row 1 (RS): Sl 1, work in pat to 7 (7, 9) sts beyond Seed St center, ssk, turn.

Row 2: Sl 1, work in pat to 7 (7, 9) sts beyond Seed St center, p2tog, turn—21 (21, 25) sts.

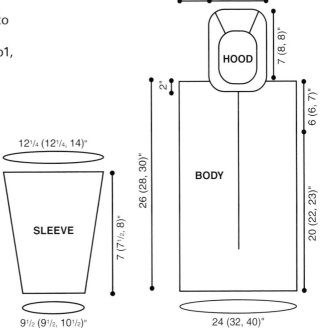

3 (4, 5)" 6¼ (7¾, 10)"

7 (8, 8)"

HOOD

6 (6, 7)"

2"

12¼ (12¼, 14)"

26 (28, 30)"

BODY

20 (22, 23)"

7 (7½, 8)"

SLEEVE

9½ (9½, 10½)"

24 (32, 40)"

HAPPY BABY BLANKIE

DESIGN BY KATHARINE HUNT

WHAT'S IN THE BAG

Patons Astra (DK weight; 100% acrylic; 133 yds/50g per ball): 4 balls Happy Days variegated #88713 (A)

Patons Astra (DK weight; 100% acrylic; 161 yds/50g per ball): 3 balls hot blue #08742 (B), 2 balls school bus yellow #02941 (C)
Size 6 (4mm) needles or size needed to obtain gauge

SKILL LEVEL

■■■□ INTERMEDIATE

FINISHED SIZE

Approx 25½ x 33 inches (not including border)

GAUGE

24 sts and 35 rows= 4 inches/10cm in pat st. To save time, take time to check gauge.

PATTERN STITCHES

Slip Stitch (multiple of 8 sts + 1)
Row 1 (RS): With A, knit.
Row 2: With A, k1, *p1 wrapping yarn twice, k5, p1 wrapping yarn twice, k1; rep from * to end.
Row 3: With B (C), k1, *sl 1 (dropping extra wrap), k5, sl 1 (dropping extra wrap), k1; rep from * to end.
Rows 4 and 6: With B (C), p1, *sl 1, p5, sl 1, p1; rep from * to end.
Row 5: With B (C), k1, *sl 1, k5, sl 1, k1; rep from * to end.
Row 7: With A, k1, *drop slipped st off needle to front of work, k2, pick up dropped st and knit it; k1, sl 2, drop next slipped st off needle to front of work, pass the 2 sts just slipped back to LH needle, pick up dropped st and knit it; k2, sl 1; rep from * across, ending last rep with k1 instead of sl 1.
Row 8: With A, k3, *p1, k1, p1, k2, sl 1,

k2; rep from * to last 6 sts, p1, k1, p1, k3.
Row 9: With A, knit.
Row 10: With A, k3, *p1, wrapping yarn twice, k1, p1 wrapping yarn twice, k5; rep from * to last 3 sts, k3.
Row 11: With B (C), k3, *sl 1 (dropping extra wrap), k1, sl 1 (dropping extra wrap), k5; rep from * to last 6 sts, sl 1 (dropping extra wrap), k1, sl 1 (dropping extra wrap), k3.
Rows 12 and 14: With B (C), p3, *sl 1, p1, sl 1, p5; rep from * to last 6 sts, sl 1, p1, sl 1, p3.
Row 13: With B (C), k3, *sl 1, k1, sl 1, k5; rep from * to last 6 sts, sl 1, k1, sl 1, k3.
Row 15: With A, k1, *sl 2, drop next slipped st

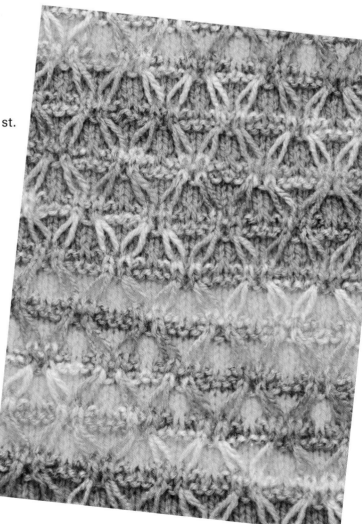

"Knitters are the only people who consider waiting in line an opportunity."

off needle to front of work, pass the 2 sts just slipped back to LH needle, pick up dropped st and knit it; k2, sl 1, drop next slipped st off needle, k2, pick up dropped st and knit it, k1; rep from * to end.

Row 16: With A, k1, *p1, k2, sl1 wyif, k2, p1, k1; rep from * to end.

Rep Rows 1–16 for pat.

Saw Tooth Edging
Row 1 (RS): K2, yo, k2tog, yo, k3—8 sts.
Row 2 and all WS rows to Row 10: Knit.
Row 3: K2, yo, k2tog, yo, k4—9 sts.
Row 5: K2, yo, k2tog, yo, k5—10 sts.
Row 7: K2, yo, k2tog, yo, k6—11 sts.

Row 9: K2, yo, k2tog, yo, k7—12 sts.
Row 11: K2, yo, k2tog, yo, k8—13 sts.
Row 12: Bind off 6 sts, k6—7 sts.

Rep Rows 1–12 rows to desired length, ending with Row 11.
Final Bind-off row: Bind off 6 sts, k1, turn, k2, turn, bind off rem sts.

PATTERN NOTE
Only 1 yarn is used per row; the color pattern is created by slipping stitches up several rows. The stripes are formed by alternating B and C in series of pattern repeats.

BLANKET
With A, cast on 145 sts.
Knit 2 rows.
*With A and B, work 2 [16-row] reps of Slip St pat.
With A and C, work 2 [16-row] reps of Slip St pat.
Rep from * 3 times.
With A and B, work 2 [16-row] reps of Slip St pat.
With A, knit 3 rows.
Bind off kwise on WS.

FINISHING
Weave in ends.
Block to finished measurements.

EDGING
With B, cast on 7 sts.
Work Saw Tooth border until it is long enough to go around perimeter of blanket; leave sts on needle.
With RS facing, using B, and beg on lower left side approx 1½ inches (or the length of 1 saw tooth), sew border around the edges of blanket. Adjust the border length, if necessary, to make it fit at the end. Sew border ends tog. ■

A-DORABLE A-LINE RUFFLED JUMPER

DESIGN BY LAURA NELKIN

WHAT'S IN THE BAG

Schaefer Yarn Lola (worsted
   weight; 100% merino
   superwash wool; 280 yds/4
   oz per skein): 1 (1, 2, 2) skeins
   Sophia Smith
Size 7 (4.5mm) 16-inch and 24-inch circular
   needles or size needed to obtain gauge
Size 6 (4mm) 16-inch circular needle or 1
   size smaller than that needed to obtain
   gauge
Stitch holders, 1 long, 2 short
Stitch markers, 1 in CC for beg of rnd

SKILL LEVEL
■■□□ EASY

SIZES
Infant's 6–12 months (12–18 months, 2T, 3T)
Instructions are given for smallest size, with
larger sizes in parentheses. When only 1
number is given, it applies to all sizes.

FINISHED MEASUREMENTS
Chest: 17¾ (20½, 22¼, 24) inches
Length from shoulder: 14½ (17, 20, 22½) inches

GAUGE
18 sts and 28 rnds = 4 inches/10cm in pat st
with larger needle.
To save time, take time to check gauge.

PATTERN STITCHES
Slip Stitch (worked in rnds on multiple of 4 sts)
Rnd 1: *K3, sl 1; rep from * around.
Rnd 2: Knit
   Rep Rnds 1 and 2 for pat.

Slip Stitch (worked in rows on multiple of
4 sts)
Row 1: *K3, sl 1; rep from * across.
Row 2: Purl.
   Rep Rows 1 and 2 for pat.

PATTERN NOTE
Change to 16-inch circular needle when
stitches no longer fit comfortably on 24-inch
circular needle.

DRESS
Ruffle
Cast on 232 (248, 264, 280) sts; place marker
for beg of rnd and join, taking care not to
twist sts.
Rnd 1: *Ssk, [yo] twice, k2tog; rep from *
around.
Rnd 2: *K1, [k1, p1] in double-yo, k1; rep from *
around.
   Rep [Rnds 1 and 2] 3 times.
Next rnd: *[K2tog] 28 (30, 32, 34) times, k2; rep
from * around—120 (128, 136, 144) sts.

Next rnd: K60 (64, 68, 72), place marker for side seam, knit to end of rnd.

Body
Work 5 (7, 9, 9) rnds in Slip St pat.
Dec rnd: *K1, ssk, knit to 3 sts before marker, k2tog, k1, slip marker; rep from * once—116 (124, 132, 140) sts.

Continue working established Slip St pat and rep Dec rnd [every 10th rnd] 0 (0, 1, 8) time(s), [every 8th rnd] 0 (3, 6, 0) time(s), [every 6th rnd] 3 (5, 1, 0) time(s) and [every 4th rnd] 6 (0, 0, 0) time(s)—80 (92, 100, 108) sts.

Work even in established Slip St pat until piece measures 9¾ (11½, 13½, 15½) inches from bottom edge, ending with Rnd 1.

Divide for armholes
Next rnd: Removing markers, k36 (42, 46, 50), bind off 7 sts, [1 st rem on RH needle], k32 (38, 42, 46) and slip to holder for front, bind off 7 sts.

BACK
Row 1 (RS): Work in pat to end of row, turn—33 (39, 43, 47) sts.
Row 2: Purl.
Dec Row: K1, ssk, work in pat to last 3 sts, k2tog, k1—31 (37, 41, 45) sts.

Continue in established pat working Dec row [every 4th row] 2 (3, 3, 3) more times—27 (31, 35, 39) sts.

Work even until armholes measure 3¾ (4½, 5½, 6) inches, ending with a WS row.

Shape back neck
Row 1 (RS): Work 5 (6, 7, 8) sts, place center 17 (19, 21, 23) sts on a holder, attach 2nd ball of yarn and work in pat to end.
Row 2: Working both shoulders at once with separate balls of yarn, purl across.
Row 3: Work to 3 sts before neck, k2tog, k1; k1, ssk, work to end—4 (5, 6, 7) sts each shoulder.

Work in pat until armholes measure 4¾ (5½, 6½, 7) inches, then slip shoulder sts to holders.

FRONT
Slip sts from holder to needle and work as for back until armholes measure 1¼ (2, 3, 4) inches, ending with a WS row.

Tip Here's a great idea for needle storage: place one of each size circular needle into a zippered CD case. You'll never be without the size you need again!

Shape front neck
Row 1 (RS): Work 7 (8, 10, 11) sts, place center 13 (15, 15, 17) sts on a holder, attach 2nd ball of yarn and work to end.
Row 2: Working both shoulders at once with separate balls of yarn, purl across.
Row 3: Work to 3 sts before neck, k2tog, k1; k1, ssk, work to end—6 (7, 9, 10) sts each shoulder.

Rep [Rows 2 and 3] 2 (2, 3, 3) times—4 (5, 6, 7) sts each shoulder.

Work in St st until armholes measure same as for back.

FINISHING
Graft front and back shoulders tog using Kitchener st. Sew side seams.

EDGINGS
With smaller needle, pick up and knit approx 52 (62, 76, 86) sts around armhole; purl 1 rnd then bind off. Rep on 2nd armhole.

With smaller needle, pick up and knit approx 62 (66, 70, 74) sts around neckline (including sts from holders); purl 1 rnd, then bind off.

Weave in all ends.

Block to finished measurements. ■

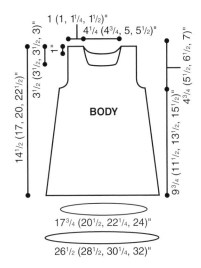

1 (1, 1¼, 1½)"
4¼ (4¾, 5, 5½)"
3½ (3½, 3½, 3)"
1"
3½ (3½, 3½, 3)"
14½ (17, 20, 22½)"
4¾ (5½, 6½, 7)"

BODY

9¾ (11½, 13½, 15½)"

17¾ (20½, 22¼, 24)"

26½ (28½, 30¼, 32)"

LITTLE SAILOR CAMI AND SOAKER PANTS

DESIGNS BY LAURA ANDERSSON

WHAT'S IN THE BAG

Crystal Palace Yarns Merino 5 (worsted weight; 100% superwash wool; 110 yds/50g per ball): 2 (3, 3) balls each flag blue #5230 (A) and baby blues #2302 (B)

4 MEDIUM

Size 5 (3.75mm) 16-inch circular needle
Size 8 (5mm) double-point (set of 4) and 16-inch circular needles or size needed to obtain gauge
Stitch marker
Stitch holders or waste yarn

SKILL LEVEL

■■□□ EASY

SIZES
Infant's 0–6 (6–12, 12–18) months Instructions are given for smallest size, with larger sizes in parentheses. When only 1 number is given, it applies to all sizes.

FINISHED MEASUREMENTS
Shirt Circumference: 18¼ (21¼, 24½) inches
Shirt Length: 9¾ (10½, 12) inches
Soakers Circumference (waist): 18 (20½, 23½) inches

GAUGE
21 sts and 29 rnds = 4 inches/10cm in St st using larger needle.
To save time, take time to check gauge.

PATTERN STITCH
Textured Pat (multiple of 4 sts)
Rnd 1: [P2, k2] around.
Rnd 2: [K2, p2] around.
Rep Rnds 1 and 2 for pat.

SPECIAL TECHNIQUES
Knitted Cast-On: Make a slip knot and put on needle. K1 into slip knot and put resulting st on LH needle; *k1 into new st and put resulting new st on LH needle; rep from * until all sts are cast on.
3-Needle Bind-Off: With WS tog and needles parallel, using a 3rd needle, *knit tog the first st on front needle and the first st on back needle; rep from * to end. Turn and bind off pwise.

PATTERN NOTES
Shirt is worked in the round, then split for armholes.

Soakers are worked in the round from the top down, then split for leg shaping.

When working color pattern, do not carry yarn not in use more than 3 stitches; if necessary, catch stranded yarn with working yarn to anchor floats.

Watch tension when working color pattern; if necessary, go up 1 needle size to maintain correct gauge.

SHIRT

BODY
With larger circular needle and A, and using knitted method, cast on 96 (112,128) sts; place marker and join, taking care not to twist sts.

"What I like to do is make travel knitting 'kits.' I find a nice soft, see-through container. I put my entire project inside—the pattern, needles, a spare larger or smaller set of needles, scissors and yarn including an extra ball, just 'in case.'"

Purl 1 rnd.
Work 4 rnds in K2, P2 Rib; cut A.
With B, work 7 rnds in K2, P2 Rib.
Work 2 (4, 4) rnds in Textured pat.
Work 6 (10, 16) rnds in St st.
Work 4 rnds Textured pat.
Work 22 rnds following Chart, then cut A.
With B, work 2 (4, 6) rnds in Textured pat.
Knit 1 rnd, ending 5 (6, 7) sts short of marker.

DIVIDE FOR FRONT & BACK
Row 1 (RS): Bind off 10 (12, 14) sts, k38 (44, 50) and put on holder for back, bind off 10 (12, 14) sts, knit to end—38 (44, 50) sts.

Front armhole shaping
Purl 1 row.
Dec row (RS): K1, ssk, knit to last 3 sts, k2tog, k1—36 (42, 48) sts.

Continue in St st rep Dec row [every RS row] twice more, ending with a WS row—32 (38, 44) sts.

Front neck
Next row (RS): K8 (11, 14) sts, join a 2nd ball of B and bind off center 16 sts, knit to end.

Working both sides at once, continue in St st

dec 1 st at each neck edge [every row] 2 (3, 4) times—6 (8, 10) sts each shoulder.

Work even until armholes measure 3 inches, then place shoulder sts on holders; cut yarn.

BACK
With WS facing, slip back sts to needle and join A.

Work armhole shaping same as for front.
Work even until armholes measure 2 inches.

Back neck
Next row (RS): K6 (8, 10) sts, join a 2nd ball of B and bind off center 20 (22, 24) sts, knit to end.

Working even until armholes measure same as for front; leave sts on needle.

FINISHING
With B, join shoulder seams using 3-Needle Bind-Off.

Armhole edging
With larger dpns and B, beg at underarm, pick up and knit 44 sts evenly around armhole.

Work 2 rnds in K2, P2 Rib. Cut B.
With A, work 1 rnd K2, P2 Rib.
Bind off pwise.

Neck edging

With larger dpns and A, beg at left shoulder, pick up and knit 70 (76, 80) sts evenly around neck.
Bind off pwise.

FINISHING

Weave in all ends.
Block to finished measurements.

BABY SHORTS/SOAKERS

BODY

With smaller needle and B, cast on 94 (108,124) sts; place marker for beg of rnd and join, taking care not to twist sts.
Work 7 rnds in K2, P2 Rib; cut B.
With A, work 7 rnds in K2, P2 Rib.
Change to larger needle and work in St st until piece measures 7¼ (7½, 7¾) inches.

DIVIDE FOR LEGS

Next rnd: Knit to 3 (4, 5) sts before marker; bind off 6 (8, 10) sts; k41 (46, 52) sts and slip to waste yarn to hold for back; bind off 6 (8, 10) sts; knit to end—41 (46, 52) sts.

Front leg shaping

Purl 1 row.
Next row (RS): K1, [ssk] 3 times, knit to last 7 sts, [k2tog] 3 times, k1—35 (40, 46) sts.
Next row: Purl.
Rep [last 2 rows] 0 (1, 2) time(s)—35 (34, 34) sts.
Next row (RS): K1, [ssk] twice, knit to last 5 sts, [k2tog] twice, k1—31 (30, 30) sts.

Next row: Purl.
Rep [last 2 rows] 4 (3, 2) times—15 (18, 22) sts.
Next row (RS): K1, ssk, knit to last 3 sts, k2tog, k1—13 (16, 20) sts.
Next row: Purl.
Rep last 2 rows 0 (1, 0) time(s)—13 (14, 20) sts.
Place rem sts on holder.

Back leg shaping

Work as for front; leave sts on needle.
Join to front crotch sts using 3-Needle Bind-Off.

FINISHING
Leg edging

With dpns and B, pick up and knit 42 (46, 50) sts around each leg opening.
Bind off loosely pwise.
Weave in all ends. Block to finished measurements. ■

COLOR KEY
■ Knit with A
■ Knit with B

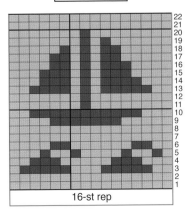

16-st rep

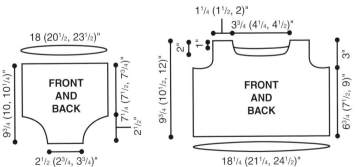

18 (20½, 23½)"

FRONT AND BACK

9¾ (10, 10¼)"

7¼ (7½, 7¾)"

2½"

2½ (2¾, 3¾)"

1¼ (1½, 2)"

3¾ (4¼, 4½)"

2"   1"

FRONT AND BACK

9¾ (10½, 12)"

6¾ (7½, 9)"

3"

18¼ (21¼, 24½)"

TONAL TRIANGLES KID'S PULLOVER

DESIGN BY AMY MARSHALL

WHAT'S IN THE BAG

Classic Elite Premiere (DK
  weight; 50% pima cotton/50%
  tencel; 108 yds/50g
  per hank): 3 (4, 5, 5, 6)
  hanks admiral blue #5210 (A); 2 (2, 3, 3,
  4) hanks natural #5216 (B); 2 (2, 3, 3, 3)
  hanks pastoral peri #5207 (C)
Size 6 (4mm) straight and 16-inch circular
  needles or size needed to obtain gauge
Stitch marker
Bobbins (optional)

SKILL LEVEL

■■■□ INTERMEDIATE

SIZES

Child's 2 (4, 6, 8, 10) Instructions are given for
smallest size, with larger sizes in parentheses.
When only 1 number is given, it applies to all
sizes.

FINISHED MEASUREMENTS

Chest: 21¾ (24¾, 27½, 30½, 33½) inches
Length: 14½ (16, 17½, 19, 20½) inches

GAUGE

22 sts and 26 rows = 4 inches/10cm in St st.
To save time, take time to check gauge.

PATTERN STITCH

Stripe Sequence
10 rows A
4 rows B
18 rows C
4 rows B
  Rep these 36 rows as needed.

PATTERN NOTES

The front and back of sweater are worked in
separate strips which are sewn together to
make piece, after which ribbing is added at the
bottom and neck.
  When working color charts, use intarsia
technique, using separate lengths of yarn for
each colored section; bring new color up from
under old color to lock them.
  Work chart for desired size by working
only stitches and rows within colored border
indicated for size.
  When sewing strips together with mattress
stitch, maintain a 1-stitch seam allowance.

BACK
STRIP 1

With A, cast on 17 (19, 21, 23, 25) sts.
  *With A, knit 1 row, purl 1 row.
Next row (RS): K2 A, work Chart A beg and
end where indicated for size to last 2 sts, k2 A.
  Continuing to work first and last 2 sts in St st
with A, complete chart for size being worked.
  Rep from *, working Charts B, C, D, then A
once more.
  With A, knit 1 row, purl 1 row.
  Bind off.

STRIP 2

Work as for Strip 1, but work charts in
following order: B, C, D, A, B.

STRIP 3
Work as Strip 1, but work charts in following order: C, D, A, B, C.

STRIP 4
Work as Strip 1, but work charts in following order: D, A, B, C, D.

Bottom rib
Join strips with mattress st.

With C, pick up and knit 62 (70, 78, 86, 94) sts along lower edge.

Row 1 (RS): K2, *p1, k1; rep from * to end.

Continue in established rib and work 3 rows C, 4 rows B, 4 rows A.

Bind off loosely in A.

FRONT
STRIP 1
Work as for back.

STRIP 2
Work as for back through Row 0 (2, 4, 2, 4) of last chart.

Shape right neck
Next row (RS): Bind off 11 (13, 13, 15, 15) sts, work rem 6 (6, 8, 8, 10) sts in pat.

Work 1 row even.

Dec row (RS): K1, ssk, work to end of row— 5 (5, 7, 7, 9) sts.

Rep Dec row [every RS row] 4 more times— 1 (1, 3, 3, 5) st(s).

For Sizes 2 and 4: Bind off.
For Sizes 6, 8 and 10: Complete chart. With A, knit 1 row, purl 1 row. Bind off.

STRIP 3
Work as for back through Row 0 (2, 4, 2, 4) of last chart.

Shape left neck
Next row (RS): Work 6 (6, 8, 8, 10) sts in pat, bind off 11 (13, 13, 15, 15) sts.

Dec row (RS): Rejoin yarn; work to last 3 sts, k2tog, k1—5 (5, 7, 7, 9) sts.

Rep Dec row [every RS row] 4 more times— 1 (1, 3, 3, 5) st(s).

For Sizes 2 and 4: Bind off.
For Sizes 6, 8 and 10: Complete chart. With A, work 2 rows St st. Bind off.

STRIP 4
Work as for back.

Bottom Rib
Join strips with mattress st.

Note for Sizes 2 and 4 only: *Top of Strips 1 and 4 will be 6 rows longer than Strips 2 and 3.*

Work bottom rib as for back.

SLEEVES
With A, cast on 32 (36, 40, 44, 44) sts.

Row 1 (RS): K2, *p1, k1, rep from * across row.

Continue in established rib and work 3 rows A, 4 rows B, 4 rows C.

Next row (RS): Change to St st, beg Stripe sequence inc 4 sts evenly across row—36 (40, 44, 48, 48) sts.

Continuing Stripe sequence in St st, work 3 rows even.

Inc row (RS): K2, M1, knit to last 2 sts, M1, k2—38 (42, 46, 50, 50) sts.

Rep Inc row [every 4 rows] 9 (11, 12, 12, 18) more times, then [every 6 rows] 4 (4, 4, 5, 3) times—64 (72, 78, 84, 92) sts.

Work even until piece measures approx 13¼ (14¼, 14¾, 16, 17½) inches.

Bind off.

FINISHING

Weave in all ends. Block all pieces to finished measurements. Join shoulder seams.

NECKBAND

With RS facing and using circular needle and C, pick up and knit 78 (86, 86, 100, 100) sts evenly around neck opening, place marker for beg of rnd.

Working in K1, P1 Rib, work 2 rnds C, 2 rnds B, 2 rnds A.

Bind off in rib.

ASSEMBLY

Sew sleeves to body. Sew side seam and underarm seams. Weave in rem ends. ■

COLOR AND SIZE KEY
- A
- B
- C
- Size 2 13-st block
- Size 4 15-st block
- Size 6 17-st block
- Size 8 19-st block
- Size 10 21-st block

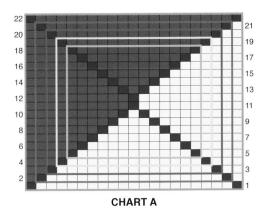

CHART A

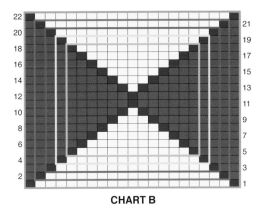

CHART B

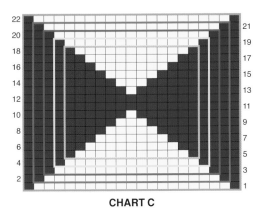

CHART C

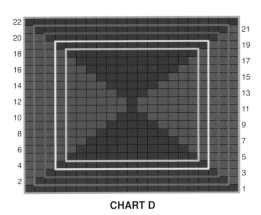

CHART D

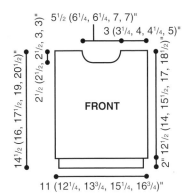

FRONT

5¹/₂ (6¹/₄, 6¹/₄, 7, 7)"
3 (3¹/₄, 4, 4¹/₄, 5)"
2¹/₂ (2¹/₂, 2¹/₂, 3, 3)"
14¹/₂ (16, 17¹/₂, 19, 20¹/₂)"
12¹/₂ (14, 15¹/₂, 17, 18¹/₂)"
2"
11 (12¹/₄, 13³/₄, 15¹/₄, 16³/₄)"

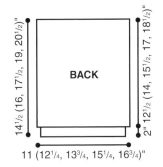

BACK

14¹/₂ (16, 17¹/₂, 19, 20¹/₂)"
12¹/₂ (14, 15¹/₂, 17, 18¹/₂)"
2"
11 (12¹/₄, 13³/₄, 15¹/₄, 16³/₄)"

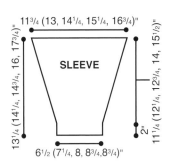

SLEEVE

11³/₄ (13, 14¹/₄, 15¹/₄, 16³/₄)"
13¹/₄ (14¹/₄, 14³/₄, 16, 17³/₄)"
11¹/₄ (12¹/₄, 12³/₄, 14, 15¹/₂)"
2"
6¹/₂ (7¹/₄, 8, 8³/₄, 8³/₄)"

GIFTY THINGS

In this chapter, you'll find an eclectic array of projects, offering a mix of fun and quirky creations, along with timeless classics. We'll keep you busy for hours on end with an inspiring collection of designs to make all of your traveling journeys memorable!

CABLE SAMPLER BABY BLOCKS

DESIGN BY DIANE ZANGL

WHAT'S IN THE BAG

Knit One Crochet Too Ty-Dy
   (worsted weight; 100% cotton;
   196 yds/100g per ball): 1
   ball blueberry fields #631 or
   pumpkin garden #541 or veranda #423
Size 7 (4.5mm) needles
Cable needle
Stitch markers
Polyester fiberfill

SKILL LEVEL
■■■□ INTERMEDIATE

FINISHED SIZE
Approx 6-inch cube

GAUGE
Specific gauge is not critical for this project;
work at a fairly tight gauge so filling does not
show through sts.

SPECIAL ABBREVIATION
Place marker (pm): Place marker on
needle to separate pats.

BLOCKS A, B AND C
Cast on 106 sts.
   Purl 1 row.
Set up pat (RS): K1, pm, work Row 1
of Chart A over next 34 sts, pm, k1,
pm, work Row 1 of Chart B over
next 34 sts, pm, k1, pm, work
Row 1 of Chart C over 34 sts,
pm, k1.
   Working edge sts and
marked sts in St st and
rem sts in established
pats, work even for 31
more rows.
   Bind off all sts kwise
on RS.
   Cut yarn.

BLOCK D
With WS facing, pick up and purl 1 st in each of
36 center sts (Chart B sts and 2 St st side sts),
going through purl 'bump' behind each bound-
off st (see Fig. 1).

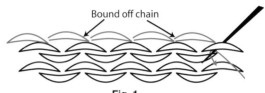

Fig. 1
PICK UP PURLWISE
Insert needle under top bar of st, wrap yarn
around needle as if to purl, pull loop through stitch.

Next row (RS): K1, work Row 1 of Chart D over
next 34 sts, k1.
   Working edge sts in St st and rem sts in pat
D, work even for 31 rows more.
   Bind off all sts kwise on RS.
   Do not cut yarn.

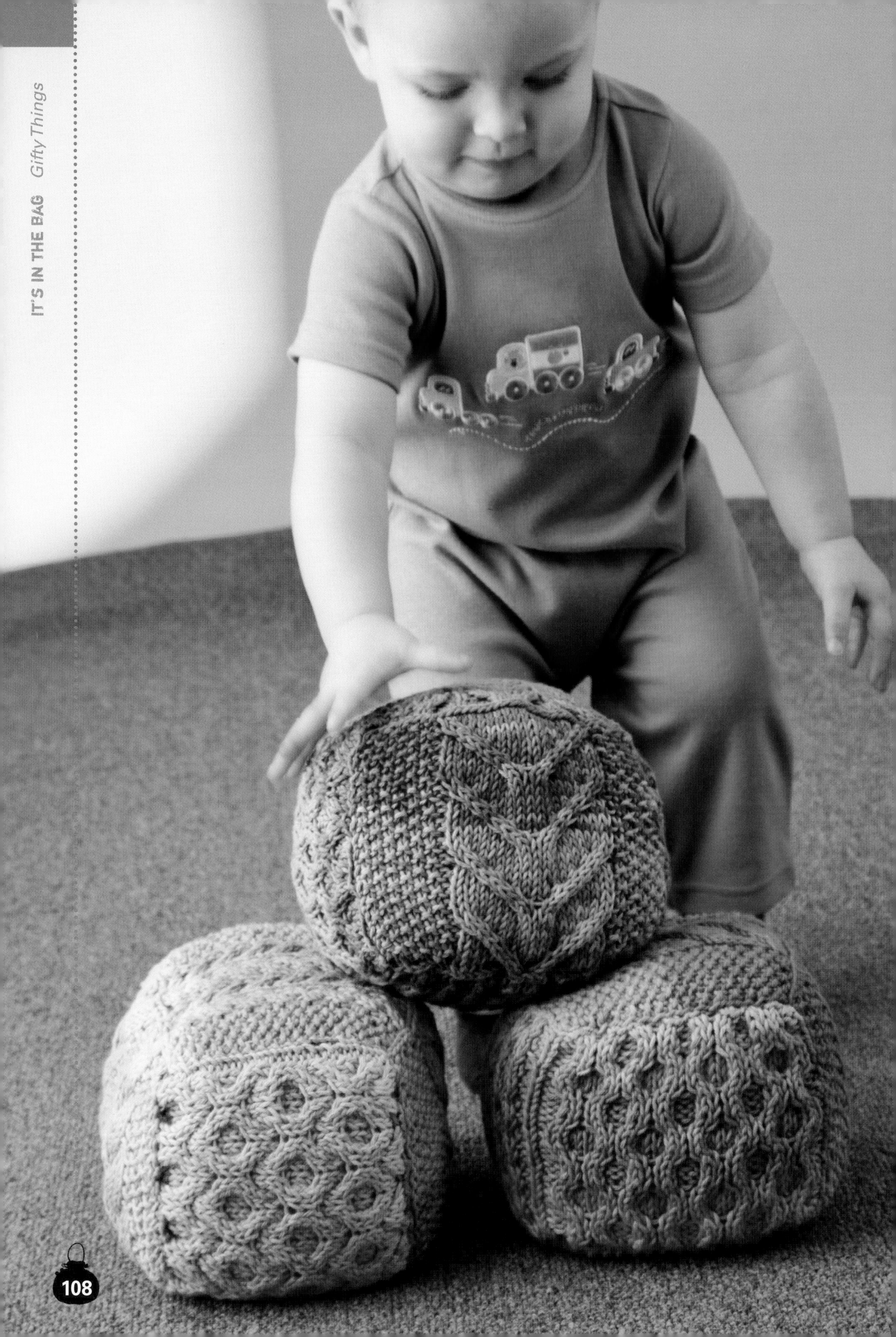

BLOCK E

With WS facing, pick up and purl 1 st in each of 36 Block D sts.

Complete as for Block D, substituting Chart E for D.

BLOCK F

With WS facing, pick up and purl 1 st in each of 36 Block E sts.

Complete as for Block D, substituting Chart F for D.

Tip If you forgot your cable needle, try a tapestry needle, a toothpick or small double-point needle.

ASSEMBLY

Weave in ends. Block piece.

Sew seams, forming a box with an open lid. Stuff with fiberfill. Sew rem seams. ■

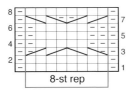

CHART A

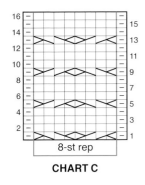

CHART C

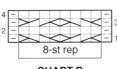

CHART B

STITCH KEY

☐ K on RS, p on WS

– P on RS, k on WS

Sl 2 to cn and hold in front, p2, k2 from cn.

Sl 2 to cn and hold in back, k2, p2 from cn.

Sl 2 to cn and hold in front, k2, k2 from cn.

Sl 2 to cn and hold in back, k2, k2 from cn.

Sl 2 to cn and hold in front, k4, k2 from cn.

Sl 4 to cn and hold in back, k2, k4 from cn.

Sl 4 to cn and hold in front, k4, k4 from cn.

Sl 4 to cn and hold in back, k4, k4 from cn.

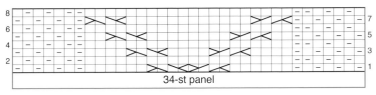

CHART D

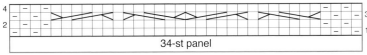

CHART E

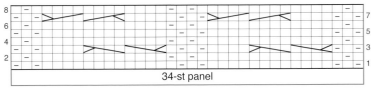

CHART F

NAUTICAL STRIPES ONESIE & SUNHAT

DESIGNS BY KARA GOTT WARNER

WHAT'S IN THE BAG

Tahki Torino (worsted weight;
100% extra fine merino wool; 94
yds/50g per ball): 2 (2, 3) balls
each light blue heather #135 (A),
cream heather #134 (B) and grey heather
#136 (C)

Size 8 (5mm) straight, double-point (set
of 4) and 16-inch circular needles or size
needed to obtain gauge

Stitch markers, 1 in CC for beg of rnd

5 (size 3) Dritz nickel-plated brass snaps

Sewing thread to match yarn

SKILL LEVEL

 INTERMEDIATE

SIZES

Onesie: Infant's 0–3 (3–6, 6–12) months
Hat: Infant's 0–6 (6–12) months Instructions
are given for smallest size, with larger sizes in
parentheses. When only 1 number is given, it
applies to all sizes.

FINISHED MEASUREMENTS

Chest: 20¾ (22, 24) inches
Total length to shoulder (hemmed): 11 (13,
15½) inches
Hat circumference: 14 (16) inches

GAUGE

19 sts and 26 rows/rnds = 4 inches/10cm in
St st.
To save time, take time to check gauge.

SPECIAL ABBREVIATIONS

Place marker (pm): Place marker on needle to
separate sections.
Make 1 Left (M1L): Insert LH needle from front
to back under the running thread between the
last st worked and next st on LH needle. With
RH needle, knit into the back of this loop.
Make 1 Right (M1R): Insert LH needle from

back to front under the running thread
between the last st worked and next st on LH
needle. With RH needle, knit into the front of
this loop.

PATTERN STITCHES

Stripe Sequence (Onesie): *Work 14 rnds/rows
St st in A, 14 rnds/rows B, 14 rnds/rows C; rep
from * to end of piece.
Stripe Sequence (Hat): *Knit 8 rnds A, 8 rnds
C, 8 rnds B; rep from * to end of piece.

PATTERN NOTES

Raglan-shaped onesie is worked in the round
from top to armholes, then divided into body
and sleeves. The body continues in the round
from armholes to crotch at which point the
piece is split at center front/back for legs
(worked back and forth in rows). Sleeves are
worked in the round.

Hat is worked from bottom to top, starting
with the brim; change to double-point needles
when stitches no longer fit comfortably on
circular needle.

ONESIE

COLLAR

With circular needle and B, cast on 54 (56, 64)
sts; pm for beg of rnd and join, taking care not
to twist sts.

Work 1½ inches in St st and on last rnd,
place raglan shaping markers as follows: K2
(3, 3) st, pm, k25 (25, 29), pm, k2 (3, 3), pm, k25
(25, 29).

Raglan yoke
Change to A and beg working 14-rnd/row
Stripe Sequence.
Inc rnd: Slipping markers, *k1, M1L, knit to 1 st
before marker, M1R, k1; rep from * around—62
(64, 72) sts.

Rep Inc rnd [every 2 (3, 3) rnds] 10 (2, 4)
times, then [every 2 rnds] 0 (9, 7) times—142
(152, 160) sts.

"Some time ago, I took a ski trip to Vermont with some friends. Happily, I was not driving. Since this was a 6 hour trip, it was, of course, a perfect opportunity to knit! My chosen projects were a ski hat and mittens that I was determined to finish before my arrival. I began to knit at warp speed, but soon after we got on our way, it started to get dark. Eventually, I couldn't see a thing! Since I was working in stockinette, I relied on my fingers to see, and by the time we made it to the resort, my hat and mittens were done. And yes, I even wove in those loose ends!"

Separate sections
Next rnd: *Knit to marker, then slip 26 (28, 29) sts to waste yarn for sleeve; knit to next marker; rep from * once—90 (96, 102) body sts rem, with 45 (48, 51) sts each front and back.

BODY
Rnd 1: Cast on 4 (4, 6) sts for underarm, work front sts, cast on 4 (4, 6) sts for 2nd underarm, work back sts, place marker for beg of rnd—98 (104, 114) sts.

Work even until piece measures 5¾ (7, 8¾) inches from armhole; cut yarn.

Shape crotch and legs
Slip first 27 (28, 32) sts and last 22 (24, 25) sts to waste yarn, splitting body in half at center

front/back—49 (52, 57) sts rem on needle.
Row 1 (RS): Reattach yarn; k2, [ssk] twice, knit to last 6 sts, [k2tog] twice, k2—45 (48, 53) sts.
Row 2: Purl.
   Rep [Rows 1 and 2] once more—41 (44, 49) sts.
   Work even until legs measure 2 (2¼, 2½) inches from beg of crotch, ending with a WS row.

Leg Hem
Turning row (RS): Purl.
   Work 3 rows in St st.
   Bind off.
   Rep for other side.

SLEEVES
Slip sleeve sts from waste yarn to double-point needles.
Row 1 (RS): Maintaining established Stripe Sequence, cast on 2 (2, 3) sts for underarm, knit across sleeve sts, cast on 2 (2, 3) sts for underarm, pm for beg of rnd and join—30 (32, 35) sts.

   Work even in St st until sleeve measures 2 (2½, 2½) inches.

Sleeve Hem
Turning rnd: Purl.
   Knit 3 rnds.
   Bind off.

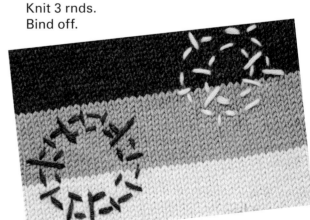

FINISHING

Sew sleeve and body sts tog at underarms.

Fold up sleeve and leg hems at turning ridge and sew to WS. With B, sew running stitch in middle of hem. With colors of choice, sew dashed circle designs randomly around hat (see Figs 1 and 2).

Fig.1
Basic Running Stitch
Thread yarn onto tapestry needle.
Starting from the WS, *draw needle up through A, then down into B; rep from *.

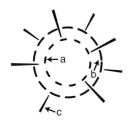

Fig.2
Dashed Circle
Work 2 concentric circles with
random rays as follows:
Thread yarn onto tapestry needle.
A: Starting from WS, draw needle up
through first stitch for smaller circle; work
Basic Running Stitch until circle is complete.
B: Work larger circle same as for A.
C: Work single short and long stitches
randomly around circles.

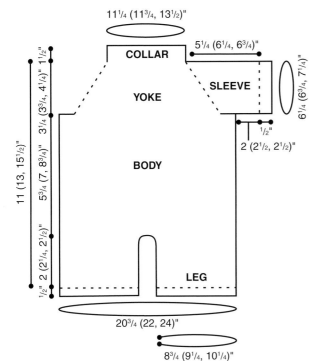

Weave in loose ends. Block to finished measurements.

Sew on 5 sets of snaps to close crotch, 1 in center crotch and 2 on each leg.

HAT

BRIM

With circular needle and A, cast on 90 (93) sts, pm every 30 (31) sts.

Knit 3 rnds.

Dec rnd: Slipping markers, *k1, k2tog, knit to 3 sts before marker, ssk, k1; rep from * around—84 (87) sts.

Purl 1 rnd for turning ridge.

Beg 8-rnd Stripe Sequence and work Dec rnd—78 (81) sts.

Knit 3 rnds.

Rep Dec rnd—72 (75) sts.

BODY AND CROWN

Maintaining Stripe Sequence, knit 14 rnds.

Rep Dec rnd on next then [every other rnd] 9 times—12 (15) sts.

Cut yarn, leaving a 6-inch tail.

Using tapestry needle, thread tail through rem sts, and pull tight.

Weave in all ends.

FINISHING

Fold up hem at turning ridge and sew to WS. With C, sew running stitch in middle of hem edge. With colors of choice, sew dashed circle designs randomly around hat (see Figs 1 and 2).

Block. ■

CUTE AS A BUTTON BABY SET

DESIGNS BY CHRISTINE L. WALTER

WHAT'S IN THE BAG

Knit One Crochet Too Babyboo
(DK weight; 55% nylon/45%
bamboo; 115 yds/50g per ball):
4 (5, 5) balls lilac #719
Size 6 (4 mm) double-point (set of 5) and
16-inch circular needles or size needed
to obtain gauge
5 (½-inch) buttons
1 yard ribbon for booties (optional)

SKILL LEVEL
■■□□ EASY

SIZES
Jacket: Newborn (3–6 months, 6–9 months)
Hat: Small/medium (medium/large)
Booties: Small/medium (medium/large)
Instructions are given for smallest size, with
larger sizes in parentheses. When only 1
number is given, it applies to all sizes.

FINISHED MEASUREMENTS
Sweater chest: 19¼ (21¼, 24¼) inches
(buttoned)
Sweater length: 10 (11, 12) inches
Hat circumference: 14 (16) inches
Foot length: 4 (5) inches

GAUGE
17 sts and 32 rows = 4 inches/10 cm in Eyelet
Lace (after blocking).
19 sts and 27 rows = 4 inches/10 cm in St st.
To save time, take time to check gauge.

SPECIAL ABBREVIATION
Knit in Front and Back of Stitch (k1f&b): K1
in front and back of st to inc 1.

PATTERN STITCH
Eyelet Lace (multiple of 3 sts + 3)
Row 1 and all WS rows: Purl.
Row 2 (RS): K2, *k2tog, yo, k1; rep from *
to last st, k1.

Row 4: K2, *yo, k1, k2tog; rep from * to last
st, k1.
Rep Rows 1–4 for pat.

PATTERN NOTE
When knitting hat, change to double-
point needles when stitches no longer fit
comfortably on circular needle.

JACKET

BACK
Cast on 42 (45, 51) sts.
Knit 5 rows.
Work in Eyelet Lace until piece measures
10 (11, 12) inches, ending with a RS row.
Bind off pwise.

RIGHT FRONT
Cast on 18 (21, 24) sts.
Knit 5 rows.
Work in Eyelet Lace until piece measures
8½ (9, 10) inches, ending with a WS row.

Neck shaping
With RS facing, continue in pat and bind off
2 sts at neck edge [every RS row] 1 (2, 3)
times—16 (17, 18) sts.
Bind off 1 st at neck edge [every RS row]
3 times—13 (14, 15) sts.
Work even in pat until piece measures same
as back, ending with a RS row.
Bind off pwise.

LEFT FRONT
Work as for right front to neck shaping, ending
with a RS row.

Tip
Plastic, sealable containers are
a great solution for organizing
projects in your car trunk. Why
not keep an extra container on hand
with a selection of yarns for future projects.

Neck shaping

With WS facing, continue in pat and bind off 2 sts at neck edge [every WS row] 1 (2, 3) times—16 (17, 18) sts.

Bind off 1 st at neck edge [every WS row] 3 times—13 (14, 15) sts.

Work even in pat until piece measures same as back, ending with a RS row.

Bind off pwise.

SLEEVES

Cast on 28 (30, 30) sts.

Knit 5 rows.

Inc row (RS): K1, k1f&b, knit to last 2 sts, k1f&b, k1—30 (32, 32 sts).

Continue in St st and rep Inc row [every 4 rows] 8 (9, 11) times—46 (50, 54) sts.

Work even until piece measures 6½ (7, 8) inches.

Bind off.

FINISHING

Weave in all ends. Block pieces. Sew shoulder seams. Mark armholes by placing markers 4¾ (5¼, 5½) inches down from shoulders on fronts and back. Sew sleeves between markers. Sew side and sleeve seams.

NECK EDGING

With RS facing, pick up and knit 47 (49, 57) sts around neck.

Knit 3 rows.

Bind off pwise on RS.

BUTTONHOLE BAND

With RS facing, pick up and knit 42 (46, 48) sts along appropriate front edge (right side for girl's sweater, left side for boy's sweater) between cast-on edge and neck edging.

Knit 3 rows.

Buttonhole row: K2 (2, 4), *yo, k2tog, k7 (8, 8); rep from * to last 4 sts, yo, k2tog, k2.

Knit 3 rows.

Bind off kwise on WS.

BUTTON BAND

With RS facing, pick up and knit 42 (46, 48) sts along opposite front edge.

Knit 8 rows.

Bind off kwise on WS.

Weave in ends.

HAT

BODY

Using dpns or short circular needle, cast on 60 (66) sts; place marker for beg of rnd and join, taking care not to twist sts.

Rnds 1, 3, 5: Purl

Rnds 2, 4, 6: Knit.

Rnd 7: *K2tog, yo, k1; rep from * around.

Rnd 8: Knit.

Rnd 9: *Yo, k1, k2tog; rep from * around.

Rep Rnds 6–9 until hat measures 4 (4½) inches.

SHAPE CROWN

Rnd 1: *K4, k2tog; rep from * around—50 (55) sts.

Rnd 2 and all even-numbered rnds: Purl.

Rnds 3 and 5: Knit.

Rnd 7: *K3, k2tog; rep from * around—40 (44) sts.

Rnd 9: Knit.

Rnd 11: *K2, k2tog; rep from * around—30 (33) sts.

Rnd 13: *K4, k2tog; rep from * to last 0 (3) sts, k0 (3)—25 (28) sts.

Rnd 15: *K3, k2tog; rep from * last 0 (3) sts, k0 (3)—20 (23) sts.
Rnd 17: *K2, k2tog; rep from * around—15 (18) sts.
Rnd 19: *K1, k2tog; rep from * around—10 (12) sts.
Rnd 21: *K2tog; rep from * around—5 (6) sts.
Cut yarn leaving a 6-inch tail.

With tapestry needle, thread tail through rem sts, pull tight and secure to WS.

Weave in ends.

BOOTIES

CUFF/HEEL
Cast on 27 (33) sts.

Knit 4 rows.

Beg with Row 2, work 11 (15) rows in Eyelet Lace.

Next row (RS): K18 (22) sts, turn, leaving rem sts unworked.

Next row: K9 (11) sts, turn, leaving rem sts unworked.

Working on center 9 (11) sts, knit 12 (16) rows.

Next row (RS): K9 (11), pick up and knit 7 (9) sts along left side of flap, knit across rem 9 (11) sts, turn—25 (31) sts.

Next row: K25 (31), pick up and knit 7 (9) sts along right side of flap then knit rem 9 (11) sts—41 (51) sts.

SHAPE FOOT
Row 1 (RS): K1, k2tog, k15 (19), k2tog, k1 (3), k2tog, k15 (19), k2tog, k1—37 (47) sts.
Rows 2 and 4: Knit.
Row 3: K1, k2tog, k13 (18), k2tog, k1, k2tog, k13 (18), k2tog, k1—33 (43) sts.
Row 5: K1, k2tog, k11 (16), k2tog, k1, k2tog, k11 (16), k2tog, k1—29 (39) sts.

Bind off kwise on WS.

Cut yarn, leaving a long tail.

FINISHING
Sew seam from toe/sole to top cuff. Weave in ends.

Optional: Thread ribbon through eyelets closest to foot and tie in bow. ∎

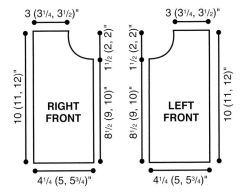

RIGHT FRONT
3 (3¼, 3½)"
1½ (2, 2)"
10 (11, 12)"
8½ (9, 10)"
4¼ (5, 5¾)"

LEFT FRONT
3 (3¼, 3½)"
1½ (2, 2)"
10 (11, 12)"
8½ (9, 10)"
4¼ (5, 5¾)"

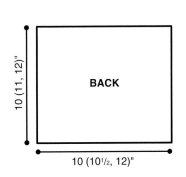

BACK
10 (11, 12)"
10 (10½, 12)"

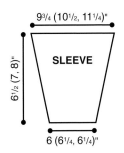

SLEEVE
9¾ (10½, 11¼)"
6½ (7, 8)"
6 (6¼, 6¼)"

DAY AT THE BEACH FLIP-FLOPS & BRACELET

DESIGNS BY ELLEN EDWARDS DRECHSLER

WHAT'S IN THE BAG

Plymouth Fantasy Linen (worsted weight; 72% mercerized cotton/17% rayon/11% linen; 130 yds/100g per skein): 1 skein brown #5

Size 5 (3.75mm) double-point needles (flip-flops)
Size 3 (3mm) double-point needles (bracelet)
Stitch holder
Beading needle (with large eye)
Toggle set (bracelet)
Pair of thong sandals
Assorted beads (size E and larger) with large holes (the number you need may vary depending upon the size of your beads and the size of your flip-flops—sample flip-flops required approx 56 inches of strung beads; bracelet required approx 55 beads)

SKILL LEVEL
■■□□ EASY

FINISHED SIZE
As desired by knitter

GAUGE
Gauge is not critical for this project.

SPECIAL ABBREVIATION
Bring Up Bead (BUB): Slide up a bead and work next st.

PATTERN NOTES
If you want your flip-flops to match, divide the skein into 2 balls and string

beads in same order onto each ball of yarn.

If you have a large bead or a long bead, work the adjacent stitches without a bead to allow more room for the bigger bead.

Beads should sit between stitches and show on the purl side of the fabric.

If you run out of pre-strung beads, you can add beads to the non-working end of the yarn.

Make the bracelet tight because the weight of the beads will cause the bracelet to stretch out over time.

FLIP-FLOPS

With beading needle, thread variety of beads onto approx 56 inches of yarn.

TOE THONG
Leaving a long tail and using larger needles, cast on 7 sts.
Row 1 (WS): Knit 1 row, weaving in yarn end as you knit.
Row 2 (RS inc row): P1, M1, purl to last st, M1, p1—9 sts.
Row 3: K3, [BUB, k1] 3 times, k3.
Rep Inc row [every RS row] 4 times, and *at the same time*, gradually inc the number of beads being used on WS rows to 7 per row, placing them in the center of the row—17 sts.
Work even until toe thong measures approx 1½ inches, ending with a WS row.

STRAP 1
Next row (RS): P9, slip rem 8 sts to holder.
Leaving the first and last 2 sts bead-free, and bringing up a bead between each of the center 5 sts on WS rows, work even in rev St st on the 9 sts until knitted beaded material is approx the

"If you really want people to stare, try knitting at the gym. I usually take a small, light-weight project. I place my yarn in a small, sporty bag, which hangs off the elliptical machine. I place the instructions on the machine's control panel, and I'm ready to workout!"

length of your sandal strap (for the model, strap measures 6 inches).

Work 4 rows without beads.

Bind off and cut yarn, leaving a very long tail for sewing.

STRAP 2

Slip sts from holder to needle.

Working as for Strap 1, inc 1 st on first row—9 sts.

Complete as for Strap 1.

FINISHING

Place the toe thong portion of the fabric (purl side out) around the sandal thong, then sew sides tog with mattress st.

Using tail, sew edges of 1 strap tog to encase the sandal strap; rep on other strap.

Weave in all ends.

BRACELET

With beading needle, thread approx 55 beads onto yarn.

Thread 1 end of jewelry toggle.

Using smaller needles, cast on 4 sts.

Knit 1 row, sliding the toggle in between the 3rd and 4th sts.

Purl 1 row, weaving in the tail as you work.

Continue in St st, sliding up beads between each st on knit rows.

Work even until piece measures slightly less than your wrist circumference.

Measure off enough yarn for 3 additional rows and a bind off row, then cut the yarn.

Thread the other end of the toggle set onto the tail.

Work 2 sts, slide up the toggle, work rem 2 sts.

Work 2 more rows without beads.

Bind off.

Weave in ends. ■

ANDREA BEADED CUFFS

DESIGNS BY LAURA NELKIN

WHAT'S IN THE BAG

Schaefer Yarn Andrea (lace weight; 100% cultivated silk; 1093 yds/3.5 oz per skein): 1 skein in Laura Ingalls Wilder and Greenjeans or 40 yds of any lace weight yarn

1 SUPER FINE

Size 0 (2mm) needles or size needed to obtain gauge

Size 1 (2.25mm) double-point needles or 1 size larger than that needed to obtain gauge

Size 8/0 seed beads (approx 8g)

Size C/2 (2.75) crochet hook

Dental floss threader

Crochet hook

Slide clasp (optional)

SKILL LEVEL

 ■■■☐ INTERMEDIATE

SIZES

Extra-small (small, medium, large) Instructions are given for smallest size, with larger sizes in parentheses. When only 1 number is given, it applies to all sizes.

FINISHED MEASUREMENTS

Length: 5½ (6½, 7½, 8½) inches
Width: 1¼ inches (Beaded Twist Cuff);
1¾ inches (Diamond Cuff)

GAUGE

Beaded Twist Cuff: 48 sts and 44 rows = 4 inches/10cm with smaller needles.
Diamond Cuff: 52 sts and 48 rows = 4 inches/10cm with smaller needles.
To save time, take time to check gauge.

SPECIAL TECHNIQUE

Provisional Cast-On: With crochet hook and waste yarn, make a chain several sts longer than desired cast-on. With knitting needle and project yarn, pick up indicated number

of sts in the "bumps" on back of chain. When indicated in pattern, "unzip" the crochet chain to free live sts.

PATTERN NOTE

If you don't want to work I-cord loops and beaded clasps to close the cuff, purchase a sew-on clasp or decorative hook and eye to finish your cuff. If you do this, work 2nd short end with plain attached I-cord.

BEADED TWIST CUFF

Using dental floss threader, thread 54 (66, 78, 90) beads onto yarn.
    With smaller needles, cast on 12 sts.
    Knit 2 rows.
    Work Beaded Twist chart 9 (11, 13, 15) times.
    Knit 2 rows.
    Bind off.
    Thread 52 (64, 76, 88) additional beads onto yarn.
    Continue with I-cord instructions below.

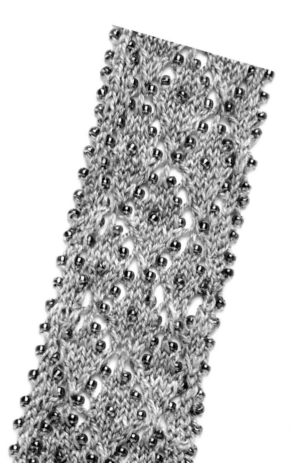

DIAMOND CUFF

Using dental floss threader, thread 135 (162, 189, 216) beads onto yarn.

With smaller needles, cast on 17 sts.

Knit 2 rows.

Work Diamond chart 5 (6, 7, 8) times.

Knit 2 rows.

Bind off.

Thread 58 (70, 82, 94) additional beads onto yarn.

Continue with I-cord instructions below.

I-CORD

Note: Instructions are given for Beaded Twist Cuff with Diamond Cuff instructions in parentheses.

With dpn and beg at top LH corner, work a 2-st attached beaded I-cord along the outside edge of the cuff as follows: Using provisional method, cast on 2 sts onto 1 dpn, and with same dpn, pick up (but do not knit) 1 st from edge of cuff—3 sts on needle.

Row 1: K1 with bead, skp, pick up 1 st from edge (but do not knit); slide sts to other end of dpn—3 sts.

Row 2: K1, skp, pick up 1 st from edge (but do not knit); slide sts to other end of dpn—3 sts.

Rep Rows 1 and 2 all the way down one long side of the cuff.

When you reach the first short side, discontinue the use of beads and continue the attached I-cord.

Resume using beads along the other long side of the cuff.

On the 2nd short side, create loops to fasten the cuff as follows: Discontinue using beads and work 2 (3) rows of attached I-cord.

*Work a 2-st unattached I-cord for 6 rows.

Skipping 1 st, pick up next st of edging and work attached I-cord for 5 (8) rows.

Rep from *, but finish by working only 2

(3) more rows of attached I-cord.

Unzip Provisional Cast-On; graft sts tog with live sts from beg of I-cord.

BEADED CLASPS
Make 2

String 3 beads onto yarn with a small sewing needle; leaving a 3-inch tail, go back through the beads again, creating a loop.

String 3 more beads and go back through the first 3 beads again; you will have a circle of 6 beads, with a length of yarn running through the middle of it (see Diagram).

Yarn running through middle of beaded circle

BEADED CLASP DIAGRAM

Sew beaded clasps to the opposite end of the bracelet in line with 2 loops, sewing only on the center thread. This is important so that the loop can go all the way around the "button" and catch itself.

FINISHING

Weave in ends and block. ■

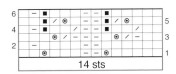

BEADED TWIST CUFF

STITCH KEY	
☐	K on RS, p on WS
−	P on RS, k on WS
⊙	Yo
⟋	K2tog
⟍	Ssk
⅄	S2KP2
✳	Slip up 1 bead and K1
⊙	Slip up 1 bead and Yo
■	No stitch

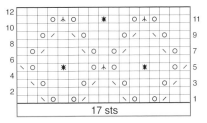

DIAMOND CUFF

> **Tip**
> Here's an idea for this incredibly portable and quick project you can throw in your purse: Wind off enough yarn for each cuff, string the beads, and place the yarn along with short needles, notions, and copy of the chart cut down to size and taped onto an index card into a plastic sandwich bag.

EASY AS 1-2-3 BRAIDED BELT

DESIGN BY JULIE GADDY

WHAT'S IN THE BAG

Knit One Crochet Too Wick
  (worsted weight; 53% soy/47%
  polypropylene; 120 yds/50g per
  ball): 1 ball painted daisies #565

(4 MEDIUM)

Size 4 (3.5mm) double-point needles (2)
  or size needed to obtain gauge
Waste yarn or 3 safety pins
2 D-rings or O-rings with at least 1¾₁₆ inch
  inside diameter
1 yd of ⅜ inch grosgrain ribbon and
  matching sewing thread (optional)

SKILL LEVEL

 INTERMEDIATE

SIZES

Woman's small/medium (medium/large)
Instructions are given for smaller size, with
larger size in parentheses. When only 1
number is given, it applies to both sizes.
Directions for custom sizing are also included
following other sizes.

FINISHED SIZE

1 x 29-33 (35-40, custom) inches

GAUGE

24 sts and 56 rows = 4 inches/10cm in Double-
Knitting.
Gauge is not critical to this project.

PATTERN STITCH

Double-Knitting (even number of sts)
Row 1: *Sl 1 wyif, k1; rep from * across.
Rep Row 1 for pat.

SPECIAL TECHNIQUE

4-St I-Cord: *K4, do not turn, slip sts back to LH
needle; rep from * until cord is desired length.

PATTERN NOTES

The gauge for the belt is significantly tighter
than the recommended gauge for the yarn.

This is to give the belt more body.
  Size M/L takes the entire ball. If you are making
a custom size and plan to fit waist size larger
than 40 inches, you will need a second ball.

BELT

Flap and Tab
Cast on 6 sts.
  Work 10 rows in St st, ending with a WS row.
Set-up row: *Yo, k1; rep from * across—12 sts.
  Work in Double-Knitting for 5 (6) inches.
  For custom size, knit until belt measures 5
inches from beg of double-knit section.

Divide for I-Cord

Divide sts into 3 groups of 4 sts and slip 2nd
and 3rd groups to a safety pin or waste yarn.
  *Work 4-st I-cord for 35 (43) inches; slip sts
to safety pin or waste yarn.
  Cut yarn leaving tail approx 2 yds long to use
for adjusting length of cords when braiding.
  Rep from * for the rem 2 groups of 4 sts.
  For custom size, knit I-cord 1½ times the
length of the completed braid.

BRAID

Lay belt on a flat surface and braid the 3 cords,
making a firm braid to minimize stretching
during wear; braid should measure 22 (27)
inches or 10 inches less than finished waist
measurement. Adjust length of cords by
adding or subtracting rows of I-cord.

TAB

Slip the 12 sts to 1 dpn.

> **Tip**
> Here's a great way to be an
> "inconspicuous knitter": If you're
> working on a small project, why
> not try 12-inch circular needle? Simply
> pull out the portion you're working on, and
> then when you're done, coil it up, and place it
> back in your purse at a moment's notice. Don't
> worry, no one will notice!

Work in Double-Knitting for 10 (11) inches. For custom size, make tab 10 inches long.

Slip the dpn out of the sts; the knit tube will open.

Slip the front (knit) sts onto 1 dpn the back (purl) sts onto another dpn.

Hold the 2 dpns parallel and graft the sts tog using the Kitchener st (page 166).

FINISHING
Attach rings by sliding onto St st flap and folding flap to WS of belt. Sew neatly in place.

Stabilize the braid (optional): To keep the braided section of the belt from stretching out of shape while wearing, cut a piece of grosgrain ribbon the length of the braided section plus 2 inches. Fold under ½ inch on each end. Using coordinating sewing thread, sew folded ends of ribbon to double knit section of belt. Tack braid to ribbon at intervals as desired. ■

ORIENT EXPRESS EYE PILLOW

DESIGN BY DAWN LEESEMAN

WHAT'S IN THE BAG

Rowan Classic Yarns Pure Silk
   DK (DK weight; 100% silk,
   137 yds/50g per skein): 1 ball
   tranquil #00156
Size 5 (3.5mm) needles
Size 6 (4mm) needles or size needed to
   obtain gauge
100 #6 Czech glass beads in hematite
Size #10 steel crochet hook or size to fit
   through opening of bead
Size E/4 (3.5mm) crochet hook
Sewing needle
¼ yd fabric for lining
Thread to match fabric
1¼–1½ cups raw rice
Aromatherapy herbs or oils

SKILL LEVEL

 ■■□□ EASY

FINISHED SIZE

8½ x 4 inches

GAUGE

22 sts and 36 rows = 4 inches/10cm in beaded
Seed st with smaller needles.
22 sts and 32 rows = 4 inches/10cm in St st
with larger needles.
To save time, take time to check gauge.

SPECIAL ABBREVIATION

Place bead on next st and purl (PBP): Place a
bead onto steel crochet hook. With hook facing
you, insert the hook into the next st on LH
needle, pull the loop through the bead, replace
the st with bead onto the LH and purl.

PATTERN NOTES

It's a good idea to purchase extra beads
because some center holes may be misshapen.
When using eye pillow, keep non-beaded side
next to eyes.

BEADED PIECE

With smaller needles, cast on 47 sts.
Row 1 (RS): K1, *p1, k1; rep from * across.
Row 2: K1, *PBP, k1; rep from * across.
Row 3: K1, p1, k1; rep from * across.
Row 4: K1, PBP, k1, *p1, k1; rep from * to last
2 sts, PBP, k1.
   Rep Rows 3 and 4 until piece measures
4½ inches, ending with Row 4.
   Work Rows 1 and 2 once more.
   Bind off all sts in pat.

PLAIN PIECE

With larger needles, cast on 47 sts.
   Work in St st until piece measures 4½ inches.
   Bind off all sts.

ASSEMBLY

Weave in all ends.
   Place rice in a bowl, add desired herbs or
oils, set aside.
   Using knitted piece as template, cut 2 pieces
from lining fabric, each ½ inch wider and
longer than knitted piece. With RS of fabric tog
and beg on long side edge, using matching
thread, sew ¼-inch seam around 3 sides. Turn
right-side out and fill with scented rice; sew
across open end.
   With WS of St st and beaded pieces tog and
using larger crochet hook, beg at corner of
long side of rectangle, work sc through both
layers around 3 sides of the rectangle; insert
rice pouch; work sc across last side to close;
do not turn.
   Work 1 rnd reverse sc around all 4 sides,
fasten off. ■

"Just to make sure I'm not 'knit-less,' I always keep extra yarn and needles in tow just in case."

FANCIFUL FELTED PURSE

DESIGN BY PHYLLIS SANDFORD

WHAT'S IN THE BAG

Plymouth Galway Worsted
(worsted weight; 100% wool;
210 yds/100g per ball): 2 balls
purple #132 (A)

Plymouth Galway Worsted Highland
Heather (worsted weight; 100% wool;
210 yds/100g per ball): 1 ball each green
#728 (B) and blue-gray #732 (C)
Size 13 (9mm) needles or size needed to
obtain gauge
Sharp sewing needle
Sewing thread to match yarn
Beads of choice
Beading thread
Beading needle
Large snap

SKILL LEVEL

■□□□ BEGINNER

FINISHED SIZE

10½ inches wide x 10 inches long

PRE-FELTING GAUGE

12 sts and 14 rows = 4 inches/10cm in St st.
Exact gauge is not critical; make sure your sts
are loose and airy.

PURSE

With A, cast on 136 sts.
Work in St st until piece measures approx
20 inches.
Bind off.
Fold fabric in half vertically.
With A, sew side and bottom seams.

LEAVES

With B, cast on 75 sts.
Work in St st until piece measures approx
6½ inches.
Bind off.

FLOWER

With C, cast on 75 sts.
Work in St st until piece measures approx
6½ inches.
Bind off.

STRAP

With A, cast on 80 sts.
Work 10 rows in St st.
Bind off.
With WS out and using A, sew cast-on and
bound-off edges tog.
Turn right side out.

FELTING

Felt bag, strap, flower and leaf fabric following
felting instructions on page 167. When bag
reaches finished measurements or desired
size, gently rinse all pieces in the sink. Roll
the bag in a towel and squeeze out the excess
water. Roll strap between your hands to shape.
Let all pieces dry thoroughly.

ASSEMBLY

Sew ends of strap to inside of bag.

Cut 3 leaf shapes from the green fabric.

Cut 5 petal shapes and center circle for flower.

Arrange leaves, petals and flower center on front of bag as desired.

Using sharp needle and matching thread, referring to photo, sew to front of bag, starting with leaves and ending with center circle.

Using beads of choice, beading needle and beading thread, referring to photo, sew a row of beads along the top edge of the bag.

Sew 2nd row of beads approx 1 inch below first. Sew beads to leaves. Sew large bead in center of flower.

With sharp needle and thread, sew large snap to center of WS of bag, approx 1½ inches from top or positioned as desired. ■

Tip Keep a "knitting bag within a knitting bag". This is great for air travel. Since space is at a minimum, bring your mini bag on the plane, and keep a larger bag in your suitcase.

CHICO'S SWEATER

DESIGN BY SHIRLEY MACNULTY

WHAT'S IN THE BAG

- Moda Dea Sassy Stripes (light worsted weight; 100% acrylic; 147 yds/50g per ball):1 ball swish #6952
- Size 4 (3.5mm) straight and double-point needles (set of 4)
- Size 5 (3.75mm) needles or size needed to obtain gauge
- Small piece of contrasting yarn for a marker

SKILL LEVEL

 EASY

SIZE

Small, to fit a 2–4 pound miniature dog such as a miniature Chihuahua.

FINISHED MEASUREMENTS

Chest: 11 inches
Length: 11 inches

GAUGE

22 sts and 30 rows = 4 inches/10cm in St st with larger needles.
To save time, take time to check gauge.

SPECIAL ABBREVIATION

Make 1 (M1): Insert LH needle from front to back under the running thread between the last st worked and next st on RH needle; knit into the back of resulting loop.

PATTERN NOTE

This sweater begins at the neck.

SWEATER

With smaller needles, cast on 48 sts.

Work in K1, P1 Rib for 1½ inches, ending with a WS row.

Inc row (RS): With larger needles, k1, M1, knit to last st, M1, k1—50 sts.

Continue in St st rep Inc row [every other row] 3 more times, ending with a WS row—56 sts.

Leg openings

Row 1 (RS): K10, bind off 4 sts, k28, (this includes st rem from bind off), bind off 4 sts, k10 (this includes st rem from bind off).

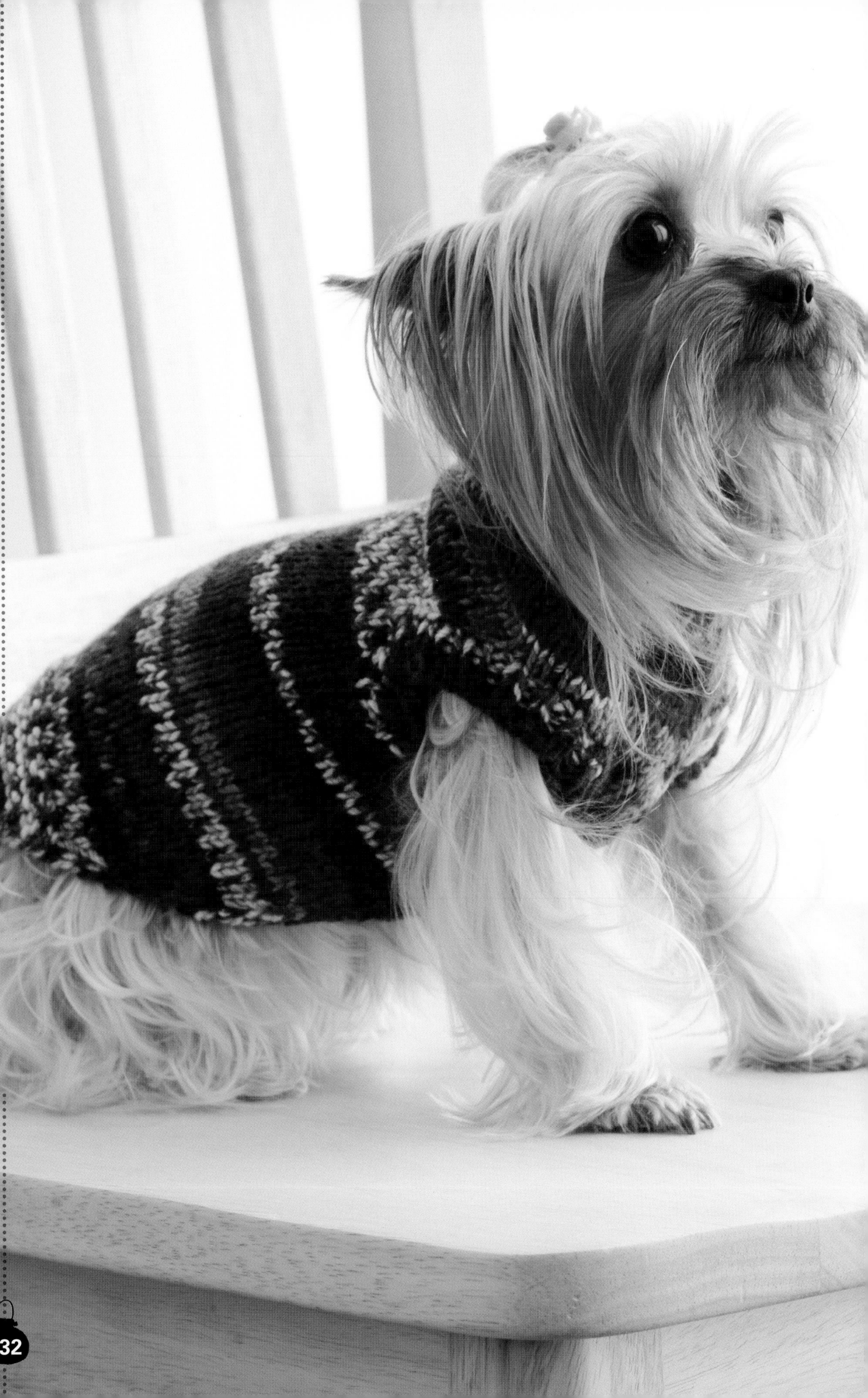

Row 2: Working all 3 sections at once, p10, attach 2nd ball of yarn, p28, attach 3rd ball of yarn, p10.

Row 3: First section: k1, M1, knit to last 3 sts, k2tog, k1; middle section: k1, ssk, knit to last 3 sts, k2tog, k1; last section: k1, ssk, knit to last st, M1, k1—10 sts in first and last sections, 26 sts in middle section.

Row 4: Purl.

Rep [Rows 3 and 4] twice—10 sts in first and last sections; 22 sts in middle section.

Work 4 rows even in St st.

Inc row (RS): First section: knit to last st, M1, k1; middle section: k1, M1, knit to last st, M1, k1; last section: k1, M1, knit to end—11 sts in first and last sections; 24 sts in middle section.

Continue in St st and rep Inc row [every RS row] twice more, ending with a WS row— 13 sts in first and last sections, 28 sts in middle section.

Next row (join sections): K13, cast on 4 sts, knit across middle section, cast on 4 sts, knit to end—62 sts.

Next row: Purl.

Shape back

Row 1 (RS): K1, ssk, knit to last 3 sts, k2tog, k1—60 sts.

Row 2: K1, purl to last st, k1.

Row 3: Knit.

Row 4: Rep Row 2

Rep [Rows 1–4] 9 more times—42 sts.

Dec row (RS): K1, ssk, knit to last 3 sts, k2tog, k1—40 sts.

Next row: Knit.

Rep [last 2 rows] 9 more times—22 sts.

Bind off as to knit.

Leg ribbing

With dpn, pick up and knit 32 sts around leg opening, dividing sts onto 3 needles.

Work 5 rnds in K1, P1 Rib.

Bind off in rib.

Rep for other leg opening.

FINISHING

Block to finished measurements. Sew seam, beg at neck ribbing and end at back shaping. Weave in all ends. ■

Tip With a small, compact purse, you can knit a stitch or two standing in line at the supermarket or even at a cocktail party!

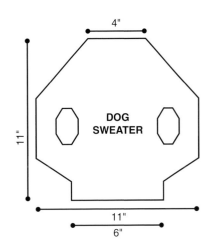

DOG SWEATER

4"
11"
11"
6"

FRILLY PRILLY PONCHO

DESIGN BY JEAN CLEMENT

WHAT'S IN THE BAG

Berroco Pure Merino Heather
(worsted weight;100% extra fine
merino wool; 92 yds/50g per
ball): 3 balls Tyrolean Alps #8616(A)

Berroco Jasper (worsted weight; 100% fine
merino wool; 98 yds/50g per hank): 3
hanks copper silk #3810 (B)

Size 9 (5.5mm) 16- and 24-inch circular
needles or size needed to obtain gauge

Stitch markers, 1 in CC for beg of rnd

Stitch holders or waste yarn

SKILL LEVEL

 INTERMEDIATE

SIZE

To fit medium-size dog (25–30 lbs)

FINISHED MEASUREMENTS

Neck circumference: approx 13 inches
Back length: approx 16 inches

GAUGE

20 sts and 30 rows = 4 inches/10cm in Navaho
Basket stitch.
To save time, take time to check gauge.

PATTERN STITCHES

K3, P1 Rib (worked in rnd on multiple of 4 sts)
Rnd 1: K1, *p1, k3; rep from * to last 3 sts, p1, k2.
  Rep Rnd 1 for pat.

K3, P1 Rib (worked flat on multiple of 4 sts + 5)
Row 1 (WS): K1, p1, k1, *p3, k1; rep from * to
last 2 sts, p1, k1.
Row 2 (RS): K2, *p1, k3; rep from * to last 3 sts,
p1, k2.
  Rep Rows 1 and 2 for pat.

Stripe Pattern (in rib)
Work 4 rnds/rows A, 2 rnds/rows B, 2 rnds/
rows A, 2 rnds/rows B.
  Rep these 10 rnds/rows for stripe pat.

Navaho Basket (multiple of 4 sts + 5)
Row 1 (RS): With A, knit.
Row 2 (WS): With A, purl.
Row 3: With B, k1, *k1, sl 1 wyif; rep from * last
st, k1.
Row 4: With B, purl.
Row 5: With A, k1, *sl 1 wyif, k1; rep from * to
last st, k1
Row 6: With A, purl.
Rows 7 and 9: With B, k2, *sl 1, k3; rep to last 3
sts, sl 1, k2.
Rows 8 and 10: With B, k1, p1, *sl 1, p3; rep to
last 3 sts, sl 1, p1, k1.
Rows 11–16: Rep Rows 1–6.
Rows 17 and 19: With B, k1, *k3, sl 1; rep from
* to last 4 sts, k4.
Rows 18 and 20: With B, k1, *p3, sl 1; rep from
* to last 4 sts, p3, k1.
  Rep Rows 1–20 for pat.

PATTERN NOTES

Carry unused color up side edge, catching it
every couple rounds to secure.

The back length can be adjusted by
working fewer or more, full or partial repeats
of the Navaho Basket pattern. To determine
the correct length for your dog, measure
from the base of dog's back neck to hip bones.
The shaping decreases for the dog's hind
quarters should begin at hip bones. The
body will also look best if the decreases are
begun on Row 1 or 11 of the Navaho
Basket pattern.

PONCHO

Collar and Front Panel

With shorter circular needle and A, cast on 64
sts; place marker for beg of rnd and join, taking
care not to twist sts.

Counting cast-on as first rnd of Stripe pat,
work 20 rnds in Stripe pat, ending with A.

Cut B, remove beg of rnd marker and turn to
beg working back and forth.

Next row (WS): With A, work 45 sts in
established rib, then place rem 19 sts on
holder for back neck.

"We travel with our dogs in a 22-foot trailer, and I'm usually good about making sure my knitting projects stay safe. However, we once made a trip to Tennessee, and I wasn't so careful. When we arrived at our destination, we parked and visited friends. During our absence, one of the dogs jumped up onto the bathroom counter and somehow managed to turn the water faucet on. Of course, my knitting bag that had been sitting on the counter was now floating in the middle of the trailer. Since that day I've never let my knitting bag out of my sight!"

Continuing in established rib and Stripe pat, work 40 rows.

Cut B.

Next row (RS): With A, work in established pat.

Body

Change to longer needle.

Next row (RS): With RS facing and using A, pick up and knit 27 sts along left edge of front panel (approx 2 sts for every 3 rows), knit 19 sts from holder, pick up and knit 27 sts along right edge of front panel; place 45 front panel sts on holder—73 sts on needle.

Next row (WS): K1, purl to last st, k1. Rejoin B and beg with Row 3, work in Navajo Basket pat until body measures 16 inches, ending with Row 10 or 20.

Set-up row (RS): Working in established pat, k19, k2tog, place marker, k31, place marker, ssk, k19—71 sts.

Next row: Work in established pat, purling the dec sts.

Dec row (RS): Work to 2 sts before marker, k2tog, slip marker, work 31 sts, slip marker, ssk, work to end—69 sts.

Rep Dec row [every RS row] 9 times, purling all dec sts on WS and ending on a RS row—51 sts.

Next row (WS, dec): Work to 2 sts before first marker, ssp, work center 31 sts, p2tog, work to end—49 sts.

Continue to dec [every row] 8 times—33 sts.

Border

Rnd 1 (RS): With A, k2, [p1, k3] 7 times, p1, k2; pick up 105 sts along body edge (approx 3 sts for every 4 rows), work 45 held front panel sts in established pat; pick up 105 sts along body

edge, place marker for beg of rnd and join—288 sts.

Work K3, P1 Rib as established for 8 rnds, alternating 2 rnds A and 2 rnds B, and *at the same time*, continue to dec every rnd at markers—272 sts.

With A, work 4 rnds even, then bind off in rib.

FINISHING

Weave in ends; block gently. ■

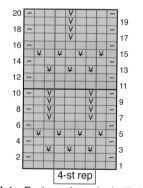

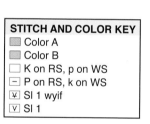

STITCH AND COLOR KEY
- Color A
- Color B
- □ K on RS, p on WS
- − P on RS, k on WS
- ⅄ Sl 1 wyif
- ⌵ Sl 1

Note: Each row is worked with 1 color only. Use the color (A or B) that is the first color in row.

NAVAHO BASKET

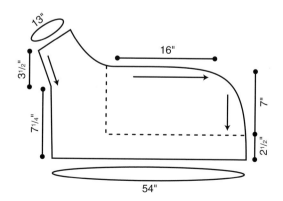

LUXURIOUS LACE COLLAR

DESIGN BY JOËLLE MEIER RIOUX FOR CLASSIC ELITE YARNS

WHAT'S IN THE BAG

Classic Elite Yarns Blithe (DK weight; 100% baby camel; 128 yds/25g per hank): 1 hank sage #C10459

Size 6 (4mm) needles or size needed to obtain gauge

Size E/4 (3.5mm) crochet hook

One 2-inch toggle button

SKILL LEVEL

■■■□ INTERMEDIATE

FINISHED SIZE

6 x 21 inches

GAUGE

23 sts and 28 rows = 4 inches/10cm in St st.
To save time, take time to check gauge.

SPECIAL ABBREVIATIONS

Decrease 3, left-leaning (Dec3L): Sl 1k, k3tog, psso.

Decrease 3, right-leaning (Dec3R): K3tog, sl st from RH back to LH needle and pass second st on LH needle over first. Sl st back to RH needle.

Decrease 4 (Dec4): Ssk, k3tog, pass 2nd st on RH needle over first st.

Knit 1 or make a bobble (k1/MB): Either k1 or make a bobble (see Pattern Notes).

Make Bobble (MB): Knit into the [front, back] twice, then front again of the same st; turn; p5, turn; k5, turn; p2tog, k1, ssp, turn; sk2p.

Place marker (pm): Place a marker on needle to separate pats.

PATTERN STITCHES

Right Edge Panel (5-st panel)
Row 1 (RS): Sl 1k, k2, yo, k2tog.
Row 2: Knit.
   Rep Rows 1 and 2 for pat.

Leaf Panel (13-st panel)
Row 1 (RS): [K1, yo] twice, Dec3L, yo, k1, yo, Dec3R, [yo, k1] twice.
Row 2 and all WS rows: Purl.
Row 3: K1, yo, k3, yo, Dec4, yo, k3, yo, k1.
Row 5: K1, yo, ssk, k1, k2tog, yo, k1, yo, ssk, k1, k2tog, yo, k1.
Row 7: K1, yo, ssk, k1, k2tog, yo, k1/MB, yo, ssk, k1, k2tog, yo, k1.
Row 8: Purl.
   Rep Rows 1–8 for pat.

Center Panel (7-st panel)
Row 1 (RS): K1, yo, k2tog, k2, yo, k2tog.
Row 2: Knit.
   Rep Rows 1 and 2 for pat.

Left Edge Panel (5-st panel)
Row 1 (RS): K1, yo, k2tog, k2.
Row 2: Sl 1k, k4.
   Rep Rows 1 and 2 for pat.

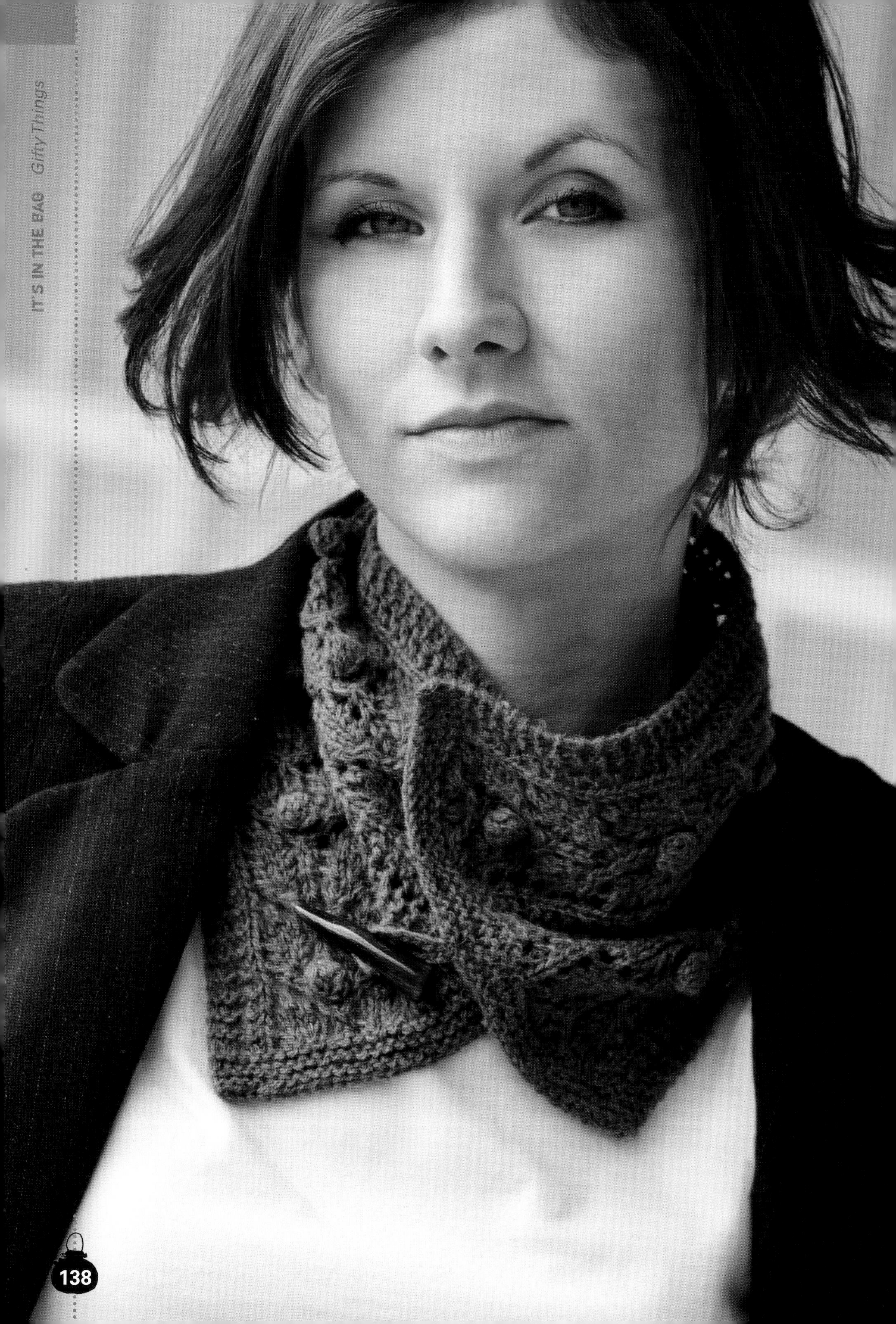

PATTERN NOTES

A bobble is worked every other Row 7 of Leaf Panels, alternating between the 2 panels; otherwise, knit the stitch.

Slip first stitch of every row as to knit.

A chart for the Leaf Panel is provided for those preferring to work from charts.

COLLAR

Cast on 43 sts.

Knit 6 rows.

Set-up row (WS): Sl 1, k4, p13, k7, p13, k5.

Establish pat (RS): Work Row 1 of Right Edge Panel, pm, work Row 1 of Leaf Panel, work Row 1 of Center Panel, pm, work Row 1 of Leaf Panel, pm, work Row 1 of Left Edge Panel.

Work even in established pats until piece measures 18½ inches from beg (measure garter st at center, not stretched), ending with Row
5 of Leaf Panel.

Knit 5 rows.

Bind off all sts as to knit.

FINISHING

Block to measurements, being careful not to flatten bobbles. With crochet hook, ch 15 and attach ends of chain to center panel on cast-on edge, forming a loop. Sew button to center panel on opposite end, approx 2
inches in from edge. ■

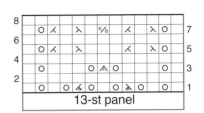

Tip

Prepare a "knitting emergency travel kit" for your car. Purchase a small plastic case in which to keep your essentials. You can easily store this under a seat or in the trunk.

13-st panel

LEAF PANEL

STITCH KEY

☐ K on RS, p on WS
⊙ Yo
☒ Dec3L
☒ Dec3R
△ Dec4
☒ Ssk
☒ K2tog
K/B K1/MB

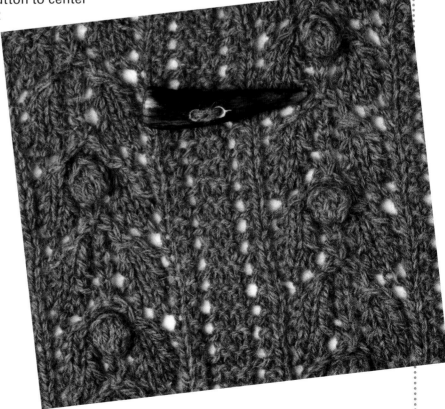

HOME ADORNMENTS

If you want to add some character to your abode, the creations to follow will be just what you've been searching for. So pack up that knitting bag you love with a "new favorite" today!

RUSTIC BASKET WEAVE TABLE RUNNER

DESIGN BY CELESTE PINHEIRO

WHAT'S IN THE BAG

Mission Falls 1824 Wool (worsted weight; 100% merino superwash; 85 yds/50g per ball): 3 balls each stone #002 (A), amethyst #023 (B) and curry #013 (C); 2 balls each russet #010 (D), thyme #016 (E) and denim #021 (F)
Size 8 (5mm) needles or size needed to obtain gauge

SKILL LEVEL
■□□□ BEGINNER

FINISHED SIZE
14 x 90 inches

GAUGE
19 sts and 26 rows = 4 inches/10cm in Basket Weave pat.
To save time, take time to check gauge.

PATTERN STITCH
Basket Weave (multiple of 8 sts + 3)
Rows 1 and 3 (WS): K4, *p3, k5; rep from * to last 7 sts, p3, k4.

Row 2 (RS): P4, *k3, p5; rep from * to last 7 sts, k3, p4.
Row 4: Knit.
Rows 5 and 7: *P3, k5; rep from * to last 3 sts, p3.
Row 6: *K3, p5; rep from * to last 3 sts, k3.
Row 8: Knit.
 Rep Rows 1–8 for pat.

PATTERN NOTE
A chart of the Basket Weave pattern is provided for those preferring to work from chart.

TABLE RUNNER
With A, using long-tail method, cast on 69 sts.
Row 1 (WS): K1, work Basket Weave pat to last st, k1.

 Maintaining first and last st in garter st, continue Basket Weave pat, and *at the same time*, work stripe pat as follows: 1 more row A, 8 rows E, 20 rows B, 12 rows C, 4 rows F, 12 rows A, 4 rows D, 8 rows B, 20 rows E, 4 rows F, 12 rows C, 12 rows A, 8 rows B, 20 rows D, 4 rows E, 12 rows C, 4 rows F, 12 rows A, 4 rows D, 8 rows E, 20 rows B, 4 rows F, 12 rows C,12 rows A, 8 rows E, 4 rows D, 20 rows F,

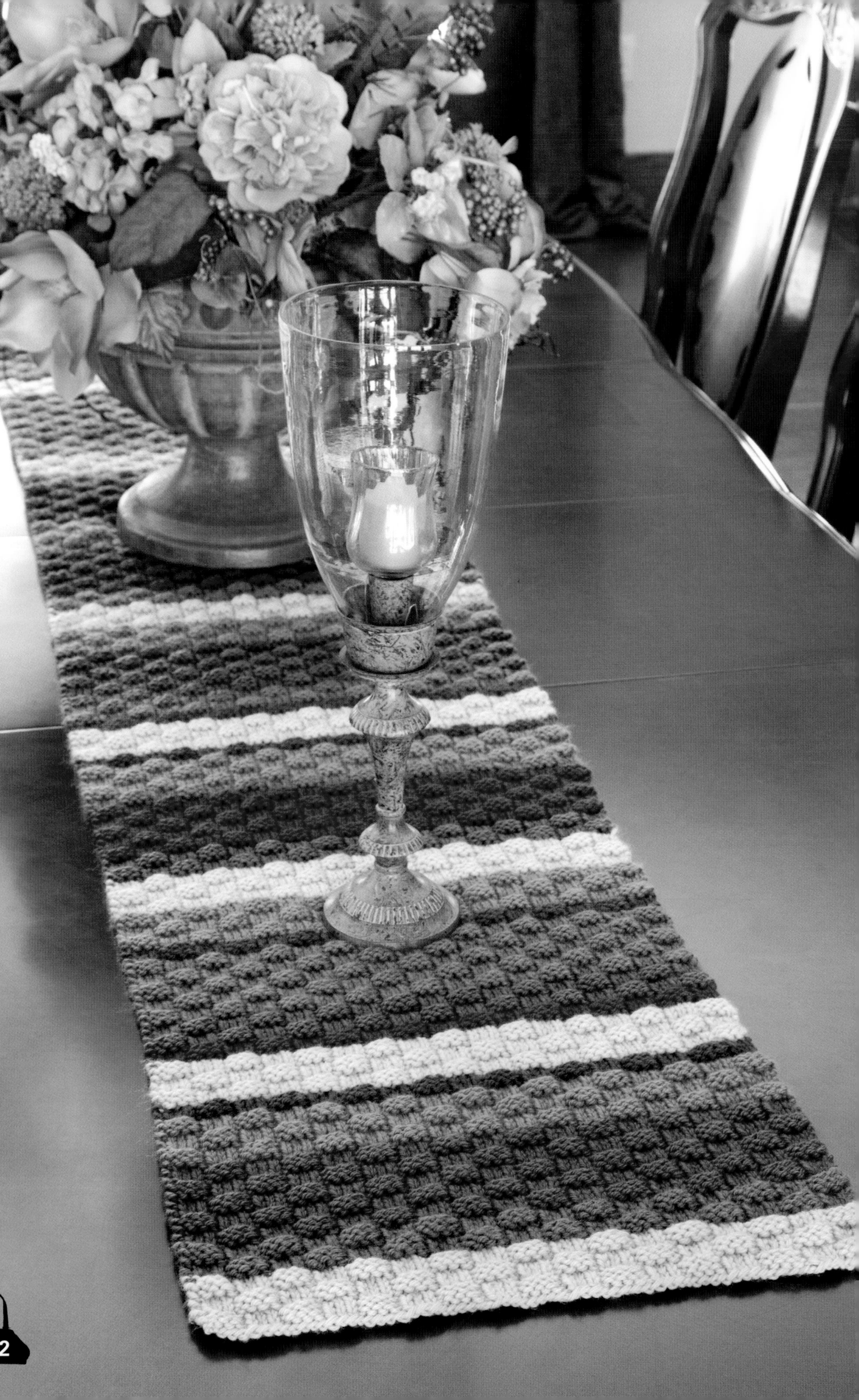

"When traveling, I like to work on projects that call for a variegated yarn. It's fun to see the gradual flow of one color after another, creating a surprising pattern. If I'm in the car, I don't have to glance down so much—and I don't get car sick either!"

4 rows B, 12 rows E (center stripe), 4 rows B,
20 rows F, 4 rows D, 8 rows E, 12 rows A,
12 rows C, 4 rows F, 20 rows B, 8 rows E,
4 rows D, 12 rows A, 4 rows F, 12 rows C,
4 rows E, 20 rows D, 8 rows B, 12 rows A,
12 rows C, 4 rows F, 20 rows E, 8 rows B,
4 rows D, 12 rows A, 4 rows F, 12 rows C,
20 rows B, 8 rows E, 12 rows A.
   Bind off with A.
   Weave in ends. Block as necessary. ■

STITCH KEY
☐ K on RS, p on WS
⊟ P on RS, k on RS

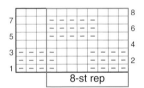

BASKET WEAVE

PRETTY PASTELS LAP BLANKET

DESIGN BY KATHARINE HUNT

WHAT'S IN THE BAG

Plymouth Encore Worsted (worsted weight; 75% acrylic/25% wool; 200 yds/100g per ball): 4 balls off-white #240 (A); 1 ball each green #1232 (B), light purple #958 (C), rust #456 (D), and earth #6002 (E)

Size 8 (5mm) needles or size needed to obtain gauge

Size E/4 (3.5mm) crochet hook

SKILL LEVEL

■■■☐ INTERMEDIATE

FINISHED SIZE

Approx 40 x 41 inches

GAUGE

24 sts and 26 rows = 4 inches/10cm over Cable panel.

To save time, take time to check gauge.

BLANKET

Cable Panel
Make 5

With A, cast on 21 sts.
Work Cable Panel chart for 260 rows (13 reps).
Bind off.

Zigzag Panel 1
Make 2

With B (D), cast on 31 sts.
Work Zigzag Panel chart for 260 rows (13 reps).
Bind off.

Zigzag Panel 2
Make 2

With C (E), cast on 31 sts.
Beg on Row 11, work Zigzag Panel chart for 260 rows (13 reps).
Bind off.

FINISHING

Sew panels tog in following color order: A, B, A, C, A, D, A, E, A.
Weave in all ends.
Block blanket lightly to measurements.

144

WAR
AND PEACE

EDGING

With crochet hook and A, work 2 rows of sc across top of blanket, fasten off.
Rep on bottom edge. ∎

Tip Never dig down to the bottom of your bag again for that long lost tape measure! Keep your knitting essentials in a clear makeup bag for easy access.

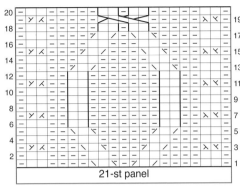

CABLE PANEL

21-st panel

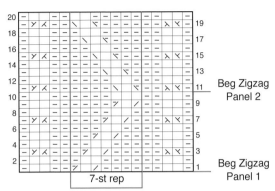

ZIGZAG PANEL

7-st rep

Beg Zigzag Panel 2

Beg Zigzag Panel 1

STITCH KEY

- ⊟ P on RS, k on WS
- ☐ K on RS, p on WS
- Sl 1 to cn and hold in back, k1, k1 from cn
- Sl 1 to cn and hold in front, k1, k1 from cn
- Sl 2 to cn and hold in front, p1, k2 from cn
- Sl 1 to cn and hold in back, k2, p1 from cn
- Sl 2 to cn and hold in front, k3, k2 from cn

LACED-UP CABLES AFGHAN

DESIGN BY SUZANNE ATKINSON

WHAT'S IN THE BAG

Plymouth Galway Chunky
(bulky weight; 100% wool;
123 yds/100g per ball): 13
balls maroon #12 (A), 11 balls
charcoal gray #704 (B), 3 balls olive
heather #750 (C)
Size 10 (6.mm) needles
Size I/9 (5.5mm) crochet hook
Cable needle

5 BULKY

SKILL LEVEL

◼◼◻◻ EASY

FINISHED MEASUREMENTS

52 x 64 inches

GAUGE

22 sts and 22 rows = 4¾ inches/12cm in
Cable Pat (i.e. width of one cable panel).
To save time, take time to check gauge.

SPECIAL ABBREVIATIONS

Cable 6 Forward (C6F): Sl next 3 sts to cn
and hold in front, k3, k3 from cn.
Make 1 (M1): Insert LH needle from
front to back under the running thread
between the last st worked and next
st on RH needle; knit into the back of
resulting loop.

PATTERN STITCH

Cable Panel (22-st panel)
Row 1 (RS): K5, p3, k6, p3, k5.
Row 2: K8, p6, k8.
Row 3: K2, yo, ssk, k1, p3, C6F, p3, k1,
k2tog, yo, k2.
Row 4: Rep Row 2.
    Rep Rows 1–4 for pat.

PATTERN NOTES

Afghan is worked as separate cable
panels; the panels are joined by
lacing crocheted chains through
eyelets in the panels and joining at ends.
    A chart for the Cable Panel is provided for
those preferring to work from charts.

AFGHAN

Make 11 Cable Panels (6 in A and 5 in B)
    Cast on 20 sts.
    Knit 2 rows.
Next row: K2, yo, ssk, k12, k2tog, yo, k2.
    Knit 2 rows.
Next row: K9, M1, k2, M1, k9—22 sts.
    Work [Rows 1– 4 of Cable pat] 49 times,
ending with Row 4.
Next row: K8, k2tog, k2, k2tog, k8—20 sts.
    Knit 3 rows.

Next row: K2, yo, ssk, k12, k2tog, yo, k2.
Next row: Knit.
  Bind off.

FINISHING

Weave in all ends. Block cable panels.

  With crochet hook and C, make 22 8-ft lengths of chain st.

  Lay cable panels side by side on large flat surface alternating colors (A, B, A, B, etc. ending with A).

  Using crocheted chains, join adjacent panels as for lacing sneakers, using 2 crochet chains for each join, beg at first eyelet in each panel and alternating eyelets to end of panel. Let 8 inches of each crochet chain extend beyond afghan for tying together in a bow at each end of afghan.

  Weave single crocheted chain through eyelets at each side panel edge as follows: *pull chain through first eyelet from RS to WS; go around outer edge, then pull chain from RS to WS through next eyelet; rep from * to end (see photo). ∎

Tip

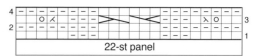
When working with multiple colors of yarn, instead of traveling with large unnecessary skeins, wind off small balls of only the colors you'll need.

CABLE PANEL

STITCH KEY
☐ K on RS, p on WS
⊟ P on RS, k on WS
⊙ Yo
⟩ Ssk
⟨ K2tog
⟩━━⟨ C6F

SPIRALED I-CORD SEAT COVER

DESIGN BY SHIRLEY MACNULTY

WHAT'S IN THE BAG

Trendsetter Yarns Viva (bulky
  yarn; 65% new wool/20%
  acrylic/15% polyamide; 55
  yds/50g per skein): 6 skeins
  cask & cleaver #814
Size 13 (9mm) 16 inch circular needle
  or size needed to obtain gauge
Size K (6.5mm) crochet hook

(5 BULKY)

SKILL LEVEL
■■□□ EASY

FINISHED SIZE
Diameter: Approx 17½ inches
(including edging)

GAUGE
12 sts and 12 rnds = 4 inches/10cm in St st in
an I-cord tube.
To save time, take time to check gauge.

PATTERN NOTES
Most of pattern is worked as a 4-stitch I-cord;
at the very end, it is gradually decreased to
1 stitch.

Each skein of the designated yarn yields
approximately 2¼ yards of I-cord.

Some may find it easier to sew the I-cord
together as they knit, sewing after every
12 inches or so, then resuming knitting.

SEAT COVER
Cast on 4 sts.
Rnd 1: K4, do not turn; slide sts to opposite end
of needle pulling yarn tightly behind work.

Rep Rnd 1 until cord measures approx
12 yds or desired length.
Next rnd: K1, k2tog, k1—3 sts.
Next 3 rnds: Work as for Rnd 1 on 3 sts.
Next rnd: K2tog, k1.
Next 3 rnds: Work as for Rnd 1 on 2 sts.
Next rnd: K2tog.
Next 3 rnds: Work as for Rnd 1 on 1 st.
  Fasten off.

FINISHING
Thread tapestry needle with an 18-inch piece
of project yarn.

With RS facing, and beg at cast-on end,
sew I-cord into a round flat coil using whip
st, catching 1 st on each side of the I-cord
tube. You should have 2 knit sts (1 from
each section of I-cord being sewn tog)
traveling tog in a straight line around
the top side of the piece. Every few sts,
skip 1 of the sts on the outer I-cord so
that the cover will lie flat. Add new
sewing yarn as necessary.

When finished sewing, work 1
rnd of dc around outside edge.
Weave loose ends into I-cord
tubes.

Wet-block piece, pulling it as
necessary to get it to lie flat. Put
between towels and cover with
heavy weights (such as large
books). Allow to dry thoroughly. ■

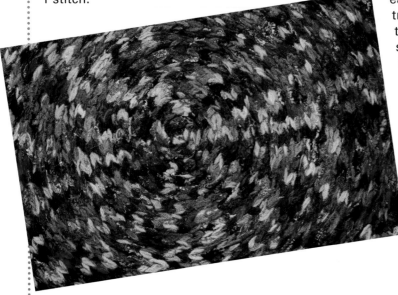

"Once many years ago, we were out in our little boat. We suddenly came to a stop, and lo and behold we got stranded on a sandbar. Luckily I had some knitting with me—we had to wait three hours for the rising tide to set us free!"

KNIT, THEN WEAVE, PLACE MATS

DESIGN BY COLLEEN SMITHERMAN

WHAT'S IN THE BAG

Lily Sugar 'n Cream (worsted weight; 100% cotton; 120 yds/71g per skein): 1 skein each cornflower blue #00083 (A) and soft ecru #01004 (B)

Size 8 (5mm) 29-inch circular needle
Size 11 (8mm) needles or size needed to obtain gauge
Size N/15 (10mm) crochet hook
5 stitch holders

SKILL LEVEL

■■□□ EASY

FINISHED SIZE

Approx 12½ x 17½ inches, not including fringe

GAUGE

14 sts and 15 rows = 4 inches/10cm in St st with larger needles (before weaving).
17 sts and 13 rows = 4 inches/10cm (after weaving).
To save time, take time to check gauge.

SPECIAL TECHNIQUE

Provisional Cast-On: With crochet hook and waste yarn, make a chain several sts longer than desired cast-on. With knitting needle and project yarn, pick up indicated number of sts in the "bumps" on back of chain.

When indicated in pattern, "unzip" the crochet chain to free live sts.

PATTERN NOTE

Each place mat is made from 5 narrow knit panels which are joined by weaving horizontal stripes across all 5 panels.

PLACE MAT

Panels
Make 5 (3 with A, 2 with B)

Using provisional method and A, cast on 15 sts.
Work 41 rows of St st.
Cut yarn and put sts on holder.

Weave panels together

With RS facing and cast-on edges at the bottom, lay panels side by side in the following sequence: A, B, A, B, A.
Thread yarn needle with A; do not cut yarn.

152

Beg with the bottom row and working to top row, work 2 rows of weaving through each row of knitting as described below:

*Beg at the outer A panel (right side if right-handed, left side if left-handed), weave needle and yarn horizontally across the knit row going under the left leg of every st, connecting all 5 panels as you weave; cut yarn, leaving a 3-inch tail at each side edge.

Thread the needle again, and weave needle and yarn across the same row again, going under the right leg of every st; cut yarn, leaving a 3-inch tail at each side edge.

Smooth out the weaving after each row so the width measures 17½ inches and weaving is uniform.

Rep from *, weaving twice in each row of knitting, creating stripes as follows: with A, weave 26 more rows through 13 rows of knitting; with B, weave 28 rows through 14 rows of knitting; with A, weave 28 rows through 14 rows of knitting.

Top border
Transfer sts from all holders to smaller needle—75 sts.

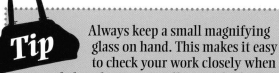

Tip Always keep a small magnifying glass on hand. This makes it easy to check your work closely when needed, and it is especially useful when working in less than ideal lighting.

With RS facing and using A, bind off all sts kwise.

Bottom border
Unzip Provisional Cast-On from each panel and transfer all live sts to smaller needle.

With RS facing and using A, bind off all sts kwise.

FINISHING
Weave in all knitting tails to WS.

Steam lightly, squaring up corners and sides.

Using overhand knots, tie weaving yarn tails tog 2 at a time close to place mat edges.

Trim fringe to 1 inch on both sides. ■

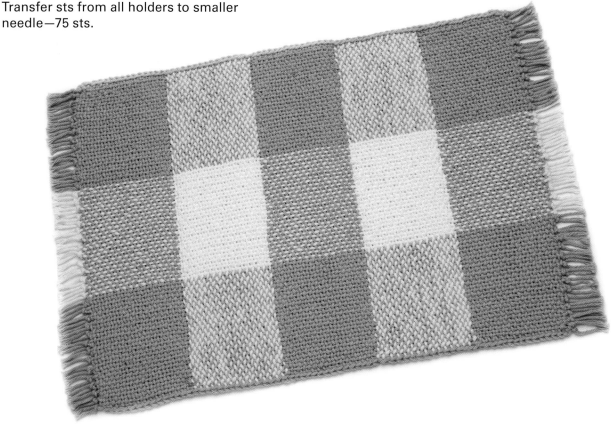

EARTH TONES AFGHAN

DESIGN BY PAULINE SCHULTZ

WHAT'S IN THE BAG

Patons SWS (worsted weight;
  70% wool/30%soy; 110 yds/80g
  per ball): 15 balls natural earth
  #70013
Size 9 (5.5mm) needles or size needed to
  obtain gauge
Latch hook or large crochet hook
Stitch markers

4 MEDIUM

SKILL LEVEL
■■□□ EASY

FINISHED SIZE
Approx 43 x 60 inches

GAUGE
15 sts and 18 rows = 4 inches/10cm Indian
Cross pat.
To save time, take time to check gauge.

SPECIAL TECHNIQUE
Crochet Cast-On: Make slip knot on crochet
hook. *Hold crochet hook vertically in front
of and at right angles to the needle with
the needle point facing right. Take the yarn
under the needle, up and across the front
of the crochet hook. Pull yarn through
loop—new st on needle. Rep from * as
required. Slip loop from crochet hook to
needle to form the last st.

SPECIAL ABBREVIATIONS
Knit 1 with 4 Wraps (K1W4): Insert
needle into next st and wrap yarn
loosely 4 times around the needle, then
knit the st.
Cross 8 Left (C8L): Sl 8 pwise, dropping
all extra wraps (8 long sts result);
insert LH needle into the 2nd 4 of these
8 long sts and pass them to the left
over the first 4 (4 sts on LH needle,

4 sts on RH needle); sl 4 sts from RH back to
LH needle; knit the 8 crossed sts.
Cross 4 Left (C4L): Sl 4 pwise dropping all
extra wraps (4 long sts result); insert LH needle
into the 2nd 2 of these 4 long sts and pass
them to the left over the first 2 (2 sts on LH
needle and 2 sts on RH needle); sl 2 sts from
RH to LH needle; knit the 4 crossed sts.
Place marker (pm): Place a marker on needle
to separate pats.

PATTERN STITCH

Indian Cross (multiple of 8 sts)
Rows 1–4: Knit.
Row 5: K1W4 in each st.
Row 6: [C8L] 4 times.
Rows 7–10: Knit.
Row 11: Rep Row 5.
Row 12: C4L, [C8L] 3 times, C4L.
Rep Rows 1–12 for pat.

AFGHAN

Left Panel

Crochet cast on 39 sts.
Knit 3 rows.
Set-up pat (RS): K5, pm, work 32 sts in Indian Cross pat, pm, k2.
Working edge sts in garter st and sts between markers in Indian Cross pat, work 25 reps of Indian Cross, then work Rows 1–6 of pat once more.
Knit 6 rows.
Bind off as to purl to last st, place this st on waste yarn for holder; cut yarn leaving a 6-inch tail and draw through next to last st.

Right Panel

Crochet cast on 39 sts.
Knit 3 rows.
Set-up pat (RS): K2, pm, work 32 sts in Indian Cross pat, pm, k5.
Work as for left panel to bind-off.
Slip first st to waste yarn for holder, bind off rem sts as to purl; cut yarn, leaving a 6-inch tail.

Center Panels
Make 2

Crochet cast on 36 sts.
Knit 3 rows.
Set-up pat (RS): K2, pm, work 32 sts in Indian Cross pat, pm, k2.
Work as for left panel to bind-off.
Slip first st to holder, bind off sts to last st, place this st on waste yarn for holder; cut yarn leaving a 6-inch tail and draw through next to last st.

FINISHING

Weave in all ends, except for the 3 (6-inch) tails.
Unravel sts on holders down through cast-on row.
Wet block each panel to measure

Tip Just roll up the strip you're working on, secure it with a needle or long stitch holder and away you go. You can even stash an extra ball of yarn inside!

10 x 60 inches (not including the side loops), using pins or blocking wires threaded through side loops to keep them straight.
When pieces are dry, join right panel to center panel using a crochet or latch hook as follows: insert hook through bottom left-side center panel loop; *catch the bottom loop of the right panel and draw through loop on hook; catch next center panel loop and draw through loop on hook; rep from * until last loop is on hook, then thread the 6-inch bind-off tail through it and fasten off securely.
Join rem panels as above. ■

LUXEMBOURG LACE PLACE MATS

DESIGN BY CHRISTINE L. WALTER

WHAT'S IN THE BAG

Knit One Crochet Too 2nd Time Cotton (worsted weight; 75% recycled cotton/25% acrylic; 180 yds/100g per skein): 1 skein ochre #485

Size 8 (5mm) 24-inch circular needle or size needed to obtain gauge

SKILL LEVEL

 EASY

FINISHED SIZE

Approx 13½ x 17 inches

GAUGE

16 sts and 26 rows = 4 inches/10cm in combination of garter st and lace pat.
To save time, take time to check gauge.

SPECIAL ABBREVIATION

Place marker (pm): Place a marker on needle to separate pats.

PATTERN STITCH

Lace Pat (9-st panel)
Row 1 (RS): K1, [k2tog, yo] 3 times, k2.
Row 2: Purl.
Row 3: K2, [k2tog, yo] twice, k3.
Row 4: Purl.
  Rep Rows 1–4 for pat.

PLACE MAT

Cast on 55 sts.
  Knit 7 rows.
Next row: K5, pm, k9, pm, [k3, pm, k9, pm] 3 times, k5.
Set-up row (RS): Slipping markers, k5, work Lace pat over next 9 sts, [k3, work Lace pat over next 9 sts] 3 times, k5.

Continue pats as established, working 5 edge sts and 3 sts between each lace panel in garter st, until piece measures 16 inches, ending with Row 3 of lace pat.
  Removing markers on first row, knit 8 rows. Bind off very loosely on WS.

FINISHING

Weave in ends. Block as necessary. ∎

 **Tip** Take your knitting for a walk—place a small project, a short circular needle and a small ball of yarn in your fanny pack, and get moving!

BAMBOO BATH MAT

DESIGN BY CECILY GLOWIK MACDONALD

WHAT'S IN THE BAG

Classic Elite Wool Bam Boo (DK
weight; 50% wool/50% bamboo;
118 yds/50g per ball): 5 balls
each artichoke green #1672 (A)
and celery #1681 (B); 1 ball sachet
#1605 (C)

3 LIGHT

Size 10 (6mm) needles or size needed to
obtain gauge

SKILL LEVEL

■■□□ EASY

FINISHED SIZE

18 inches x 24 inches

PRE-FELTED GAUGE

16 sts and 24 rows = 4 inches/10cm in garter st
with 2 strands held tog.
To save time, take time to check gauge.

PATTERN NOTES

Bath mat is made of 9 separate rectangles of
one size and 9 separate rectangles of another
size that are then sewn together before felting.
All pieces are worked with 2 strands of yarn
held together.

BATH MAT

Large Rectangles
Make 9
With 1 strand each of A and B held tog, cast
on 25 sts.

Knit 44 rows.
Bind off.

Small Rectangles
Make 9
With 1 strand each of A and B held tog, cast
on 25 sts.
Knit 20 rows.
Bind off.

ASSEMBLY
Panels
Make 3
With tapestry needle and double-strand of C,
whip stitch the pieces tog so that seam sts are
visible.

*Sew the bound-off edge of a small
rectangle to the cast-on edge of a large
rectangle; sew the bound-off edge of the
large rectangle just used to the cast-on edge
of a new small rectangle; rep from * once,
then sew the bound-off edge of the last small
rectangle used to the cast-on edge of 1 more
large rectangle.

With tapestry needle and double-strand of B,
sew panels together along the long sides; the
middle panel is sewn
in facing the opposite
direction of the 2 side
panels (see Diagram).
Weave in ends.

FELTING

Follow basic felting
instructions on page
167 until finished
measurements are
obtained or piece is
desired size. Tumble dry
low, remove when still
damp. Shape and lay
flat to dry. ■

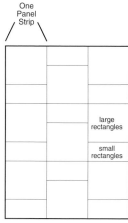

One
Panel
Strip

large
rectangles

small
rectangles

DIAGRAM

Tip Create knitting needle "bouquets"
by placing your needles in
decorative vases and tins around
the house. This not only adds character to
your surroundings, but it will be easy to grab
your needles and head out the door.

GENERAL INFORMATION

STANDARD ABBREVIATIONS

[ ] work instructions within brackets as many times as directed
( ) work instructions within parentheses in the place directed
** repeat instructions between the asterisks as directed
* repeat instructions following the single asterisk as directed
approx approximately
beg begin/beginning
CC contrasting color
ch chain stitch
cm centimeter(s)
cn cable needle
dec decrease/decreases/decreasing
dpn(s) double-point needle(s)
g gram
inc increase/increases/increasing
k knit

k2tog knit 2 stitches together
LH left hand
lp(s) loop(s)
m meter(s)
M1 make one stitch
MC main color
mm millimeter(s)
oz ounce(s)
p purl
pat(s) pattern(s)
p2tog purl 2 stitches together
psso pass slipped stitch over
rem remain/remaining
rep repeat(s)
rev St st reverse stockinette stitch
RH right hand
rnd(s) rounds
RS right side
skp slip, knit, pass stitch over—one stitch decreased
sk2p slip 1, knit 2 together, pass slip stitch over the knit 2

together; 2 stitches have been decreased
sl slip
sl 1k slip 1 knitwise
sl 1p slip 1 purlwise
sl st slip stitch(es)
ssk slip, slip, knit these 2 stitches together—a decrease
ssp slip, slip, purl these 2 stitches together through the back loops [or tbl]—a decrease
st(s) stitch(es)
St st stockinette stitch/stocking stitch
tbl through back loop(s)
tog together
WS wrong side
wyib with yarn in back
wyif with yarn in front
yd(s) yard(s)
yfwd yarn forward
yo yarn over

SKILL LEVELS

●□□□ **BEGINNER**
Projects for first-time knitters using basic knit and purl stitches. Minimal shaping.

●●□□ **EASY**
Projects using basic stitches, repetitive stitch patterns, simple color changes and simple shaping and finishing.

●●●□ **INTERMEDIATE**
Projects with a variety of stitches, such as basic cables and lace, simple intarsia, double-point needles and knitting in the round needle techniques, mid-level shaping and finishing.

●●●● **EXPERIENCED**
Projects using advanced techniques and stitches, such as short rows, Fair Isle, more intricate intarsia, cables, lace patterns and numerous color changes.

STANDARD YARN WEIGHT SYSTEM
Categories of yarn, gauge ranges and recommended needle sizes

Yarn Weight Symbol & Category Names	1 SUPER FINE	2 FINE	3 LIGHT	4 MEDIUM	5 BULKY	6 SUPER BULKY
Type of Yarns in Category	Sock, Fingering, Baby	Sport, Baby	DK, Light Worsted	Worsted, Afghan, Aran	Chunky, Craft, Rug	Bulky, Roving
Knit Gauge* Ranges in Stockinette Stitch to 4 inches	21–32 sts	23–26 sts	21–24 sts	16–20 sts	12–15 sts	6–11 sts
Recommended Needle in Metric Size Range	2.25–3.25mm	3.25–3.75mm	3.75–4.5mm	4.5–5.5mm	5.5–8mm	8mm
Recommended Needle U.S. Size Range	1 to 3	3 to 5	5 to 7	7 to 9	9 to 11	11 and larger

* GUIDELINES ONLY: The above reflect the most commonly used gauges and needle sizes for specific yarn categories.

INCHES INTO MILLIMETERS & CENTIMETERS (Rounded off slightly)

inches	mm	cm	inches	cm	inches	cm	inches	cm
1/8	3	0.3	5	12.5	21	53.5	38	96.5
1/4	6	0.6	5 1/2	14	22	56	39	99
3/8	10	1	6	15	23	58.5	40	101.5
1/2	13	1.3	7	18	24	61	41	104
5/8	15	1.5	8	20.5	25	63.5	42	106.5
3/4	20	2	9	23	26	66	43	109
7/8	22	2.2	10	25.5	27	68.5	44	112
1	25	2.5	11	28	28	71	45	114.5
1 1/4	32	3.2	12	30.5	29	73.5	46	117
1 1/2	38	3.8	13	33	30	76	47	119.5
1 3/4	45	4.5	14	35.5	31	79	48	122
2	50	5	15	38	32	81.5	49	124.5
2 1/2	65	6.5	16	40.5	33	84	50	127
3	75	7.5	17	43	34	86.5		
3 1/2	90	9	18	46	35	89		
4	100	10	19	48.5	36	91.5		
4 1/2	115	11.5	20	51	37	94		

KNITTING NEEDLES CONVERSION CHART

U.S.	0	1	2	3	4	5	6	7	8	9	10	10 1/2	11	13	15
Metric(mm)	2	2 1/4	2 3/4	3 1/4	3 1/2	3 3/4	4	4 1/2	5	5 1/2	6	6 1/2	8	9	10

CROCHET HOOKS CONVERSION CHART

U.S.	1/B	2/C	3/D	4/E	5/F	6/G	8/H	9/I	10/J	10 1/2/K	N
Continental(mm)	2.25	2.75	3.25	3.5	3.75	4.25	5	5.5	6	6.5	9.0

GLOSSARY

bind-off—used to finish an edge

cast-on—process of making foundation stitches used in knitting

decrease—means of reducing the number of stitches in a row

increase—means of adding to the number of stitches in a row

intarsia—method of knitting a multicolored pattern into the fabric

knitwise—insert needle into stitch as if to knit

make 1—method of increasing using the strand between the last stitch worked and the next stitch

place marker—placing a purchased marker or loop of contrasting yarn onto the needle for ease in working a pattern repeat

purlwise—insert needle into stitch as if to purl

right side—side of garment or piece that will be seen when worn

selvage (selvedge) stitch—edge stitch used to make seaming easier

slip, slip, knit—method of decreasing by moving stitches from left needle to right needle and working them together

slip stitch—an unworked stitch slipped from left needle to right needle, usually as if to purl

wrong side—side that will be inside when garment is worn

work even—continue to work in the pattern as established without working any increases or decreases

work in pattern as established—continue to work following the pattern stitch as it has been set up or established on the needle, working any increases or decreases in such a way that the established pattern remains the same

yarn over—method of creating a stitch by wrapping the yarn over the right needle without working a stitch

BASIC STITCHES

Garter Stitch

When working back and forth, knit every row. When working in the round on circular or double-point needles, knit one round then purl one round.

Stockinette Stitch

When working back and forth, knit right-side rows and purl wrong-side rows. When working in the round on circular or double-point needles, knit all rounds.

Reverse Stockinette Stitch

When working back and forth, purl right-side rows and knit wrong-side rows. When working in the round on circular or double-point needles, purl all rounds.

Ribbing

Ribbing combines knit and purl stitches within a row to give stretch to the garment. Ribbing is most often used for the lower edge of the front and back, the cuffs and neck edge of garments.

The rib pattern is established on the first row. On subsequent rows the knit stitches are knitted and purl stitches are purled to form the ribs.

READING PATTERN INSTRUCTIONS

Before beginning a pattern, read through it to make sure you are familiar with the abbreviations that are used.

Some patterns may be written for more than one size. In this case the smallest size is given first, and others are placed in parentheses. When only one number is given, it applies to all sizes.

You may wish to highlight the numbers for the size you are making before beginning. It is also helpful to place a self-adhesive sheet on the pattern to note any changes made while working the pattern.

MEASURING

To measure pieces, lay them flat on a smooth surface. Take the measurement in the middle of the piece. For example, measure the length to the armhole in the center of the front or back piece, not along the outer edge where the edges tend to curve or roll.

GAUGE

The single most important factor in determining the finished size of a knit item is the gauge. Although not as important for flat, one-piece items, it is important when making a clothing item that needs to fit properly.

It is important to make a stitch gauge swatch at least 4 inches square with recommended patterns and needles before beginning.

Measure the swatch. If the number of stitches and rows are fewer than indicated under "Gauge" in the pattern, your needles are too large. Try another swatch with smaller-size needles. If the number of stitches and rows is more than indicated under "Gauge" in the pattern, your needles are too small. Try another swatch with larger-size needles.

Continue to adjust needle sizes until correct gauge is achieved.

WORKING FROM CHARTS

When working with more than one color or combination of stitches in a row, sometimes a chart is provided to help follow the pattern. On the chart each square represents one stitch. A key is given indicating the color or stitch represented by each color or symbol in the box.

When working in rows, odd-numbered rows are usually read from right to left and even-numbered rows from left to right.

For color-work charts, rows beginning at the right represent the right side of the work and are usually knit. Rows beginning at the left represent the wrong side and are usually purled.

When working in rounds, every row on the chart is a right-side row and is read from right to left.

USE OF ZERO

In patterns that include various sizes, zeros are sometimes necessary. For example, k0 (0,1) means if you are making the smallest or middle size, you would do nothing, and if you are making the largest size, you would k1.

INTARSIA

In certain patterns there are larger areas of color within the piece. Since this type of pattern requires a new color only for that section, it is not necessary to carry the yarn back and forth across the back. For this type of color change, a separate ball of yarn or bobbin is used for each color, making the yarn available only where needed. Bring the new yarn being used up and around the yarn just worked; this will "lock" the colors and prevent holes from occurring at the join.

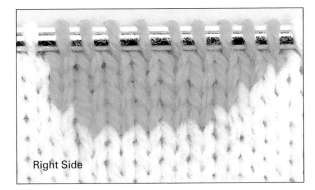

Right Side

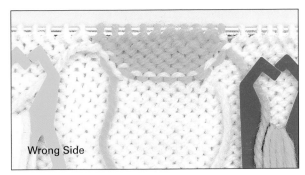

Wrong Side

SEAM FINISHES
Mattress Seam

This type of seam can be used for vertical seams (like side seams). It is worked with the right sides of the pieces facing you, making it easier to match stitches for stripe patterns. It is worked between the first and second stitch at the edge of the piece and works best when the first stitch is a selvage stitch.

To work this seam, thread a tapestry needle with matching yarn. Insert the needle into one corner of work from back to front, just above the cast-on stitch, leaving a 3-inch tail. Take needle to edge of other piece and bring it from back to front at the corner of this piece.

Return to the first piece and insert the needle from the right to wrong side where the thread comes out of the piece. Slip the needle upward under two horizontal threads and bring the needle through to the right side.

Cross to the other side and repeat the same process "down where you came out, under two threads and up."

Continue working back and forth on the two pieces in the same manner for about an inch,

then gently pull on the thread pulling the two pieces together. (Photo A)

Photo A

Complete the seam and fasten off. Use the beginning tail to even-up the lower edge by working a figure 8 between the cast-on stitches at the corners. Insert the threaded needle from front to back under both threads of the corner cast-on stitch on the edge opposite the tail, then into the same stitch on the first edge. Pull gently until the figure 8 fills the gap. (Photo B)

Photo B

When a project is made with a textured yarn that will not pull easily through the pieces, it is recommended that a smooth yarn of the same color be used to work the seam.

Garter Stitch Seams

The "bumps" of the garter stitch selvage nestle between each other in a garter stitch seam, often producing a nearly reversible seam. This is a good seam for afghan strips and blocks of the same color. Starting as for the mattress seam, work from bump to bump, alternating sides. In this case you enter each stitch only once.

Matching Patterns

When it comes to matching stripes and other elements in a sweater design, a simple method makes things line up perfectly:

Begin the seam in the usual way.

Enter the first stitch of each new color stripe (or pattern detail) on the same side as you began the seam; i.e. the same side as your tail is hanging.

KITCHENER STITCH

This method of grafting with two needles is used for the toes of socks and invisible joins. To graft the edges together and form an unbroken line of stockinette stitch, divide all stitches evenly onto two knitting needles—one behind the other. Thread yarn into tapestry needle. Hold needles with wrong sides together and work from right to left as follows:

Step 1: Insert tapestry needle into first stitch on front needle as to purl. Draw yarn through stitch, leaving stitch on knitting needle.

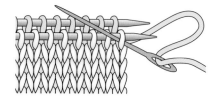

Step 2: Insert tapestry needle into the first stitch on the back needle as to purl. Draw yarn through stitch and slip stitch off knitting needle.

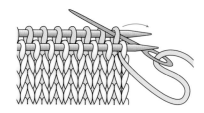

Step 3: Insert tapestry needle into the next stitch on same (back) needle as to knit, leaving stitch on knitting needle.

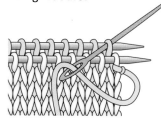

Step 4: Insert tapestry needle into the first stitch on the front needle as to knit. Draw yarn through stitch and slip stitch off knitting needle.

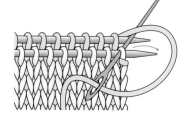

Step 5: Insert tapestry needle into the next stitch on same (front) needle as to purl. Draw yarn through stitch, leaving stitch on knitting needle.

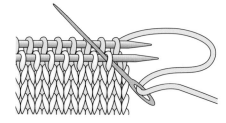

Repeat Steps 2 through 5 until one stitch is left on each needle. Then repeat Steps 2 and 4. Fasten off. Grafted stitches should be the same size as adjacent knitted stitches.

FRINGE

Cut a piece of cardboard half as long as fringe length specified in instructions plus ½ inch for trimming. Wind yarn loosely and evenly around cardboard. When cardboard is filled, cut yarn across one end. Do this several times, then begin fringing. Wind additional strands as necessary.

Single Knot Fringe

Hold specified number of strands for one knot together, fold in half. Hold project to be fringed with right side facing you. Use crochet hook to draw folded end through space or stitch indicated from right to wrong side.

Pull loose ends through folded section.

Draw knot up firmly. Space knots as indicated in pattern instructions.

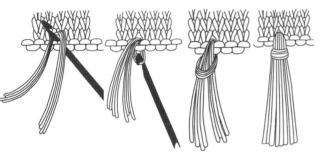

Single Knot Fringe

KNITTING WITH BEADS

Threading beads onto yarn is the most common way to knit with beads.

Step 1: Before beginning to knit, thread half of the beads onto your skein of yarn using a bead threader. As you work, unwind a small quantity of yarn, each time sliding the beads towards the ball until needed. Pass the yarn through the loop of the threader and pick up beads with the working end of the needle.

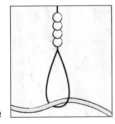

Step 2: Slide the beads over the loop and onto the yarn.

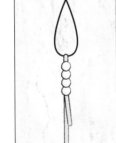

FELTING INSTRUCTIONS
The Felt Formula

Felting is not a precise science. Wool felts when exposed to water, heat and agitation, but each element is hard to control precisely. As a result, each individual project may vary in the way it felts.

Felting can be done in the sink, but washing machines get the job done more quickly. Each washing machine is different, and the rate at which specific machines felt a piece will

vary. So, be sure to follow the specific felting instructions of the piece you are making, and check your piece several times during the felting process to make sure you are getting the desired results.

The felting process releases fibers which can clog your washing machine. Therefore, you may want to place items in a zippered pillowcase before putting them in the washing machine. Also, adding other laundry, such as jeans, when felting will increase the amount of agitation and speed up the process. Be careful not to use items that shed fibers of their own, such as towels.

Felting Facts

Felting a knit or crochet piece makes it shrink. Therefore, the piece you knit must start out much larger than the finished felted size will be. Shrinkage varies since there are so many factors that affect it. These variables include water temperature, the hardness of the water, how much (and how long) the piece is agitated, the amount and type of soap used, yarn brand, fiber content and color.

You can control how much your piece felts by watching it closely. Check your piece after about 10 minutes to see how quickly it is felting. Look at the stitch definition and size to determine if the piece has been felted enough.

How to Felt

Place items to be felted in the washing machine along with one tablespoon of dish detergent and a pair of jeans or other laundry. (Remember, do not felt projects with other clothing that release their own fibers.) Set washing machine on smallest load and use hot water. Start machine and check progress after ten minutes. Check progress more frequently after piece starts to felt. Reset the machine if needed to continue the agitation cycle. Do not allow machine to go to spin cycle; rapid spinning can cause creases in the felted fabric that may be very difficult to get out later. As the piece becomes more felted, you may need to pull it into shape.

When the piece has felted to the desired size, rinse it by hand in warm water. Remove the excess water either by rolling in a towel and squeezing.

Block the piece into shape, and let air dry. Do not dry in clothes dryer. For pieces that need to conform to a particular shape (such as a hat or purse), stuff the piece with a towel to help it hold its shape while drying. Felted items are very strong, so don't be afraid to push and pull it into the desired shape. It may take several hours or several days for the pieces to dry completely.

After the piece is completely dry, excess fuzziness can be trimmed with scissors if a smoother surface is desired, or the piece can be brushed for a fuzzier appearance.

3-NEEDLE BIND-OFF

Use this technique for seaming two edges together, such as when joining a shoulder seam. Hold the live edge stitches on two separate needles with right sides together.

With a third needle, knit together a stitch from the front needle with one from the back.

Repeat, knitting a stitch from the front needle with one from the back needle once more.

Slip the first stitch over the second.

Repeat knitting, a front and back pair of stitches together, then bind one pair off.

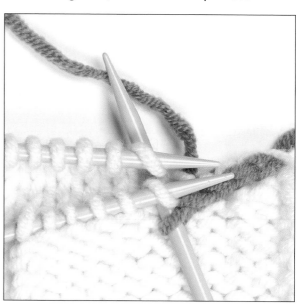

EMBROIDERY STITCHES

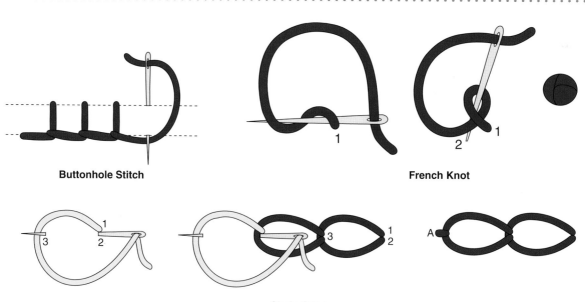

Buttonhole Stitch

French Knot

Chain Stitch

KNITTING BASICS

CAST ON

Leaving an end about an inch long for each stitch to be cast on, make a slip knot on the right needle.

Place the thumb and index finger of your left hand between the yarn ends with the long yarn end over your thumb, and the strand from the skein over your index finger. Close your other fingers over the strands to hold them against your palm. Spread your thumb and index fingers apart and draw the yarn into a "V."

Place the needle in front of the strand around your thumb and bring it underneath this strand. Carry the needle over and under the strand on your index finger.

Draw through loop on thumb.

Drop the loop from your thumb and draw up the strand to form a stitch on the needle.

Repeat until you have cast on the number of stitches indicated in the pattern. Remember to count the beginning slip knot as a stitch.

CABLE CAST-ON

This type of cast on is used when adding stitches in the middle or at the end of a row.

Make a slip knot on the left needle. Knit a stitch in this knot and place it on the left needle. Insert the right needle between the last two stitches on the left needle. Knit a stitch and place it on the left needle. Repeat for each stitch needed.

KNIT (K)

Insert tip of right needle from front to back in next stitch on left needle. Bring yarn under and over the tip of the right needle.

Pull yarn loop through the stitch with right needle point.

Slide the stitch off the left needle. The new stitch is on the right needle.

PURL (P)

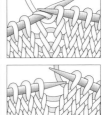

With yarn in front, insert tip of right needle from back to front through next stitch on the left needle. Bring yarn around the right needle counterclockwise. With right needle, draw yarn back through the stitch.

Slide the stitch off the left needle. The new stitch is on the right needle.

BIND-OFF

Binding off (knit)

Knit first two stitches on left needle. Insert tip of left needle into first stitch worked on right needle and pull it over the second stitch and completely off the needle.

Knit the next stitch and repeat. When one stitch remains on right needle, cut yarn and draw tail through last stitch to fasten off.

Binding off (purl)

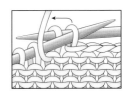

Purl first two stitches on left needle. Insert tip of left needle into first stitch worked on right needle and pull it over the second stitch and completely off the needle.

Purl the next stitch and repeat. When one stitch remains on right needle, cut yarn and draw tail through last stitch to fasten off.

INCREASE (INC)
Two stitches in one stitch
Increase (knit)
Knit the next stitch in the usual manner, but don't remove the stitch from the left needle. Place right needle behind left needle and knit again into the back of the same stitch. Slip original stitch off left needle.

Increase (purl)
Purl the next stitch in the usual manner, but don't remove the stitch from the left needle. Place right needle behind left needle and purl again into the back of the same stitch. Slip original stitch off left needle.

INVISIBLE INCREASE (M1)
There are several ways to make or increase one stitch.

Make 1 with Left Twist (M1L)
Insert left needle from front to back under the horizontal loop between the last stitch worked and next stitch on left needle.

With right needle, knit into the back of this loop.

To make this increase on the purl side, insert left needle in same manner and purl into the back of the loop.

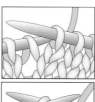

Make 1 with Right Twist (M1R)
Insert left needle from back to front under the horizontal loop between the last stitch worked and next stitch on left needle.

With right needle, knit into the front of this loop.

To make this increase on the purl side, insert left needle in same manner and purl into

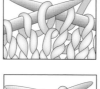

the front of the loop.

Make 1 with Backward Loop over the right needle
With your thumb, make a loop over the right needle.
Slip the loop from your thumb onto the needle and pull to tighten.

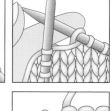

Make 1 in top of stitch below
Insert tip of right needle into the stitch on left needle one row below.

Knit this stitch, then knit the stitch on the left needle.

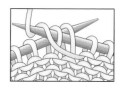

DECREASE (DEC)
Knit 2 together (k2tog)
Put tip of right needle through next two stitches on left needle as to knit. Knit these two stitches as one.

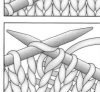

Purl 2 together (p2tog)
Put tip of right needle through next two stitches on left needle as to purl. Purl these two stitches as one.

SLIP, SLIP, KNIT (SSK)
Slip next two stitches, one at a time, as to knit from left needle to right needle.

Insert left needle in front of both stitches and work off needle together.

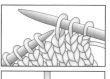

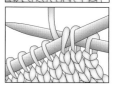

SLIP, SLIP, PURL (SSP)
Slip next two stitches, one at a time, as to knit from left needle to right needle. Slip these stitches back onto left needle keeping them twisted. Purl these two stitches together through back loops.

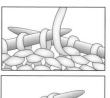

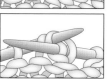

CROCHET BASICS

Some knit items are finished with a crochet trim or edging. Below are some abbreviations used in crochet and a review of some basic crochet stitches.

CROCHET ABBREVIATIONS

ch	chain stitch
dc	double crochet
hdc	half double crochet
lp(s)	loop(s)
sc	single crochet
sl st	slip stitch
yo	yarn over

CHAIN STITCH (CH)

Begin by making a slip knot on the hook. Bring the yarn over the hook from back to front and draw through the loop on the hook.

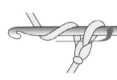

For each additional chain stitch, bring the yarn over the hook from back to front and draw through the loop on the hook.

SINGLE CROCHET (SC)

Insert the hook in the second chain through the center of the V. Bring the yarn over the hook from back to front.

Draw the yarn through the chain stitch and onto the hook.

Again bring yarn over the hook from back to front and draw it through both loops on hook.

For additional rows of single crochet, insert the hook under both loops of the previous stitch instead of through the center of the V as when working into the chain stitch.

REVERSE SINGLE CROCHET (REVERSE SC)

Working in opposite direction from single crochet, insert hook under both loops of the next stitch to the right.

Bring yarn over hook from back to front and draw through both loops on hook.

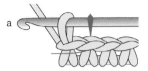

HALF-DOUBLE CROCHET (HDC)

Bring yarn over hook from back to front, insert hook in indicated chain stitch.

Draw yarn through the chain stitch and onto the hook.

Bring yarn over the hook from back to front and draw it through all three loops on the hook in one motion.

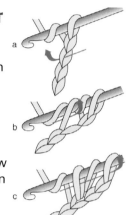

DOUBLE CROCHET (DC)

Yo, insert hook in st, yo, pull through st, (yo, pull through 2 lps) 2 times.

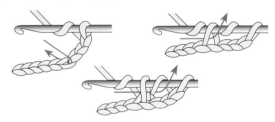

SLIP STITCH (SL ST)

Insert hook under both loops of the stitch, bring yarn over the hook from back to front and draw it through the stitch and the loop on the hook.

PICOT

Picots can be made in a variety of ways so refer to pattern for specific instructions.

Chain required number of stitches. Insert hook at base of chain stitches and through back loop of stitch, complete as indicated in pattern.

TAKE & MAKE JOURNAL

Never forget where you left off in a pattern with this template page. You can copy and carry it while you're on the road, keeping track as you go!

Date Started: _____ This Project Was Made For: _____

Travel Tips I Found Useful: _____

_____

Project Name & Page Number(s): _____

PROJECT ORGANIZER

Yarn Brand/Name	Color(s) & Dye Lot	Gauge (stitches x rows= 4 inches)
Number of Skeins/Balls Used	Needle(s)	Notions

Pattern repeat info: multiple of: _____ + _____ stitches.

Additional pattern repeat notes:

Use the spaces below to keep track of each section you're working on. For example, if you're working on the Front of a sweater, list specific notes about that section's progress. When done, check it off and move on to the next section.

PAGE/SECTION NOTES

☐

☐

☐

☐

☐

☐

☐

☐

☐

☐

☐

☐

☐

Memorable Travel Notes: _____

_____

_____

YARN & BAG RESOURCES

Many of the yarns and bags presented in this book are available in your local yarn shop. If you should have any problems purchasing them in your area, the list below will serve as a helpful resource.

YARN

ORNAGHI FILATI YARNS
Dist. by Aurora Yarns
P.O. Box 3068
Moss Beach, CA 94038
(650) 728-2730
www.aurorayarns.net

BERROCO INC.
P.O. Box 367
14 Elmdale Road
Uxbridge, MA 01569-0367
(508) 278-2527
www.berroco.com

CARON INTERNATIONAL
Customer Service
P.O. Box 222
Washington, NC 27889
www.caron.com
www.shopcaron.com
www.naturallycaron.com

CASCADE YARNS
1224 Andover Park East
Seattle, WA 98188
(206) 574-0440
www.cascadeyarns.com

CLASSIC ELITE YARNS INC.
122 Western Ave.
Lowell, MA 01851-1434
(978) 453-2837
www.classiceliteyarns.com

COATS & CLARK
(Moda Dea)
P.O. Box 12229
Greenville, SC 29612-0229
(800) 648-1479
www.coatsandclark.com
www.modadea.com

CRYSTAL PALACE YARNS
160 23rd St.
Richmond, CA 94804
(510) 237-9988
www.straw.com

REYNOLDS
Dist. by JCA, Inc.
35 Scales Lane
Townsend, MA 01469
(978) 597-8794
www.jcacrafts.com

KNIT ONE, CROCHET TOO INC.
91 Tandberg Trail, Unit 6
Windham, ME 04062
(207) 892-9625
www.knitonecrochettoo.com

MISSION FALLS
5333 Casgrain #1204
Montreal, Quebec
H2T 1X3 Canada
(877) 244-1204
www.missionfalls.com

NASHUA HANDKNITS
Dist. by Westminster Fibers Inc.
165 Ledge St.
Nashua, NH 03060
(800) 445-9276
www.nashuaknits.com
www.westminsterfibers.com

PLYMOUTH YARN COMPANY INC.
500 Lafayette St.
Bristol, PA 19007
(215) 788-0459
www.plymouthyarn.com

PRISM ARTS INC.
2595 30th Ave. North
St. Petersburg, FL 33713
(727) 321-1905
www.prismyarn.com

ROWAN
Dist. by Westminster Fibers Inc.
165 Ledge St.
Nashua, NH 03060
(800) 445-9276
www.knitrowan.com
www.westminsterfibers.com

SCHACHENMAYR
Dist. by Westminster Fibers Inc.
165 Ledge St.
Nashua, NH 03060
(800) 445-9276
www.schachenmayr.us
www.westminsterfibers.com

SCHAEFER YARN COMPANY LTD.
3514 Kelly's Corners Road
Interlaken, NY 14847
(607) 532-9452
www.schaeferyarn.com

SPINRITE LP
(Lily Sugar n' Cream, Patons)
320 Livingstone Ave. S.
Listowel, ON
N4W 3H3 Canada
(888) 368-8401
www.spinriteyarns.com
www.sugarncream.com
www.patonsyarns.com

TAHKI STACY CHARLES INC.
70-30 80th St. Building 36
Ridgewood, NY 11385
(800) 338-YARN (9276)
www.tahkistacycharles.com

TRENDSETTER YARNS
16745 Saticoy St. Suite #101
Van Nuys, CA 91406
(800) 446-2425
www.trendsetteryarns.com

BAGS

ATENTI
2336 Mountain Ave.
La Crescenta, CA 91214
(818) 248 8459
www.atenti.net
Disks Satchel, Page 38
Kiss Me Doctor Bag,
   Page 140

DELLA Q
2637 2nd Ave. N.
Seattle, WA 98109
(877) 733-5527
www.dellaq.com
Eden Cotton Project Bag,
   Page 1.
Molly, Page 6
Rosemary, Page 176

LANTERN MOON
7911 N.E. 33rd Drive,
   Suite 140
Portland, OR 97211
(800) 530-4170
www.lanternmoon.com
Calypso, Cover.
Garden Taffeta in silver,
   Page 173.
Libby, Page 106 and
   Back Cover.

NAMASTE, INC.
9025 Eton Ave. Suite B
Canoga Park, CA 91304
(818) 717-9134
www.namasteneedles.com
Needle Binder, Page 66.

PHOTO INDEX

Little Sailor Cami &
Soaker Pants, 98

Tonal Triangles Kids'
Pullover, 102

GIFTY THINGS

Cable Sampler
Baby Blocks, 107

Nautical Stripes
Onesie & Sunhat, 110

Cute as a Button
Baby Set, 114

Day at the Beach Flip-
Flops & Bracelet, 118

Andrea Beaded Cuffs,
121

Easy as 1-2-3
Braided Belt, 124

Orient Express
Eye Pillow, 126

Fanciful Felted Purse,
128

Chico's Sweater, 131

Frilly Prilly Poncho, 134

Luxurious Lace Collar,
137

HOME
ADORNMENTS

Rustic Basket Weave
Table Runner, 141

Pretty Pastels Lap
Blanket, 144

Laced-Up Cables
Afghan, 147

Spiraled I-Cord
Seat Cover, 150

Knit, Then Weave,
Place Mats, 152

Earth Tones Afghan, 155

Luxembourg Lace
Place Mats, 158

Bamboo Bath Mat, 160

175

SPECIAL THANKS

This book would not be a success without the talents of the following designers. We would like to thank them for contributing their imaginative designs to help make this book possible.

Laura Andersson
Little Sailor Cami & Soaker Pants, 98

Kate Atherley
European Tour Set, 42

Suzanne Atkinson
Laced-Up Cables Afghan, 147

Kathryn Beckerdite
Harlequin Socks, 29

Cheryl Beckerich
Little Miss Hat & Purse, 10

Laura Bryant for Prism Yarn
Gossamer Capelet, 35; Simply Stripes Scarf, 22

Jean Clement
Frilly Prilly Poncho, 134

Ellen Edwards Drechsler
Day at the Beach Flip-Flops & Bracelet, 118

Julie Gaddy
Easy as 1-2-3 Braided Belt, 124

Faina Goberstein
Cozy Hooded Sleeping Sack, 88

Ava Lynne Green
Casual Cotton T-Shirt, 48

Jacqueline W. Hoyle
City Girl Scarf, 24

Katharine Hunt
Baby Dearest, 80; Happy Baby Blankie, 92; Pretty Pastels Lap Blanket, 144

Melissa Leapman
Dual Texture Tunic, 39; Outback Basket Weave Pullover, 62; Saucy Stripes Pullover, 85

Dawn Leeseman
Orient Express Eye Pillow, 126

Sara Lucas
Day at the Met Mitered Wrap, 16

Cecily Glowik MacDonald
Bamboo Bath Mat, 160; Sleek & Stylish Sleeveless Top, 52; Uptown Chic Satchel, 7

Shirley MacNulty
Chico's Sweater, 131; Lacy A-Line Baby Dress, 76; Spiraled I-Cord Seat Cover, 150

Amy Marshall
Tonal Triangles Kids' Pullover, 102

Laura Nelkin
A-Dorable A-Line Ruffled Jumper, 95; Andrea Beaded Cuffs, 121

Celeste Pinheiro
Kaleidoscope Market Bag, 26; Rustic Basket Weave Table Runner, 141

Irina Poludnenko
Bodacious Bobble Hat, 85

Joëlle Meier Rioux for Classic Elite Yarns
Kathmandu Cravat, 14; Luxurious Lace Collar, 137

Phyllis Sandford
Fanciful Felted Purse, 128

Pauline Schultz
Earth Tones Afghan, 155

Colleen Smitherman
"It's a Wrap" Cabled Shrug, 58; Knit, Then Weave, Place Mats, 152

Christine L. Walter
Cute as a Button Baby Set, 114; Luxembourg Lace Place Mats, 158; Traveling Lace Beaded Shawl, 32

Kara Gott Warner
Nautical Stripes Onesie & Sunhat, 110

KyleAnn Williams
Country Roads Scarf, 19

Lois S. Young
Little Princess Dress Up Set, 70; Roundabout Ruffled Top, 67

Diane Zangl
Cable Sampler Baby Blocks, 107; Take It On the Road Tank, 55